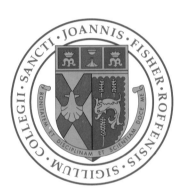

Lavery Library

St. John Fisher
College

Rochester, New York

Sí pero no

Sí pero no

Fabián Dobles
and the Postcolonial Challenge

Ann B. González

Madison • Teaneck
Fairleigh Dickinson University Press

Associated University Presses
2010 Eastpark Boulevard
Cranbury, NJ 08512

The paper used in this publication meets the requirements of the American National Standard for Permanence of Paper for Printed Library Materials Z39.48-1984.

Cataloging-in-Publication Data is on file with the Library of Congress.

To my husband, Daniel González Dobles,
and our children, Carolina, Gina, John, Daniel, and Ana Alicia,
all of whom are part of this story, too.

Contents

Acknowledgments

THIS WORK WAS SUPPORTED, IN PART, BY FUNDS PROVIDED BY THE UNIVERsity of North Carolina at Charlotte. I am also particularly grateful to Anne C. Barnhart, Latin American and Iberian Studies Librarian for Davidson Library, University of California at Santa Barbara, who carefully read my manuscript three times for Fairleigh Dickinson University Press. My thanks go to the Dobles family for providing materials and information, to my husband who acted as my first editor, and to my family, friends, and colleagues for their continued support and encouragement in what turned out to be a four-year-long project.

Sí pero no

Prologue: Critical Assumptions and Background

Wιτηιν τηε ςοντεχτ οf WESTERN LITERARY CRITICISM, CENTRAL AMERI-
can literature has been studied as part of the body of Latin American
literature or divided up into the national literatures of Guatemala,
Nicaragua, Honduras, El Salvador, Costa Rica, and sometimes Panama.[1] Prominent individual figures stand out who have been appropriated by the dominant canons of world literature: Rubén Darío
from Nicaragua and Miguel Angel Asturias from Guatemala, but
generally, the literary production from Central America has been
effectively marginalized by international critics. The Sandinista revolution in Nicaragua and the decades-long low-intensity wars in Guatemala and El Salvador in the 1970s and 1980s, however, focused
world attention on the human suffering, oppressive governmental
politics, and detrimental economics of the area.

Only then did Central American literature begin to establish itself
as a regional literature with its own history, context, and environment. Mainstream literary critics began to notice the area's cultural
production and the effects of the revolutionary agenda on the vision
of the region's artists. Central America became known especially for
its revolutionary poetry and its testimonial narratives that related
eyewitness accounts of the horrors of military oppression and the
epic civilian resistance.[2] Nobel Peace laureates, President Oscar
Arias of Costa Rica and Guatemalan Mayan Rigoberta Menchú,[3]
brought further international attention to the area, and writers like
Manlio Argueta and Claribel Alegría from El Salvador, Ernesto Cardenal, Sergio Ramírez, and Gioconda Belli from Nicaragua, and Arturo Arias and Mario Roberto Morales from Guatemala, began to be
discussed within new critical frameworks. Costa Rica, however,
tended to be left out of the critical debate[4] precisely because it has
no revolutionary poetry or *testimonios*, indeed, no military. Instead,
it has enjoyed relative stability, a generally peaceful and democratic
history, and the absence of large indigenous populations. A closer

look, however, reveals cracks in Camelot. Alternative stories that challenge official history and denounce political atrocities and social injustices perpetrated against the region's poor, ignorant, or otherwise marginalized members have a long literary history in Costa Rica as elsewhere in Central America dating back to colonial times.

One of the most outspoken critics of political and economic abuses by the metropolis is award winning novelist Fabián Dobles (1918–1997), whose work has gone largely unrecognized by traditional literary criticism (a common experience for authors from the third world). He is well known only in his own country, and even there the Costa Rican establishment tried to silence him for his left-wing political views during the conservative 1950s and early sixties.[5] In 1968, however, he was finally honored with Costa Rica's most coveted prize, El Premio Magón, awarded for a lifetime of achievement in the arts. More recently, in the 1990s a critical reevaluation of his work has begun on the national level[6] with the publication of his last novel in 1989 and his *Obras completas* in 1993. While isolated translations of some of his stories have appeared sporadically in various anthologies since 1955, more recent and intense efforts to introduce his work to international audiences have been made through significant translations into Russian, Italian, and English of his last novel, *Los años, pequeños días* (1989), and his most famous book of short stories, *Historias de Tata Mundo* (1955).

Traditionally, Dobles has been considered part of the realist movement in literature[7] and, indeed, his work exhibits most of the characteristics associated with this school imported from Europe to Latin America around the turn of the century: a mimetic representation of the world, a tone of criticism and denunciation, an agenda for political action, and a privileging of the regional. Nevertheless, this study considers Dobles' narrative corpus from a different perspective, specifically subaltern and postcolonial studies, an approach that has begun to gain acceptance within Latin American literary and cultural criticism.[8]

The particular conditions of Costa Rica's colonization and independence offer a unique spin on its narratives of resistance and subversion, and the double victimization of Central America by the successively dominant hegemonic centers, Spain and the United States, invites particular attention to the issues of language, hybridity, difference, and textual representation. Anticolonialist perspectives, as old as colonialism itself, have more recently overlapped with poststructuralist and multicultural approaches in a renewed focus on colonial discourse and its counter discourses. Theorists from Fanon to Said, Spivak, and Bhabha have enriched the debates with reference primarily to English-speaking countries affected by British imperialism in the nineteenth century (India, Africa, and the English-speaking Caribbean).[9] More recently Chicano literary scholars[10] have picked up the model to understand their unique literature. Central and South American scholars are also increasingly referring to postcolonialist perspectives to determine the sociopolitical, economic, and cultural contexts of this area's literary production that, as Gayatri Spivak says, is part of "the other story— the conjuncture that didn't catch . . . it too is a model: of the failure of decolonization that is inscribed—and not as an accident—in the most aggressive decolonization narratives."[11]

The historical differences of Spanish colonialism and independence in Central and South America contrast strikingly with the British imperial project; yet similarities in the process of subject/object formation, differential power relations, the phenomenon of neocolonialism and its nationalistic antithesis, and the colonized response of hybridized language and culture present issues that converge, parallel, and overlap contemporary postcolonialist interests. Moreover, the twentieth-century advent of North American cultural imperialism in the region adds an additional variable to the problematic of ideological and epistemic control.

The view that language is central to cultural identity is a position that informs Dobles' writing from the early 1940s—well before postcolonialism had a name in literary discourse. His aim is to legitimize Costa Rican Spanish, that is, to "decolonize"[12] it. His glossaries at the end of his early works offer a form of translation from the Costa Rican vernacular into standard academic Spanish. Moreover, his dependence on oral storytelling practices provides a forum for the silenced and subaltern voices of the Costa Rican *campesino* [peasant]. Dobles' decision to use Costa Rican Spanish in his fiction parallels the choice of important African writers to use native languages rather than European ones to tell their stories.[13]

Central America, however, suffers cultural and linguistic holdovers not only from Spanish colonialism but also from more recent economic and political dependence on the United States. Dobles' work to rescue Costa Rican Spanish from the onslaught of North American English,[14] therefore, can only really be appreciated from a postcolonial stance as part of a lifelong effort to develop a cultural

identity free of the traditional domination by Europe and the
United States. Dobles is keenly aware of the danger of internalizing
or naturalizing the dominant ideology by creating a form of neocolonial oppression through art (through, for instance, government
and economic institutions) modeled on European or North American values. His goal is to articulate a regional identity within Costa
Rican literature, to speak about and to "his" people, and he chas-
tises fellow writers for unwittingly adopting a self-denigrating position in their claim that "en Costa Rica no hay material suficiente"
[in Costa Rica there is not enough material].[15] His response to their
complaint, written in 1945, suggests a postcolonial analysis of the
artist's dilemma:

> La obra literaria se escribe por hombres. Es natural que ellos se resien-
> tan de la pobreza o se alimenten con la riqueza cultural del país donde
> han nacido . . . Pero echar la culpa de esa verdad al inocente hombre de
> la calle o al desguarnecido campesino que nada tiene que hacer con los
> problemas del oficio del novelista, viene a ser trastrocar los factores, to-
> mando el efecto por la causa. (363)

> [People write literary works. It is only natural for them to resent the cul-
> tural poverty or to be nourished by the cultural richness of the country
> in which they were born . . . But to blame this fact on the innocent man
> in the street or the landless farmer who has nothing to do with a novel-
> ist's preoccupations, is to put the cart before the horse and mistake the
> effect for its cause.]

The underlying cause, he implies, is colonialism itself, whether
Spanish or North American, whether conscious or not, and its effect
is always to silence the masses, to make them invisible and nameless,
docile and passive, to belittle their humanity and their differences,
and to render them voiceless. His intent is not to criticize Eurocentric notions but to recognize that all knowledge must be culturally
situated:

> Y no que el escritor costarricense no deba, como una obligación, estu-
> diar y leer las obras *psicoanalistas* y, vaya también, *socialistas,* del viejo
> mundo, para tomar de ellas lo que, en función de la cultura universal,
> sea aplicable a los personajes que está obligado a escribir. No se ve por
> dónde un campesino, un indio, un mulato o un obrero de San José de
> Costa Rica no implique problemas psicológicos, especiales, suyos, dife-
> rentes, aunque también iguales, al de un hombre de cultura europea o

pseudo-europea. Suena a snobismo[16] eso de despreciar lo propio para buscar el rastro de lo ajeno. (365)

[It is not that the Costa Rican writer should not, as a matter of course, study and read the *psychoanalytic* works and, indeed, the *socialist* ones from the old world and to take from them whatever of universal culture may be applicable to the characters that he must portray. I cannot see that a peasant, an Indian, a mulatto or a Costa Rican worker from San José would not imply psychological problems that are special, unique to themselves, different, although the same, as a man from European or pseudo-European culture. It sounds like "snobbism" to denigrate what is one's own in order to look for the trace of what is foreign.]

Costa Rican critic Ronald Solano, in his acute analysis of the often unstated theoretical assumptions underpinning much of the criticism on Dobles' narrative, is confused by Dobles' own views as both writer and reader of his work. He notes that Dobles is clearly aware of the extra-authorial social factors that shape his narrative: "existen fuerzas exteriores que lo determinan, que lo hacen ir en busca de una verdad que por lo mismo no posee" [outside forces exist that determine it and make it look for a truth that for that very reason it does not possess]. Nevertheless, he seems surprised by Dobles' ingenuousness regarding language:

Puesto que desconoce de manera evidente, la mediación lingüística que actúa en todo acto de lectura-escritura: según él, el autor y el lector se comunican, entran en contacto. La labor del lector es tratar de percibir, de reconocer, qué quiso expresar el escritor, qué sintió al escribir, qué verdad nos quiso transmitir acerca de la realidad.[17]

[He is evidently unaware of the linguistic mediation that takes place with every reading-writing act: according to him, the author and the reader communicate, come into contact. The task of the reader is to attempt to perceive, to recognize, what the author wanted to express, what he felt while writing, what truth he tried to transmit about reality.]

Viewed from a postcolonialist stance, however, Dobles' position regarding language makes sense. While he obviously could not foresee the contemporary critical jargon to describe his literary practice, he knew precisely what he was doing: writing in code, as he, himself, said, "en clave."[18] His medium permits communication between writer and subaltern reader, not because it is transparent, but precisely because it is not. It is a language the dominant ideology does not control; indeed, may not fully understand, that permits writer and reader to function as a team, in league against colonial domination, that is, those external social factors Dobles recognizes. Thus, Dobles' narrative becomes a game of one-upmanship aimed to resist official elitist culture and promote a national identity.

Fredric Jameson's assertion that in third world literature "the story of a private individual destiny is always an allegory of the embattled situation of the public third-world culture and society"[19] is fundamentally valid in Dobles' case and helps clarify the ideological bases sustaining his narrative. Alfonso Chase, a recent recipient of Costa Rica's Premio Magón (2000), speaks of Dobles' achievement in similar terms: "logró mezclar los intereses íntimos y personales de sus protagonistas con la marejada social que constituye la base de nuestra identidad"[20] [he was able to mix the intimate and personal interests of his protagonists with the social undercurrent that constitutes the basis of our identity]. In fact, Dobles' work has been placed by most Costa Rican critics within the context of an ongoing national discourse about what it means to be Costa Rican, what constitutes a Costa Rican literature, what qualities exemplify the Costa Rican people, and who is included in and excluded from these constructions.[21] Dobles underlines the notions of region, of personal subjectivity, and cultural identity intricately intertwined with land and family and a mythical mode of rural existence that has all but disappeared, if it ever really existed, in the urbane and technologically oriented societies of today. His representations of country people deconstruct negative stereotypes of third world "Latinos" present in Western discourse and mirrored in *costumbrista* narrative, the local color texts that were popular at the beginning of the century. As Alberto Cañas noted about his fellow writer and lifelong friend, it is no longer clear whether Dobles reflected the identity and speech of the Costa Rican *campesino* or whether the *campesino* adopted the personal and cultural identity that Dobles constructed for him in his fiction.[22]

After Edward Said's classic study on Orientalism,[23] we can no longer ingenuously speak of national or cultural identity as being anything other than a complex and often explicitly manipulated social construct. In fact, the entire notion of community or nation is, following Benedict Anderson, ultimately an imagined concept.[24] These ideas are key to reevaluating Dobles' work. If, indeed, Dobles is constructing or imagining reality rather than reflecting it, then he is not merely another tired realist to be discounted and devalued by more contemporary "boom" and "post-boom" Latin American fiction. Rather, his work can be viewed as a more deliberate and complex attempt to create a sense of difference for the Costa Rican people and to subvert the neocolonial hierarchy that automatically placed the locals in a position of inferiority.

One of the purposes of this book is to understand how Dobles contributes to this postcolonial understanding or imagination of national and cultural identity. While Dobles speaks for (and with) the subaltern and marginalized voices of his people, he, in turn, suffers a parallel silencing by dominant Eurocentric criticism. The fact that Dobles never had the political and economic machinery behind him to project his voice into the international arena does not make him a lesser writer, just an ignored one. This study intends to make him more accessible to an English-speaking audience.

My approach in this endeavor is grounded not only in postcolonial perspectives, but also in part in romantic and humanistic theories that value the force and intentions of the author,[25] a position not necessarily incongruent with postmodern and poststructuralist claims.[26] By examining an author's biography as well as the critical reaction and reception to both author and work in his own time, the literary critic speaks from a particular historical, biographical, literary, and cultural standpoint.[27] Certainly one of the objectives of this book is to understand the relationship between the man, Fabián Dobles, and the narratives he wrote. One of the contentions here is that Dobles revolutionized the prevailing trend of *costumbrista* writing in Costa Rica as well as elsewhere in Central America precisely because of his personal identification with the people he wrote about. While the *costumbristas* attempted to reflect regional idiosyncrasies as they entertained their leisure class audiences with stories of the droll ignorance and quaintness of the lower classes, "el vulgar detalle pintoresco o la simple anécdota superficial"[28] [the vulgar picturesque detail or the simple superficial anecdote], Dobles determined to project more than local color in his writing. Moreover, his primary goal was never entertainment.[29] He firmly believed that while extrinsic forces influenced his narrative, that literature could, in turn, affect human behavior. Art, for Dobles, clearly serves some ultimate purpose:

Siempre he pensado que la literatura, sin que se pueda medir hasta dónde ni cuándo ni cómo, influye en la conducta humana, para bien o para mal, y así las artes en general son parte esencial de la conciencia histórica, intelectual y moral del hombre. Para mí es tan evidente como imposible de demostración. No se puede someter a pruebas de laboratorio. Pero sí a pequeñas anecdóticas comprobaciones personales. A mí me han asegurado muchachos que después de leer mi novela *El sitio de las abras,* transformaron su visión político-social. No tengo por qué no creerles.[30]

[I have always thought that literature, without being able to measure exactly when or how, influences human behavior, for good or bad, and that the arts in general are an essential part of the historical, intellectual and moral conscience of humankind. In my mind this belief is as evident as it is impossible to demonstrate. It cannot be submitted to laboratory tests. But it can be backed up by small, personal, anecdotal proofs. Several young men have assured me that after reading my novel *El sitio de las abras,* their socio-political views were transformed. I have no reason not to believe them.]

That Dobles' work is heavily autobiographical goes without question[31] and stems from his stated intention to write himself as he writes his country: "Y si algo yo deseo intensamente . . . es que en lo que vaya escribiendo quede reflejado algo de la vida de Costa Rica y algo de mi propia vida"[32] [And if there is anything that I desire intensely . . . it is that something of Costa Rican life and something of my own life be reflected in everything I write]. Judging by reader reception, the public has never been able to make a clear distinction between the two: "El pueblo se ha sentido identificado en sus relatos y hasta con la propia vida del autor de los mismos"[33] [The Costa Rican people have identified with his stories and even with the author's own life]. Therefore, this study of the narrative of Fabián Dobles is in part founded on the theoretical standpoint that the author matters, that his authorial voice can be heard and distinguished outside the ideological precepts that always and inevitably impregnate communication, and that the author's representation of his world in his art ultimately affects and restricts the meanings we readers construct and impute to that world and to that art.

There is, in addition, another motivation for this study that is not without some theoretical significance, narcissistic though it may at first appear. As it happens, I am a niece by marriage of Don Fabián. As a United States citizen by birth and upbringing, a native English speaker who has learned Spanish as a second language, and a literary comparatist by training, I have found myself immersed in a language and a culture that is not my own and that over the years I have tried to understand and negotiate in all their complexity as both an individual and a professional. My own autobiography follows the pattern of many comparatists in that it is "the story of the traces of cultural otherness discovered within and of ambivalent interactions with otherness confronted without."[34] I have of necessity become what James Clifford terms a person who "travels cultures"; thus, the question "where are you from?" is less meaningful or provocative than "where are you between?"[35] The critical space I inhabit, this "in-betweenness," ultimately influences how I read and what I read and in this sense the work of Fabián Dobles takes on special importance, for it represents, creates, and implies a world that is completely foreign (other) to me, yet inextricably and productively linked to my own. I am at pains to understand this connection if I am ever to understand myself in relation to these others—"diferentes, aunque también iguales" [different, yet also the same]—and discover my own voice within their midst.

1

Introduction

The Central American Context

THE INTRIGUING QUESTION BENEDICT ANDERSON POSES IN HIS STUDY ON nationalism[1] is how a community imagines itself to be like other individuals they do not know and different from still other individuals they also do not know. Central America is an interesting case in point. Anderson claims that the fundamental national divisions in Latin America stem from the original colonial governmental apparatus in place at the time of independence, but the history of Central America is slightly more complicated. Strictly following Anderson, it would seem that all of Central America should have formed into one nation-state since it was under the administration of the Capitanía General de Guatemala. Costa Rica, at the time of independence, was only a province delineated by geographical boundaries, rivers to the north and south. Actually, Anderson is partially correct: Central America initially did form a centralized governmental unit as a Federation of States, but this entity was plagued by political infighting from the start. By the time Braulio Carrillo (1800–1845) took his second term of office as Costa Rica's chief of state in 1838, the federation was nearly defunct. Carrillo, in order to spare Costa Rica from becoming further embroiled in the region's problems, unilaterally declared that Costa Rica would no longer be a part of the federation.[2] Costa Rica's strong sense of difference from the rest of Central America and indeed from Latin America in general, therefore, dates back to the middle of the nineteenth century if not before and has intrigued theorists of nationalism and national identity who try to understand this phenomenon in cultural, socioeconomic, political and/or historical terms.[3]

By the beginning of the twentieth century the various countries of Central and South America had begun to view themselves as clear national entities and had produced the first truly Latin American literary movement known as modernism, heralded by Nicaraguan Rubén Darío (1867–1916). Modernism, with its emphasis on language, although officially over by the turn of the century, still had a host of imitators in Latin America, and movements from Europe (romanticism, realism, naturalism) all found followers in the Spanish-speaking Americas about this same time. Unlike Europe, where successive literary movements tended to form in response to previous ones and follow each other diachronically, differing movements in Latin America converged and coexisted synchronically in hybridized adaptations. Latin Americans tended to read more works from Europe and North America than they did from neighboring Latin American countries, another deleterious effect of colonialism. In addition, Central American publishing companies printed such few copies of books that locally written material rarely traveled beyond a country's own borders. It was far easier to find books that had been imported from Spain, Europe and the United States, although Costa Rica was not so isolated as to be ignorant of important Latin American thinkers like Peru's José Carlos Mariátegui (1894–1930), Mexico's José Vasconcelos (1882–1959), and Uruguay's José Enrique Rodó (1871–1917), prominent figures in the continental preoccupation with the definition and construction of national identity.

Central Americans also read and were familiar with prominent Latin American novels during the first third of the century and followed the prevailing trends. Psychological novels like Chilean Eduardo Barrios' (1884–1963) *El niño que enloqueció de amor* (1925) were available and, like the rest of the Western world, Central American intellectuals were profoundly impacted by the theories of Sigmund Freud. Also available were novels of the city, like Argentinean Roberto Arlt's (1900–1942) *Los siete locos* (1929) although the capitals of the Central American countries were relatively small and did not lend themselves at this time to authentic criticisms of urbanism. Undoubtedly the most widespread trend in narrative was the regional or criollist novel, represented by Argentinean Ricardo Güiraldes' (1886–1927) *Don Segundo Sombra* (1926), Colombian José Eustasio Rivera's (1889–1928) *La Vorágine* (1924), and Venezuelan Rómulo Gallegos' (1884–1969) *Doña Bárbara* (1929). Dobles clearly identifies most closely with this tendency in Spanish American prose. Finally, indigenist novels, like Bolivian Alcides Arguedas' (1879–1946) *Raza de bronce* (1919), Ecuadorian Jorge Icaza's (1906–1973) *Huasipungo* (1934), and Peruvian Ciro Alegría's (1909–1967)

El mundo es ancho y ajeno (1941) were also in the libraries of educated Central Americans.

For the most part, however, cultural similarities and differences, particularly what was happening in the field of narrative, were the product more of similar or dissimilar economic, geographic, and political challenges than of any direct influence from one Latin American writer to another. Guatemala, for example, with its large indigenous population, produced authors who were clearly preoccupied with the marginal and exploited position of the Indians. Costa Rica, on the other hand, which had never been home to large indigenous groups even before the conquest and whose few indigenous peoples disappeared into the mountains with the advent of the Spaniards,[4] typically ignored the issue altogether both in political as well as cultural terms.

The 1930s found Central America reeling economically from the international repercussions of the Great Depression and deeply influenced by the growing fascism in Europe. Except for Costa Rica, every Central American nation struggled under the dictatorial control of strong generals: Jorge Ubico in Guatemala (1931–1944), Maximiliano Hernández Martínez in El Salvador (1931–1944), Tiburcio Carías Andino in Honduras (1933–1948), and Anastasio Somoza García in Nicaragua (1937–1947). Only Costa Rica managed to retain its electoral system during this decade. What is more, it established a strong Communist Party, of which Dobles was a member. Costa Rican publishing houses were willing to back national authors who denounced local and regional social and political conditions in their work whereas other Central American writers were forced to publish their national criticisms in exile.

Central American contemporaries of Costa Rica's Fabián Dobles found themselves responding in large part to the socioeconomic and political conditions of their countries. While it has taken the advent of postmodernist criticism to legitimize the role of literature in the first world as a vehicle for social analysis, criticism, and denunciation, Latin American intellectuals have long assumed that responsibility in their narratives. As Carlos Fuentes noted in 1969, the Latin American writer is "el portavoz de quienes no pueden hacerse escuchar, que siente que su función exacta consiste en denunciar la injusticia, defender a los explotados y documentar la realidad de su país"[5] [the speaker for those who cannot make themselves heard, who feels that his specific function consists of denouncing injustice, defending the exploited and documenting the reality of his country]. Such a role in the first world is granted primarily to social scientists and the canon has been slow to recognize or give credence to literature that exposes and criticizes specific social and political conditions. In Central America, however, with censorship imposed by military dictatorships, increased economic intervention by the United States, and intensified efforts by the local oligarchies to sustain a flailing agro-export economic model, writers and intellectuals took every opportunity, including fiction, to denounce the status quo.

The most famous writer to come out of this period in Central America is clearly Guatemala's Miguel Angel Asturias (1899–1974), born almost twenty years before Dobles but unpublished until *El señor Presidente* (1946), six years after Dobles wrote his first novel, and thus, not a direct influence on his early career. According to Costa Rican critic Virginia Sandoval, however, echoes of Asturias are present in some of Dobles' later work, particularly his deaf mute Gugú in his 1967 novel, *En el San Juan hay tiburón*, a character that Sandoval compares to Asturias' idiot Pelele in *El señor Presidente*.[6] Asturias' combination of real and dreamlike sequences to portray the horrors of life under dictatorship was one of the early examples of magical realism, which by the 1960s was picked up and exploited by the so-called boom novelists[7] like Colombia's Gabriel García Márquez (1928), Mexico's Carlos Fuentes (1928), and Argentina's Julio Cortázar (1914–1984). Another Guatemalan contemporary of Dobles, who just recently died, is Mario Monteforte Toledo (1911–2003). He spent much of his life in exile precisely because of the sociopolitical agenda in his narratives that brings to the fore his country's problems. Like Dobles' work, his narrative has been compared to the regionalist novels of Eustasio Rivera and Rómulo Gallegos for his depiction of the jungle, civilization versus barbarism, and the plight of the American Indian.

In Honduras, a group of regionalist writers emerged during the early part of the century, called the Generation of 26, whose intentions were once again to identify and criticize national problems, particularly the exploitative conditions among the coastal banana plantations. While there are several representative members of this group—Marcos Carías Reyes (1905–1949), Carlos Izaguirre (1894–1956), Jorge Fidel Durón (1902–1995)—the best-known internationally is Argentina Díaz Lozano (1909–1999), winner of the Honduran National Prize in Literature (1968), the same year Dobles won his national prize for literature, El Premio Magón. She was a

prolific writer who won the North American Farrar and Rinehart literary prize for Latin American literature for her novel *Peregrinaje*,
which was immediately translated into English and published as *En-
riqueta and I* (1944). This was the same regional contest that Dobles
entered with *Aguas turbias* after he won (along with Alberto Cañas
and Yolanda Oreamuno) the national selection.[8] While Díaz Lozano's topics emphasize social conditions, she is much more of a romantic than Dobles and her language is more neutral, focusing less
on regional speech than his, certainly making her easier to translate.

El Salvador's political situation during the first half of the twentieth century was anything but open to social criticism and produced
very few novels. The one outstanding name, more or less a contemporary of Dobles and certainly an influence on him as he was on
many other writers in the region, was Salvador Salazar Arrué (1899–
1975), known as Salarrué, who became famous throughout Central
America for his short stories that reproduced the rural speech pat-
terns of children: *Cuentos de barro* (1933) and *Cuentos de cipotes*
(1945). Even more difficult to read than Dobles, Salarrué uses a
phonetic spelling that practically compels his work to be read aloud.
The other well-known name from Honduras and more of a contemporary of Dobles is Hugo Lindo (1917–1985), winner of a number
of literary prizes, but very different from Dobles and the regionalist
trend in his preference for "wide-ranging human problems more
than with social change."[9]

Nicaragua, ever since Darío, if not before, has been a land of
poets. Narrative has not been, until quite recently, a popular genre.
El Salvador's Salarrué was a noted influence on what little prose
came out of this period in Nicaragua. More important, however, are
the isolated narratives, basically short stories, produced by Nicaragua's poets, Pablo Antonio Cuadra (1912–2002) and Ernesto Cardenal (1925). Two writers of note, more for their influence on later
writers than for their actual production, are Dobles' contemporaries, Mariano Fiallos Gil (1907–1969), the father of Rosario Aguilar
(1938), a contemporary Nicaraguan novelist of merit, and José Coro-
nel Urtecho (1906–1985), who mentored many young Nicaraguan
writers, especially Gioconda Belli (1948), well-known contemporary
poet and novelist.

Nicaragua's political situation under the Somoza dynasty beginning with the resistance of Augusto Sandino, assassinated in 1934,
until the final Sandinista victory in 1979, has been much more of an
influence than any single writer on the literature of the entire Cen-

tral American region. The epic proportions of the revolution and the allegorical and binary nature of the conflicting sides, the innocence of the revolutionaries alongside the flagrant corruption of the Somoza regime, has produced narratives from the forties like Manolo Cuadra's (1908) *Contra Sandino en la montaña* (1945) up to the present with novels by Belli, Aguilar, Sergio Ramírez (1942), and Omar Cabezas (1950). Even one of Dobles' novels *En el San Juan hay tiburón* (1967) is inspired by the Nicaraguan conflict.

In Costa Rica Fabián Dobles did not emerge as an isolated figure. Rather, the convergence in 1940 of a host of new writers, including Dobles, gave rise to what has been termed the Generation of 1940. Generally considered members of this group are Carlos Luis Fallas (1909–1966), Joaquín Gutiérrez (1918–2001), Yolanda Oreamuno (1916–1956), and, of course, Fabián Dobles (1918–1997). Adolfo Herrera García (1914–1975) is also included by some critics for his 1939 novel *Juan Varela,* a short naturalistic agrarian narrative that technically inaugurates the novel of social problems in Costa Rica and whose merit, according to Alfonso Chase, resides more in its "ejemplo moral antes que en valores estrictamente literarios"[10] [moral example rather than its strict literary value]. Often included in this group because of their publications in the 1940s are two older and more experienced writers, José Marín Cañas (1904–1981) and Carlos Salazar Herrera (1906–1980). These two, however, have less in common with the others in terms of social convictions and literary style. The Generation of 1940 was a groundbreaking group of writers who did as much to create a national and cultural identity as did any political or social movement in the country. Contemporary Costa Rican writer and critic Rima de Vallbona identifies several historical and cultural events that contributed to the cultural climate of these writers:

> Tax reforms carried out by President Alfredo González Flores; the disappearance of small private property and an increase of workers answering to an overseer or boss as a result of the new latifundismo; exploitation in the banana industry by the United Fruit Co., which led to a strike in 1934; an awakening of the anti-imperialist consciousness of the Costa Rican people; the founding of the Communist Party as a vehicle to encourage the organization of the proletariat and its participation in the politics of the nation.[11]

She also notes the incentives to this new group of writers of the founding of the Editorial Costa Rica and the University of Costa Rica as well as the competition sponsored by Farrar and Reinhart for the best Latin American novel. Not without significance was *El Repertorio Americano* (1919–1959), one of the most important and influential journals of the twentieth century, which originated in Costa Rica under the direction of Joaquín García Monge and published well-known contemporary writers from all over Latin America, in addition to writers from Costa Rica.

Nevertheless, the competition to find a novel to represent Costa Rica for the Farrar and Reinhart prize, more than anything else, marked the emergence of a new social consciousness and approach to literature in Costa Rica.[12] Except for *Juan Varela* (1939), the group published the bulk of its work in the decade after 1940. In those ten years Carlos Luis Fallas published his scathing attack on the United Fruit Company and North American imperialism in *Mamita Yunai* (1941) as well as another novel, *Gentes y gentecillas* (1947). Yolanda Oreamuno wrote two novels, *La ruta de su evasión* published in 1949 and her never published first novel, *Por tierra firme*. (This was the novel that shared the triple first prize in 1940 with novels by Dobles and Marín Cañas. She later destroyed all existing copies.) Joaquín Gutiérrez published two novels, *Manglar* in 1947 and *Puerto Limón* in 1950, also about the banana plantation industry. Dobles, by far the most prolific writer of the group, published four: *Ese que llaman pueblo* (1942), *Aguas turbias* (1943), *Una burbuja en el limbo* (1945), and *El sitio de las abras* (1950)—all dealing with the problems of Costa Rica's *campesino*.

This group of young writers shared a common upbringing—all but Carlos Luis Fallas came from upper-class families. They shared a social consciousness and leftist political convictions. They had all sympathized with the Republicans against Franco in the Spanish Civil War, were deeply affected by World War II, and applauded the creation of the Communist Party in Costa Rica that later became the Vanguardist Party in 1943. More importantly, along with their social denunciation, they were intent on revolutionizing the narrative in Costa Rica, both in terms of theme and forms of expression. Oreamuno concentrated on urban problems and the disintegration of the family; eventually she left Costa Rica's stifling (for her) environment and moved to Mexico. Joaquín Gutiérrez, who depicted life on the Atlantic coast, also did most of his writing from Chile where he lived for years. It was Dobles, however, writing from home, who raised the *campesino* from an object of manners to a problematized subject and ultimately to a mythical icon, merging the Costa Rican self-image once and for all with the land itself. Dobles did more in his narrative than merely denounce social problems; he created a new way for Costa Ricans to see themselves and a new language for them to hear themselves. Before Dobles and the Generation of 1940, Costa Rican authors like Aquileo Echeverría (1866–1909), Magón (1864–1936), Carmen Lyra (1888–1949), and Joaquín García Monge (1881–1958) limited the notion of nationhood to the oligarchy of the Central Plateau, specifically San José. Locality served as a backdrop for their narratives of manners and customs of the era. It took the Generation of 1940, however, to integrate the rural communities from the mountains and the coastal areas and to project the *campesino* as a sympathetic actor onto land that was more than background scenery, but rather an integral part of the life of the people and by extension the life of any Costa Rican fictional character.

Fabián Dobles' narrative has been variously termed social realism, literature of denunciation, and "realismo expresivo" [expressive realism],[13] and Dobles along with the Generation of 1940, has been credited with being an instrumental part, if not the leader, of a revolution in Costa Rican letters. The evolution from *costumbrismo* to a so-called transparent rendering of reality, in which the author's voice is clearly empathetic with the subjects he represents, is, indeed, a clear sign of a change in ideological values, a move away from art for art's sake designed to entertain the elite at the expense of the image of the country bumpkin, to art as social praxis designed to raise class consciousness and foment political action in the service of social change.

The rhetorical strategy Dobles employs is to subvert the binary opposition of "We" (the elite, the powerful, the rich, the educated, "Olimpo"[14]—positive subjectivity) and "They" (the *campesino*, the poor, the naive, the ignorant—negative otherness) by switching the identification of We/They. The "We" becomes the *campesino*, a fundamentally univocal or monologic entity with positive connotations (humility, simplicity, honesty, generosity, intelligence, strength) versus the displaced "They," also a monologic voice, imbued with negative values (arrogance, artifice, duplicity, selfishness). The resulting constructs call attention not only to the unequal power relations between rich and poor but also to the colonial structure implicit in those relations (oppressor/oppressed).

Dobles' rhetorical strategy is double voiced: on the one hand, he encourages the view that his language is transparent, a window to

reality, a faithful and authentic representation of the social and psychological problems experienced by the countryside's poor, the sub-
alterns, for whom he claims to speak. Under this assumption, he
does not have to defend a position or urge a particular course of
action. He merely "describes" the situation, "shows" rather than
"tells" and allows the outrage of his audience to take its natural
course. On the other hand, however, he clearly calls attention to the
language he uses, drawn from the vernacular, from oral tradition,
uneducated speech, and regional dialect conflated with a most "un-
countryfied" lyricism and poetical deployment of metaphor and
image. Dobles is successful in this two-pronged rhetorical attack
against colonial and neocolonial ideology precisely because the language he uses supports the illusion of reality that he constructs. His
language becomes paradoxically both transparent and opaque, apparently revealing reality through itself yet ably constructing a code
for national identity from "Costa Rican" speech, a medium that is
identifiably and superficially Castilian but no longer under the control of the Spanish Royal Academy of the Language.[15] That is, Dobles subverts the language of the dominant classes by creating an
alternative language that is politically charged.

As Edmundo Desnoes points out, "Language carries ideology
longer than social institutions,"[16] which makes Dobles' coup in his
nation's literary history all the more surprising. Desnoes feels
trapped in Spanish with its binary system of values "sí and no,"
"todo and nada" [all and nothing] claiming, "Makes no difference
whether you speak Spanish through the streets of Quito, Havana,
Mexico City, Madrid, or Managua—you're caught."[17] Dobles would
surely disagree. Spanish is not monologic; even its seemingly fundamental grammatical and structural "essence" is radically challenged
and vexed by regional variations. Language, like knowledge, is culturally situated. By foregrounding Costa Rican speech, Dobles implicitly privileges regional values and subverts the binary opposition
of "sí/no" replacing it with "sí *pero* no" [yes *but* no]. Costa Rican
speech is full of these paradoxical phrasings—"lo mismo pero diferente" [the same but different], "diferentes pero también iguales"
[different but also the same], "definitivamente que sí . . . o no)
[definitely yes . . . or no]—that are the outward signs of an implicit
resistance to official speech or "el lenguaje culto" [cultured lan-
guage], the subversion of language and power by seeming to agree
while disagreeing. What Bruce-Novoa claimed for Chicano literature
might very well be said of Dobles' language: it "attempts to guide

[Costa Ricans] toward their own center where they can recuperate those positive values upon which can be based a cultural renaissance."[18]

Dobles intuitively sensed these possibilities of language, and from his first work on, strove to imitate and recreate *campesino* speech. The hybridized Spanish he employs functions as a political act of resistance against the cultured Spanish of the colonizer, upper class, and creole oligarchy. By giving voice to the subaltern, Dobles ultimately gives voice to the nation.

THE LIFE AND TIMES OF FABIÁN DOBLES (1918–1997)

Fabián Dobles was born on 17 January 1918, the same year as famous Mexican novelist Juan Rulfo, in San Antonio de Belén, a small country town in the province of Heredia, Costa Rica. His father, Dr. Miguel Dobles Sáenz, was trained in medicine at the turn of the century at the University of New York. Upon his return to Costa Rica at age thirty-five, he asked an acquaintance, Mr. Santiago Rodríguez, for permission to wed his daughter, Carmen Rodríguez Solera, but since the girl was only fifteen years old, Don Santiago made the doctor wait another year. The marriage between Don Miguel and Doña Carmen produced five children (Carmen, Alicia, Rosario, Susana, and Miguel), and after a ten-year hiatus, produced five more (Margarita, Fabián, Alejo, Alvaro, and Marielos). Don Miguel was fond of referring to the two groups as the Old Testament and the New Testament.[19] Between the two groups, the couple had a little girl, María Lourdes, who was born with a genetic defect and died before she was three months old, a traumatic blow to Fabián's mother. Of the Old Testament group, the oldest son, Miguel, took over the family farm, and the four girls married and dedicated themselves to home and family. The New Testament group, to which Fabián belongs, was a very different bunch: all became professionals. Margarita studied educational psychology and counseling and was the first Costa Rican to earn a Ph.D. from Stanford University, California. Afterward, she worked from 1959 to 1973 in Venezuela as technical advisor for the Ministry of Education and the National Council of Universities. Alvaro became a well-known architect and worked for years with the International Development Bank in Washington. Alejo became a first-rate, nationally recognized sculptor, and Marielos, the baby, earned a bachelor's degree and license to practice social work.

Dr. Miguel Dobles, who worked as *el Médico del Pueblo* [Town Doctor] in the governmental Public Health Program, was a pioneer in the field of rural medicine. Despite the urging of various friends and family, he consistently refused to go to the capital to practice medicine where he undoubtedly would have made more money. His vocation to work with the poor was unwavering, and it is the figure of this upright, self-assured, and rigorously Catholic man who made the strongest initial impression on Fabián. In fact, later in Dobles' life he credits his father with first imbuing him with social and political sensitivity, which ultimately took the form of firm left-wing convictions and an undying support of socialism.

The fact that the children grew up in the country, (Fabián particularly remembers Atenas, a city in the province of Alajuela, where the children went to school), gave the future writer an intimate knowledge of rural people and problems, though he could hardly have called himself a *campesino*, well-trained as he was at home in art, music, literature, mathematics, and science. Fabián experienced the best of both worlds as a child, what his sister Margarita called "una infancia mágica" [a magical childhood][20] that, according to his friend and admirer, Father Resti Moreno, resulted in "las dotes de verdadero intelectual y la inclinación cercana y amorosa hacia el campesino y la tierra y, en general, el mundo de los pobres"[21] [the gifts of a true intellectual and the close and loving relationship with country people and the land, and in general, with the world of the poor]. Fabián, however, always the realist, remembers childhood with qualified nostalgia (the *sí pero no* attitude he manipulates so well) :

> Si yo tuviera que elegir una Costa Rica de las tantas que he conocido, me quedaría con la de mi infancia . . . pero no es cierto. Vivía rodeado de tísicos y tuberculosos, las gentes se nos morían a los 40 años, estábamos por completo indefensos ante la enfermedad y la pobreza.[22]

> [If I had to choose one Costa Rica from all the ones I have known, I would pick that of my childhood . . . but no, that's not true. I was surrounded by people who suffered from tuberculosis, by people who died by the time they were 40; we were completely defenseless against sickness and poverty.]

Fabián's mother was well educated for the time, having finished secondary school, and, like most young ladies of her day, was trained

Publicity picture for Dobles' first novel, ca. 1942.

Dobles with his wife Cecilia.

Dobles at work on a manuscript, ca. 1960.

in piano. Fabián remembers that she gave him his first piano lessons. She was profoundly religious and Fabián recalls her with affection and respect despite the fact that his communication with her
was less than adequate, a psychological and personal issue he takes
up again in his seventies in his last novel, *Los años, pequeños días*
(1989).

By the time Fabián entered primary school he already knew how
to read as well as milk cows and ride bareback.[23] At home he had
access to a small library that included the classics, *Don Quijote*, and
the Bible, as well as works by national authors: Luis Dobles Segreda
(his father's cousin), Carmen Lyra,[24] Magón,[25] Aquileo J. Echeverría,
and Isaías Gamboa as well as some foreign authors. Fabián remembers the importance of the arts in his formative years: "Yo me crié
en una familia donde el toquecillo mágico de la música y la literatura estaba muy presente"[26] [I was raised in a family where the magic
touch of music and literature was ever present].

The Dobles family, while not rich, was comfortable. Fabián remembers wanting a tricycle, for example, but never getting one. Es-
sentials, however, were always provided, "comíamos bonito, siempre
carnita y huevo, eso sí"[27] [we used to eat well, always meat and eggs,

Dobles at the presentation of his *Obras Completas*, 1993.

at the very least]. Furthermore, all ten survived into old age despite a serious typhoid epidemic in the 1920s that decimated the country's poor and almost killed his sister Alicia, (my mother-in-law). Despite the state of medicine at the time, more like magic than science, "magia y presencia psíquica" [magic and psychic presence], Fabián credits his father with the survival of the family: "mi papá debe haber sido muy buen médico porque todos pegamos"[28] [my father must have been a very good doctor because all of us made it].

In 1929 the Great Depression hit Costa Rica especially hard. Fabián was only eleven but already helping his father keep track of patients and accompanying the doctor on his rounds. He remembers passing a funeral procession for a child and hearing his father say, "Fabiancito, se me mueren de hambre" [Fabiancito, they're dying on me of hunger], a remark that made such an impression on him that he recalls it often in interviews and includes it *verbatim* later in a short story and again in a novel. The central themes of poverty, hunger, malnutrition, and death, fundamental in almost all of his narrative production, stem from this period. What stayed with him over the years was his father's desperation that as a doctor he could do nothing: "Hambre es la peor enfermedad de nuestro pueblo"[29] [Hunger is the worst illness of our people].

For secondary school, Dobles went to the capital, San José, where he lived with his aunt, his mother's oldest sister. He entered Colegio Seminario, run by German priests, and then switched to Liceo de Costa Rica where he graduated in 1935 as a *Bachiller* in Literature and Science and where he later went back to teach in 1957. At fourteen he read *Don Quijote*, which never ceased to influence him over his lifetime, and at sixteen he attempted to memorize the *Larousse Dictionary*. He stopped after memorizing from *A* to *G* only because the exercise seemed futile, but his ability to memorize, his concern with detailed recollection, and his fascination with language are clearly present at this early age even in this misguided enterprise.

His high-school years acquainted him with important authors and with two young and influential professors, Isaac Felipe Azofeifa and Carlos Monge Alfaro, two of the canonical names in the development of Costa Rican literature.[30] He also met and formed a lifelong friendship with Isabel Carvajal, later known as Carmen Lyra, another icon in Costa Rican literature. Fabián first became aware of his vocation to write during his adolescence, after producing some lyric poetry and a few short stories. Especially important, not only for Fabián but also for all the young writers of the period (Yolanda Oreamuno, Elizabeth Odio, and Isabel Carvajal), was Joaquín García Monge, founder and editor of *Repertorio Americano*, an influential literary magazine of the period that circulated both nationally and internationally.

During Fabián's adolescence Dr. Dobles became extremely ill and retired on a small pension, severely limiting the family economically. Fabián and his brothers, Alejo and Alvaro, were all still in high school. Margarita, who had just been named to a teaching position in the Escuela Normal, and her older sister, Susana, who earned a small income from sewing, helped put the three younger brothers through school.

Soon after his graduation from high school in 1935, Fabián entered law school at the University of Costa Rica and began six years of study graduating with a *Bachiller* in Law in 1941. He continued his study toward the next degree, the *Licenciatura* in Law, but never finished. He remembers that in Costa Rica at that time, there were few choices in higher education: law, agronomy, and pharmacy. His family could not afford to send him abroad to medical school, and he could never see himself as a pharmacist "llenando papelitos" [filling out little forms]. The University of Costa Rica had not yet opened other majors like philology, philosophy, and history, and would not until 1940. Looking back, he thought he might even have enjoyed studying science. While he read law he also worked in the legal section of the Patronato Nacional de Infancia [the National Child Protection Agency] until 1942, turning his entire meager salary over to his mother.[31] In 1942, he married Cecilia Trejos, started a family, and began work at the newly created Caja Costarricense de Seguro Social [Costa Rican Social Security Agency] where he did his most prolific writing until he, along with many other government employees, were summarily fired after the 1948 Civil War.

The decade prior to the Civil War in Costa Rica was an interesting political moment in the country. President Dr. Rafael Angel Calderón Guardia had initiated broad social reforms, one of which was the creation of the Social Security system in a masterfully handled and unorthodox alliance between the government, the Communist Party, and the local Catholic Church. The country had suffered the banana strike of 1934, immortalized in Carlos Luis Fallas' important novel *Mamita Yunai* (1941) and from a distance, but with vested interest, the country watched the painful Spanish Civil War (1936–1939) and the rise and fall of Nazism and fascism during World War II (1940–1945).

Fabián was reading international writers like Thomas Mann, Marcel Proust, William Faulkner, and Hermann Hesse as well as Latin Americans: Ciro Alegría, Jorge Icaza, Mario Azuela, and Eduardo Mallea. In addition, he wrote his thesis on family law based on his experience in PANI (Patronato Nacional de la Infancia). Ironically, he was never able to take the time off from work to defend it. Years later he rediscovered the manuscript among other old papers and subsequently buried it underneath the house he was building in the country. During this decade he began feverishly writing fiction: *Aguas turbias* (written in 1940, published in 1943); *Ese que llaman pueblo* (1942); *Una burbuja en el limbo* (1946); a collection of short stories, *La rescoldera* (1947); as well as essays published in local newspapers. What is more, he was teaching part time at the University of Costa Rica and the now defunct Universidad Obrera [Workers University].

In competition with eighteen novels, Dobles' first novel *Aguas turbias,* won first place in a controversial decision that awarded three first-place prizes.[32] The other two first-place awards went to *Pedro Ar-*

náez by José Marín Cañas, an older, more experienced writer, and *Por tierra firme* by Yolanda Oreamuno, who was also of Fabián's generation. Two other novels in this same competition were highly recommended by the panel of distinguished judges:[33] *El valle nublado* by Abelardo Bonilla (later well-known for his *Historia y antología de la literatura costarricense,* 1957) and *11 Grados latitud norte* by León Pacheco, another prominent figure in Costa Rican letters. *Mamita Yunai* by Carlos Luis Fallas was disqualified for having had sections previously published. With these six novels, 1940 became a watershed year in the development of Costa Rican narrative.

The revolutionary change that many critics credit Dobles with initiating and that moved Costa Rican narrative away from traditional *costumbrista* writing and for the first time problematized the situation of the *campesino* was beginning to be noticed both inside Costa Rica and abroad. As early as 1945, Dobles was recognized as an important writer by an American critic: "Fabián Dobles is an accomplished writer with more than ordinary ability at plot construction . . . [His novels] have interest beyond the localness of their scenes, and their social significance is certainly as apparent as that of *The Grapes of Wrath* or *Tobacco Road.*"[34]

This same watershed year for the Costa Rican novel, 1940, also saw the foundation of the Centro para el Estudio de los Problemas Nacionales [the Center for the Study of National Problems] formed by a group of young university students from middle-class backgrounds. Fabián was a member and until 3 October 1941, formed part of the editorial board for the group's official journal *Surco.*[35] During this period an unusual alliance formed between the official party, el Partido Republicano Nacional [National Republican Party] of Calderón Guardia and the Communist Party, both opposed to government by the conservative national oligarchy. In the Center for the Study of National Problems, a subgroup began to form that was also opposed to government by the oligarchy but that was fiercely anticommunist. This group ultimately backed a young businessman, José Figueres Ferrer, in his successful fight to depose Calderón in 1948 and restructure Costa Rica's government. Fabián, who had begun to lean increasingly to the left, backed Calderón's government in the short but violent Civil War of 1948, and suffered both immediate and long-term consequences for his alliance with the losing side.

With the triumph of José (Don Pepe) Figueres and what later became his new party Liberación Nacional [National Liberation], supporters of Calderón Guardia and the communists were forced out of government institutions. Dobles was imprisoned twice, once for a month and a half for reading his poems over the radio during the fighting to encourage the government troops, and again later for a week for allegedly hiding weapons.[36] But worse and more long-lasting were the economic problems caused by the loss of his job. He was not alone, of course, and remembers:

> miles de costarricenses . . . Pero los trabajadores manuales a quienes echaron . . . se podían defender más. Conseguían trabajo. Pero a los intelectuales, nos va muy feo. Porque uno no tiene otro modo de trabajar que con la cabeza.[37]

> [thousands of Costa Ricans . . . But the manual laborers they fired . . . recovered more quickly. They found work. But intellectuals don't do as well. Because we have no other means of working but with our heads.]

During the fifties, the country entered a period of extreme conservatism that severely affected Dobles' artistic production as well as his reputation as a novelist: "En 1953–54–55 nos encontramos en Costa Rica quienes perdimos en la guerra civil de 1948 . . . en un estado de ostracismo casi equivalente a un destierro intra-fronteras"[38] [In 1953–54–55, those of us who lost in the 1948 Civil War found ourselves . . . in a state of ostracism almost equivalent to exile within our own national borders]. The irony is that Dobles claims never to have been an important member of the Center for the Study of National Problems, or much of an activist for the Communist Party: "No tengo vocación política . . . Mi vocación eran mis letras. Amo la palabra"[39] [I have no political vocation . . . My vocation was always my writing. I love words]. There was no one more surprised than he when Abelardo Bonilla classified his novels as "Marxist"[40] in his *Historia de la literatura costarricense* (1957). Years later, Dobles still quarrels with the label, this time in reference to Anderson Imbert: "Un comentarista y escritor muy conocido, argentino, catalogó en un libro sobre literatura latinoamericana como obras marxistas (¡Qué tontería más grande!) mis novelas. Stalin nos hubiera mandado fusilar a ambos"[41] [One well-known Argentinean critic and writer in his book on Latin American literature labeled my novels as Marxist. (How ridiculous!) Stalin would have ordered both of us shot]. On the contrary, Dobles has insisted throughout his life on the personal nature of his convictions:

si usted capta en mi escritura una actitud de denuncia y afán de influir
emocional e intelectualmente en los lectores para que sientan y piensen
en determinado sentido social, humano, político o como quiera llamar-
lo, esto se me dio como un asunto totalmente personal. Ni el partido ni
nadie me lo pidió o sugirió.[42]

[If you detect in my writing a critical stance and an attempt to influence
my readers emotionally and intellectually to feel and think in a certain
way socially, humanly, politically or however you want to call it, this came
about as a totally personal matter. Neither the party nor anyone else
asked or suggested it.]

Dobles' writing, however, never paid the bills;[43] "nunca ha vivido
de su pluma"[44] [he has never lived from his pen] and he was forced
during the decade after the war to work in whatever he could. He
sold bedspreads in the central market and ran a small artisan weaving shop from the back of his house. Later he delivered milk for
almost two years getting up at three in the morning to begin his
rounds, and finally, thanks to his brother Alvaro, a successful architect, he managed a factory for making doors and windows. Although
his continued economic difficulties severely reduced his available
time to write, his creative efforts continued. His most famous novel
El sitio de las abras won the September 15 prize in Guatemala in 1947
and was finally published there in 1950. His book of poems *Verdad
del agua y el viento* (1949) won the September 15 prize in Guatemala
in 1948, and his novel about his prison experiences, *Hombres en tres
tiempos*, later published in 1962 as *Los leños vivientes*, was stopped in
mid-printing in 1954 by the Imprenta Trejos Hnos when the director of the editorial "se enteró de su contenido"[45] [discovered what
it was about]. At this point Dobles began the Tata Mundo stories "en
clave, modo y tono totalmente distinto" [in a totally distinct code,
method and tone]. They were published in 1955 by the same editorial that had stopped publication of his earlier novel. The publisher
felt that *Historias de Tata Mundo*, however, were "INOFENSIVAS"[46]
[INOFFENSIVE].

Not only was Dobles' artistic production affected but also his reputation as a novelist. His novel *Una burbuja en el limbo* was burned.[47]
His work, along with that of Carlos Luis Sáenz and Carlos Fallas, was
removed from high-school libraries in what Fabián referred to later
as "Marcarthyismo a la costarricense"[48] [Marcarthyism Costa Rican
style]. As Moreno explains: "Luego de los sucesos de 48, su obra
escrita, inseparable de su persona, entró por el camino de la sos-

pecha"[49] [After the events of 1948 his writing, inseparable from his person, was viewed with suspicion]. Because of this inhospitable political climate, Dobles wrote essays more than anything else in the 1950s, defending his ideas about art, literature, and politics and the role of the artist. Dobles argued then as well as later that art should function "al servicio de la redención humana"[50] [for human redemption] never for art's sake alone.

The Cuban Revolution in 1959 deeply affected Costa Rica as it did elsewhere in Latin America and the world at large. While at first revolutionary ideas abounded in the country, soon, and under the continued pressure of United States policy, Costa Rica broke diplomatic relations with Cuba and became fiercely anti-Castro. The Communist Party, which had been dissolved in 1949 by a clause in the new constitution, was not legalized again until 1975. Furthermore, the new Socialist Party with Fabián as its first president was declared antidemocratic and illegal in 1960.

In 1958, he was offered a position to teach Spanish and English, first in the Napoleón Quesada High School and then in the Liceo Costa Rica, with little more training in English than some dictionaries and evening BBC radio programs. He prides himself that he always received excellent teaching evaluations and was even described by one of his evaluators as having an English accent (clearly the influence of the BBC). On 10 March 1962, after a visit to Cuba with one of his daughters, he was summarily dismissed from the Liceo Costa Rica and accused of using the classroom as a political forum. He forcefully denied such claims and published his defense in two local newspapers.[51] After the purge ("me cortaron el rabito," Dobles' colorful way of saying they fired me), the unofficial communist party helped him economically by assigning him to various duties related to arts and letters:

El Partido Vanguardia Popular, prácticamente semi-clandestino (no estaba reconocido públicamente) me empleó como corrector de pruebas y periodista en su periódico, como sustituto de director de una revista . . . Hacía boletines . . . Era un sueldito malo. Pero yo me ayudaba con traducciones . . . de inglés y hasta de francés.[52]

[The Popular Vanguard Party, practically semiclandestine (it was not officially recognized) hired me as a copy editor and reporter for its newspaper and as a substitute for its journal director . . . I did bulletins . . . It was a meager salary. But I added to it with translations . . . from English and even from French.]

He represented the party in several international peace conferences: Helsinki in 1955, Moscow in 1962, and Cuba also in 1962. Curiously, he hated traveling abroad: "se conoce, a mi no me hace feliz, estar fuera de aquí, así es. Desde que salgo voy deseando regresar"[53] [you know, I'm not happy being away from home. From the moment I leave I want to come back] and in another interview he put it more poetically: "La tierra mía me jala, me tiene aquí sembrado"[54] [My native land pulls me; I am rooted here]. He also worked during the 1960s for the Editorial Universitaria Centroamericana (EDUCA) [The Central American Universities Press].

Despite his personal and economic problems in Costa Rica, Dobles began making a name for himself outside of Central America as early as 1955, an unusual feat given the limited number of copies available in the first printings of any of his works and the tendency of the metropolis to ignore literature produced in the periphery. Nevertheless, ever since one of his stories appeared in 1955 in *Panorama del cuento centroamericano* along with stories by Quiroga, Borges, Carpentier, Cardenal, Arévalo, García Márquez, Rulfo and other famous Latin American writers, his international recognition began to grow, albeit slowly.[55] In 1962, Dobles was finally able to publish *Los leños vivientes,* and in 1967, his narrative *En el San Juan hay tiburón* won the annual Costa Rican "Aquileo J. Echeverría" prize for novel.

Finally in 1968, Fabián Dobles was awarded the most coveted national prize for achievement in the arts, El Premio Magón. He had just turned fifty. The prize included a small lifetime pension with which Dobles was able to retire to a farm in San Isidro de Heredia he had purchased earlier with the earnings from a successful lawsuit, one of the two cases he ever took to court.[56] He called his farm "El sitio de las abras" after his most famous novel. During the 1970s he began to reedit some of his works. *El sitio de las abras,* for example, was almost completely rewritten, cutting some 20 percent of the novel by paring down style and pruning language.[57] (The novel has frequently been on required high-school reading lists published by Costa Rica's Ministry of Education.) Dobles also continued to work with the Editorial Costa Rica and in 1973, was named to its editorial board along with other prestigious artists and colleagues.

The Editorial Universitaria Centroamericana (EDUCA) published an anthology of some of his best short stories, *Cuentos de Fabián Dobles* (1971), and in 1980, he was named to the Costa Rican Academy of the Language, a position he held until his death. During his work at the Editorial Costa Rica, he had an unusual experience, a "reencuentro" [reencounter] with his longtime political enemy José Figueres Ferrer, now in old age turned writer. Dobles, without a trace of resentment, wrote a sympathetic prologue to Figueres' collection of stories, *Así nacen las palabras y los cuentos* (1977) and managed to parody the opening of Cervantes' *Don Quijote de la Mancha* at the same time:

> Cuando, en el año de . . . cuyo nombre no quiero acordarme ahora, aquel don José Figueres de armas tomar escribía con balas guerra que aún se discute y un poeta de las milicias vanguardistas le disparaba octosílabos desde una radioemisora popular—como si con versos pudieran atajarse fuerzas incontrastables—, de seguro que ni el hombre de guerra ni el muchacho de pluma hubieran podido vaticinar, rompiendo barreras temporales infranqueables, que en los umbrales de un libro de este don José Figueres de hoy, en el año de 1977, el de los octosílabos vendría a descorrer telón para ofrecerles a los lectores las narraciones de don José.[58]

> [When, in the year . . . whose name I do not wish to remember, one José Figueres took up arms and wrote with bullets that are still remembered and a poet of the military vanguard shot off octosyllabic lines from a popular radio station—as if with verses these incontrovertible forces could be stopped—, surely neither the man of war nor the boy with the pen could have foretold, by breaking the impassable barriers of time, that for the introduction of a book by this same José Figueres of today, in the year 1977, the boy of the octosyllabic lines would raise the curtain to offer his readers the narratives of don José.]

More than twenty years after the publication of his last novel *En el San Juan hay tiburón* (1967), Dobles published, *Los años, pequeños días* (1989), a work quite different in style and subject matter from his earlier realistic narratives. Here, in what is clearly an autobiographical text, Dobles struggles with the personal, psychological, and existential issues that haunted him for a lifetime.

The year 1993 was a stellar one for Dobles, then seventy-five years old. Farben Grupo Editorial Norma published a third edition of *Los años, pequeños días*. In addition, the Universidad Estatal de Distancia (UNED) brought out a special volume, illustrated with watercolors by celebrated Costa Rican artist Luis Daell, of his now classic collection *Historias de Tata Mundo*. Most importantly, in the same year his *Obras completas* in five volumes, a tribute to his fifty-year literary ca-

reer, was published in a joint venture between the Editorial Universidad Costa Rica and the Editorial Universidad Nacional, sparking
renewed critical interest and evaluation of his writing.[59] One reviewer labeled him "el más lírico de los novelistas sociales, el más
social de los poetas y el mejor cuentista de la generación de 1940"[60]
[the most lyrical of the social novelists, the most social of the poets
and the best storyteller of the Generation of 1940]. A younger col-
league, however, Rodrigo Soto, wrote the most moving tribute to Fabián:

> La literatura de un país no es una cosa lineal que se construye sólo desde
> el pasado hacia el presente, depende también de la lectura y elaboración
> que cada generación hace de la tradición y el pasado. Como en su novela
> [*Los años, pequeños días*], en donde tanto peso tiene la reconciliación
> final del joven con el padre, así también yo, y creo que casi todos los
> escritores de mi generación, tuvimos que aprender a leerlos, valorarlos
> y quererlos. Pero finalmente lo hicimos.
>   Y no imagina usted la dicha que me da poder decírselo.[61]

> [A country's literature is not linear, constructed only from the past to
> the present; it also depends on the reading and elaboration that each
> generation makes of tradition and of the past. Just as in your novel (*Los
> años, pequeños días*), where the final reconciliation between a young man
> and his father is so important, I, too, and, I think, almost every writer of
> my generation, had to learn to read, value, and love them. But finally we
> did.
>   And you cannot imagine how fortunate I feel in being able to say this
> to you.]

At the age of seventy-nine, on 22 March 1997, Fabián Dobles died
at his home in San Isidro de Heredia. He was survived by his wife,
Cecilia Trejos, five daughters, numerous grandchildren, nieces and
nephews, two sisters, Margarita and Marielos, and his younger
brother Alvaro. His passing was mourned not only by his family and
friends, at home and abroad, but also by the entire country, which
offered countless tributes and memorials in his honor. Alfonso
Chase, critic and longtime friend, summed up, perhaps more co-
gently than anyone else, the importance of Fabián Dobles within
Costa Rican letters:

> Fue uno de los mejores y lúcidos escritores de Costa Rica, cuyo oficio
> abrió caminos y estableció nuevos umbrales, los cuales él traspasó con

inteligencia y sensibilidad hasta convertirse en un clásico de nuestra cultura.[62]

[He was one of the best and most lucid writers from Costa Rica, and his work opened doors and established new thresholds that he traversed with intelligence and sensitivity until he became himself a classic of our culture.]

Perhaps the most genuine tributes, however, came throughout Fabián's lifetime from some of the very people he wrote about: "personas que, sin saber quién era yo, me recomendaban leer mis novelas o mis cuentos, porque Valían la Pena"[63] [people who, without realizing who I was, recommended I read my own novels or stories because they were Worth It].

After his death, Dobles' work continues to be reedited, translated, and analyzed. He has been the subject of numerous national and international theses, critical articles, and tributes and his writing will undoubtedly continue to provoke more and varied critical response. In his own words, as he remembers all the accomplishments of his life, which included learning to swim and climb trees, play the piano "con perdón a Scarlatti y Mozart" [begging the pardon of Scarlatti and Mozart], boxing, which he gave up "cuando me quebraron la nariz" [when they broke my nose], avid soccer fan his entire life and team player until his forties, "como bailarín aficionado ni se diga. Tocador de dulzaina y tenor fracasado" [not to mention avid dancer, harmonica player and failed tenor], in addition to the numerous and various occupations he took on to feed his family over the years, he includes almost as an afterthought: "Además, y junto a toda esa práctica de haceres, he escrito algunos versos, novelas y cuentos"[64] [In addition, and together with all these other occupations, I have written some verses, novels and stories]. As Alfonso Chase wrote on the back cover of a new collection of some of Dobles' most famous stories, hand-picked for inclusion by Dobles himself shortly before his death: "Es, más que todo, la afirmación de Dobles como el más completo narrador de su generación y piedra fundamental para la construcción del universo narrativo del presente siglo"[65] [This book is, above all, the affirmation of Dobles as the most complete narrator of his generation and the cornerstone for the construction of this century's narrative universe]. It is unlikely Fabián Dobles will lose his revered place in the canon of Costa Rican literature, and with any luck ("si Dios quiere" [God willing] as the Costa Ricans say), he will be remembered elsewhere also as a noble man and a master storyteller.

2

The Early Novels

Aguas turbias. San José: Editorial Letras Nacionales, 1943; second edition, San José: Editorial Costa Rica, 1983; third edition, Heredia: EUNA, 1995.

Ese que llaman pueblo. San José: Editorial Letras Nacionales, 1942; second edition, San José: Editorial Trejos Hnos, 1968. Subsequent editions, San José: Editorial Costa Rica, 1977, 1982, 1984, 1985, 1995.

AGUAS TURBIAS

TURNING SPECIFICALLY TO DOBLES' FIRST NOVEL *AGUAS TURBIAS* [MUDDY waters], written in 1940, although not published until 1943, one contextual and biographical point needs to be emphasized. Namely, Dobles was very young, just twenty-two, and his narrative inexperience shows along with his promise. Despite overall excellent reviews of the novel, Dobles is criticized privately for technical mistakes:

> falta de unidad en la narración; exceso de dramaticidad sentimental; dispersión en los temas; exageración a ratos del lenguaje popular, aunque ciertos diálogos son lo mejor que he leído en 'tico', sin excluir a Aquileo o a Carmen Lyra; falta de madurez y realismo en ciertas relaciones humanas, especialmente las amorosas.[1]

> [lack of narrative unity; excess of sentimental drama; dispersion of themes; exaggeration at times of popular language, although certain dialogues are the best I have read in Costa Rican speech, including Aquileo or Carmen Lyra; lack of maturity and realism in certain human relationships, especially amorous ones].

Along with the criticism, however, comes the advice: "ensaye el cuento y el teatro, pero, por Dios Santo, *no deje de escribir novelas*"[2] [try to write short stories and plays, but for heaven's sake, *don't stop writing novels*]. Overall, this favorable evaluation was also the opinion of the panel of judges who awarded *Aguas turbias* one of the three first-place prizes in the contest of unpublished novels sponsored by Farrar and Reinhart.[3] Forty-three years later with the publication of the novel's second edition, Dobles remarks on the book's continued political relevance:

> Los problemas y situaciones que plantea la novela ya no son los mismos, aunque esencialmente sí. [Read: sí pero no]. Siguen pareciéndose. Porque fíjate que ahora ya no es sólo el campesino endeudado hasta la muerte, sino el país endeudado hasta la muerte.[4]

> [The problems and situations that the novel poses are no longer the same, although in essence they are. (Read: *sí pero no*).They continue to be similar. Because you can see that it is no longer just the farmer who is in debt until he dies, but the country as well].

Aguas turbias is divided into four parts and revolves around two principal characters: Moncho and Ninfa. The first part develops the character of Juan Ramón (Moncho) López, a *campesino* who makes contraband liquor (*el chirrite* in Costa Rican Spanish), and his romantic involvement with Chela, the daughter of the town's richest and most influential man. It ends with Moncho's arrest when his still (*alambique*) is discovered and his subsequent sentence to two years in jail. The second part of the novel develops the second major character, Ninfa Ledezma, a poor *campesina* who ends up living and working with Moncho's mother. The third section, which begins after Moncho is out of prison and after his former girlfriend, Chela, has married someone else, ends with the marriage of Moncho and Ninfa. The novel, following Romantic expectations, should end here, but Dobles adds a fourth section that subverts the Romantic paradigm with a naturalistic ending. Moncho and his young son die leaving Ninfa totally devastated.

Interwoven in this structural framework is the paradoxical theme of alcohol. As long as Moncho runs his still, a crime within a system where the state maintains a monopoly on the production of alcohol, he is successful both socially and economically. He is young, rebellious, irreverent and courts the most desired young lady in town (Chela). The fact that he gets drunk when he pleases makes him even more *macho* and his challenge to official culture (both in terms of liquor and language) contributes to his personal image and identity. Even after two years in prison, Moncho continues to make contraband liquor, only now with greater precautions to evade capture by the authorities.

Despite his personal and economic success, his new girlfriend Ninfa wants him to give up the contraband business and legitimize himself, that is, incorporate himself into the system. To comply with her request he must first deny his carefully constructed cultural and personal identity and take on a neocolonial one. Moncho finally agrees to a conventional life, to work his farm, abandon his still, and marry Ninfa. Ironically, however, his situation then begins to deteriorate. Instead of the "happily ever after" ending that neocolonial ideology and Romantic tradition would predict, his farm loses money; Moncho dies in an accident; the loan shark (significantly Chela's father) takes the farm from Moncho's mother and wife and leaves them homeless.

Clearly, the moral position that finds intrinsic fault in fabricating contraband alcohol has been subverted. The most transparent expression of this subversion comes from the police themselves who despise the very man who shows them the location of Moncho's still. They dub him Judas. They see nothing inherently wrong with making alcohol, "pero si es que hacer guaro no es portase mal! Hasta nosotros que somos de la ley lo sabemos"[5] [but making liquor is not bad. Even those of us who represent the law know that]. The local police make a clear distinction between behavior that is immoral and that which is merely illegal. Arresting a *contrabandista* is simply part of their job that allows them to earn "un sueldillo regular" (91) [a regular small salary]. Moncho, speaking with the rural Costa Rican dialect that Dobles represents phonetically, also conceptualizes the issue in similar terms:

> Hacer guaro no es nada malo . . . Que es contra la ley? Güeno: cuando la ley está a contra de uno, no hay más que enfrentase con la ley . . . Quién cres que hace el guaro que se vende en todo el páis? El Gobierno. Y a uno que tiene que jodese media alma pa hacelo, lo engayolan por fabricase un poquillo. No es justo eso! (181)

> [Making liquor is not bad . . . So it's against the law? Well: when the law is against a person, there's nothing else to do but oppose the law . . . Who do you think makes the liquor that's sold all over the country? The Government. And for the little guy who has to work his ass off to make it, they stick him in jail for making just a little. That's not justice.]

In spite of Moncho's apparent political and social consciousness, he renounces his illegitimate business to please Ninfa and his mother and even runs for political office (*Agente de Policía*) in an attempt to integrate himself more fully into the system. Election day exposes the complex and duplicitous function of liquor within the neocolonial system. The state, which of course maintains a monopoly on the production of alcohol, closes the bars and *cantinas* during the election under the rationale of maintaining social order. The state's directive, however, ultimately serves its own political advantage by implicitly fostering a different sort of control. By closing the bars, the state actually transfers real control of the masses to its own political party. Richer and more powerful than opposition parties, it can afford to supply the voters with alcohol under the table in exchange for their votes. It is the state's way of helping the state:

> La taberna del barrio está cerrada. Sin embargo, muy pronto en la voz de los campesinos que van a votar se siente el olor del guaro, porque en la casa que está ubicada en el lugar más vecino a la Mesa, hay una garrafa . . . Por allá, un hombre . . . habla y palmotea a todos los que salen ya apuntalados de ron. (213)

> [The tavern in the neighborhood is closed. Nevertheless, very soon you can smell the whiff of liquor in the voices of the farmers who are going to vote, because in the house closest to the voting booth there is a jug . . . Over there is a man . . . who talks and pats everyone on the back who leaves already propped up by rum.]

Moncho, who is running for office with the opposition party, has no chance of winning under such a system. Furthermore, his political loss only engenders increased economic losses and frustrations. The state, whose discourse officially supports democratic elections, hypocritically corrupts them. Neocolonial ideology, which promises economic reward for hard (legitimate) work, has no intention of delivering. Underlying this scene is the unofficial policy of *sí pero no* that the Costa Rican vernacular so accurately captures and expresses.

The question, then, becomes one of how to resist neocolonial authority—how to subvert the power structure's control not only of language but also of alcohol. Clearly, covert challenge (Moncho's still) or open affront (Moncho riding into town drunk in the middle of Mass) are viable possibilities that Dobles considers. Another possibility, however, introduced to Moncho by a left-wing political instigator, is not to drink at all. Although the other *campesinos* laugh at the revolutionary who is handing out pamphlets, Moncho befriends him

and offers him a drink—the outward cultural sign of friendship
among "men." The revolutionary thanks Moncho but explains that
he does not drink (226), a symbolic rejection of the sociopolitical
system and a method that Moncho himself has already uncon-
sciously begun to employ: "Tan rajón antes, y hora es raro hasta que
se zampe un guarazo" (177) [Such a hard drinker before, and now
he rarely takes a swig].

For the Costa Rican *campesino*, the ability to handle one's liquor is
a sign of a man's *machismo*, a fundamental part of his cultural and
sexual identity. The fact that Moncho rarely drinks now is interpre-
ted as diminished sexual prowess. Dobles' strategy, however, is to
show that this popular view of alcohol plays into the hands of the
power structure. Participating by opposition in the neocolonial utili-
zation of alcohol is still a form of participation. The trick for colonized people is to disentangle themselves from the dominant
ideology and its mechanisms of control. Consequently, Dobles offers
an alternative view through the figures of the young unnamed revolutionary, the *campesino* Moncho, and later Moncho's son. He makes
it clear that refusal to drink parallels a refusal to participate in the
system. It is a politically charged decision.

Alcohol, however, functions as a double-edged sword, a form of
control that can backfire on the ruling class. Significantly, Chela's
father, the town's money lender, is disgustingly drunk at her wedding: "Repleto su estómago de tragos . . . sufriendo de hipo. Su voz
. . . gangosa, humedecida por el licor que aun le apesta la boca"
(103) [His stomach full of alcohol . . . hiccupping. His voice . . .
thick and wet with the liquor that still stinks in his mouth]. The rest
of the guests are also drunk: "Ya bastantes hombres y unas cuantas
mujeres con el guaro subido" (101) [Already plenty of men and
even several women are tipsy]. The mention of women drinking is
also significant. Given that one cultural indicator of masculinity is
the ability to handle one's liquor, the logical consequence is that the
same behavior in women is anti-feminine. (Dobles makes full use of
this cultural myth in his next novel). The fact that at the wedding,
not only Chela's father is drunk but also everyone else, emphasizes
the binary opposition that Dobles has established between poor and
rich, moral and immoral behavior, and emphasizes the decadence
of this family and its corresponding segment of society that can so
perversely and repulsively waste and abuse liquor and food. The tension between the opulence of Chela's wedding early in the novel
and the humility of Moncho's funeral near the end is manifest:

"Llega con un jarro y una botella, para repartir guaro, que la vieja, en medio de su dolor, ordenó comprar en la pulpería, para atender como Dios manda a los presentes" (234) [He arrives with a pitcher and a bottle of *guaro* to serve drinks that the old woman, in the midst of her pain, had him buy at the corner store so that they could attend to all the guests as God requires].

Dobles' implicit parallel throughout this novel between language and alcohol is a masterful rhetorical strategy. The colonized must learn when to drink/speak, how to drink/speak, and whether to drink/speak if they are to develop a viable personal and cultural identity that can withstand, defy, challenge, and subvert traditional ideological controls. If one examines the architectonic set up of the Costa Rican *plaza* or downtown, there is a clear colonial metonymic narrative at work. Around the central square, the foundational units of society are strategically placed: the church, the school, the bank, and the *cantina* [bar]. Each of these institutions in one way or another is used to "colonize" or control (convert, educate, finance, sedate) the masses.

Alcohol, in particular, has played an important sociological role in Costa Rican culture. According to common anecdotal complaint, Costa Rica sells more *guaro* [hard liquor] than it does milk. *Guaro*, produced from locally grown sugar cane, has become a de facto national symbol. It is inscribed in songs, jokes, graffiti, stories, and maintains a presence everywhere, in parties, meetings, weddings, baptisms, and funerals. No social gathering may take place without the medium of alcohol. Like language, alcohol offers the illusion of a window through which to view the world; it functions as a medium of communication and exists as a presence in itself. Like language, alcohol has been imposed on colonial (slave) populations as a form of control. Dobles intuitively senses the possibilities for subverting the literary presence of *guaro* in much the same way he subverts official language, by culturally situating its use.

On the one hand, Costa Ricans of all classes use alcohol as a socializing agent. It functions both as a vehicle that promotes gaiety, disinhibits, and relaxes its user and as a sedative to dull emotional and physical pain. Moral constraints, however, vex its use: alcohol is held responsible for a vast variety of social miseries, and church and state hold the individual responsible for its abuse. From Dobles' left-wing sociological perspective, however, alcohol abuse is the product of exploitative social and economic conditions; that is, neither alcohol nor the individual are inherently at fault for human suffering, but rather the structure of oppression that produces misery and then provides the masses with a drug to anesthetize its pain.

In Costa Rica the state has historically played an ambiguous *sí pero no* role in regard to alcohol. On the one hand, during the historical period encompassed by *Aguas turbias,* the government held a monopoly on the production of liquor; on the other, it was also responsible for the prevention of its abuse and the treatment of alcoholism. This double view is reaffirmed by society at large in its moral and religious condemnation of alcohol as alternatively an agent that is responsible for a multitude of psychosocial problems and/or a product of those very problems versus the opinion that it facilitates recreation, relaxation, and friendship among "men."

Dobles not only plays with the thematic nuances of how drinking functions in his culture, he also manipulates it for structural and narrative ends. In one sense Dobles utilizes liquor like language to promote and carry the narrative. Drinking loosens the tongue and provides the occasion for meeting and conversing, for exchanging stories. People drink and talk, and talk about drinking. Dobles, posing as the ultimate bartender, listens, sympathizes, and then recreates.

ESE QUE LLAMAN PUEBLO

In Dobles' second novel *Ese que llaman pueblo* [what they call town] the rhetorical and thematic use of *guaro* is even keener. People not only drink throughout, but they talk about drinking, what it means, what it causes, how to handle it. Alcohol becomes a material presence, a thing in itself, not just a means to an end, and talking about it underlines a complex dialogic narrative structure. As Alvaro Quesada Soto explains in his introduction to Dobles' *Obras completas, Ese que llaman pueblo*:

> se construye como un contrapunto de various relatos yuxtapuestos que parten de un vértice central—unas fiestas cívicas en la ciudad de San José—, pero extiende sus ramificaciones a través de otras múltiples historias y recuerdos de los personajes. (18)

> [is constructed as a counterpoint to various juxtaposed stories, all connected at a central point—civic festivals in the city of San Jose—, but the novel extends its ramifications through a number of multiple stories and memories of its characters.]

The thematic presence of alcohol in these "fiestas cívicas" acts as a unifying rhetorical device. It functions at a structural level not only to encourage dialogue among the characters but also to provoke behavior that is fundamental to the development of the story. Along the way, it allows Dobles to criticize a wide range of social problems from the inhumane working conditions on the Atlantic Coast banana plantations, "Aquel infierno de jumaos" (294) [That hellhole of drunks] to the country's growing urban/rural conflicts[6] and the ever-present problems of the nation's poor.

Ese que llaman pueblo received good reviews in all of its various editions. Dobles was praised for capturing "la esencia del alma nacional"[7] [the essence of the national soul], for dignifying "lo que es por naturaleza digno; pero que la falsa cultura de los hombres, trata de rebajar a la mera condición vulgar"[8] [what is by nature dignified; but what the falsely cultured try to reduce to mere vulgarity], and for his representation of the resigned *campesino* who stimulates the reader to action.[9] He was also diplomatically criticized, this time publicly by Abelardo Bonilla, for being too naturalistic, one-dimensional, and failing to use his authorial voice:

No puede olvidarse que la obra de arte no es una fotografía imparcial de la vida, sino un producto del autor y que éste es quien forja el plan y la unidad artística, quien siente y piensa y, en una palabra, que domina en la creación de ese mundo literario de la novela.[10]

[You cannot forget that the work of art is not an impartial photograph of life, but a product of an author, and that he is the one who forges an artistically unified plan, who feels and thinks and, in a word, controls the creation of this literary world of the novel.]

While these kinds of evaluations suffer from a certain ingenuousness regarding their own fundamental critical assumptions,[11] the point of Dobles' rhetorical attack is certainly not missed. Clearly, the multivariate and dialogic voices that no doubt exist within the categories of *campesino* and *patrones* must be masked or repressed by Dobles precisely to highlight the polemical opposition between the two groups. Nothing is "naturally" dignified or vulgar, of course; the author imbues certain situations with one or the other of those qualities; reality, as we know, is ultimately a human construct. It is the shape of this construct that is important; Dobles clearly intends to polarize his audience (he is anything but absent),[12] to take aim at the status quo and the feudal power structure that is still very much at the cultural heart of Costa Rican society.

One of the many characters in the novel is a *campesino,* Juan Manuel Anchía, who goes to the capital to recover from a failed love affair. He drinks to alleviate his loneliness and his sense of being out of place and because drinking is the expected behavior of men at these sorts of civic festivals. His use of alcohol, however, is acutely vexed. On the one hand, the popular notion exists that liquor increases a man's sensitivity: "Su cabeza está enrarecida, pero los sentimientos, con el guaro, son más afinados" (331) [His head is muddled, but his feelings, with liquor, are sharper]. On the other hand, drinking in excess exposes him to a series of situations in which he is victimized, partly because the city routinely victimizes those from the country in a form of internal colonialism and partly because Juan Manuel "está algo socao" (337) [is a little drunk]. First, Juan Manuel lends money to a complete stranger. Second, he allows two men he has just met to gamble with his money (and lose). Finally, a prostitute steals what little money he has left while he lies in an alcoholic stupor. For people from the city, Juan Manuel is just another drunken *campesino*: "Ah, el borracho! De dónde habrá salido. Ni siquiera se ha puesto zapatos" (335) [Oh, a drunk! Where in the world did he come from. He doesn't even have shoes]. Lack of shoes, the outward sign of rural origin, is only the beginning of a problem made more complex and acute by drinking.

Juan Manuel's drunkenness is the direct consequence of the sensation of friendship that *guaro* provides; it is communication (language) without words: "Es un trago de amistad que no dice palabras, pero vibra por dentro" (370) [It is a drink of friendship that does not speak words but vibrates inside]. Among "men" this feeling is particularly intense; alcohol facilitates male bonding. After a few drinks two strangers talk like old friends (290). This illusion of friendship, even intimacy, allows a complete stranger to borrow money from Juan Manuel without his having any expectation that the supposed friend will reimburse him, "Y fue por el ron. Qué gran cosa es el ron, a veces" (333) [And it was because of the rum. What a great thing rum is, sometimes]. The key expression here, however, is *a veces* [sometimes].

Although drinking seems to facilitate friendship, sharpen male sensibility, and manifest the *macho* character of the drinker, it easily slips into abuse, another matter, indeed, and one that worries not only the friends and families of drinkers, but also the drinkers themselves. Consequently, there is a great deal of talk about the dangers and consequences of too much alcohol: "un revolcadero" (290) [an upset], "enredos" (291) [complications], fights, thefts, hangovers, "lagunas mentales" (294) [mental lapses] that permit the drinker to forget everything. Then, there are the even more aggravated problems caused by chronic abuse, alcoholism, the state of being "borracho hasta los huesos" (293) [drunk to the bones]. One of Dobles' characters, the gambler who uses Juan Manuel's money, embodies this problem. He has lost his job, his wife and children, but he cannot stop drinking: "Muy a menudo se lo vio [*sic*] borracho. La araña del alcohol le tejía su red en el alma sin consistencia" (344) [Very often he was seen drunk. The spider of alcohol weaving its web in his weak soul]. Poverty intensifies the problem: "Es un vagabundo que jamás tiene dinero y cuando, sabe Dios como, lo consigue, lo bota en las cantinuchas" (351) [He's a vagabond who never has money, and when he gets some, God only knows how, he wastes it in some low-class bar]. Dobles implies, however, that the alcoholic is a case of obsession and chronic excess, a fundamentally personal problem with social ramifications.

Most Costa Ricans drink, however, because the socially perceived benefits are high. For this reason, the temptation to continue drinking is almost irresistible even when "el estómago está resentido" (334) [the stomach is upset] or when the results of excess drinking are clearly visible. Not only does alcohol make the intolerable tolerable, alleviate loneliness, sharpen the senses, and facilitate "male" friendship, but it also functions as the ultimate cultural expression of *hombría* or *machismo*. Juan Manuel, for example, remembers that his father would give him sips of *guaro* even as a child, "Si tomarse un trago es ser hombre" (355) [Having a drink makes him a man]. The on-duty policeman, once again speaking phonetically in the vernacular of Costa Rica's lower classes, is also tempted, "El es autoridad. El no puede dar mal ejemplo . . . Qué carajada es ser polecía" (331) [He represents the Law. He cannot set a bad example . . . What a shitty deal to be a policeman]. The "authority," of course, cannot drink if he is to maintain control, a clear example of how neocolonial domination functions. The problem, however, is that control mechanisms can boomerang; the policeman cannot resist the temptation to drink. The positive effects of drinking ultimately outweigh the policeman's allegiance to the neocolonial authority he serves and he indulges "al reservao, paque no me vean" (331) [discreetly, so nobody will see me]. It is, once again, a case of *sí pero no*, seeming to agree while disagreeing. Later, he buys gum to "apagar con algo el olor de lo que ha bebido" (331) [hide the odor of his drinking].

The issue of women drinking, suggested earlier in *Aguas turbias*, is presented again here with fuller ramifications. Dobles, writing long before feminist attacks on patriarchal control, indicates clearly how popular attitudes toward drinking (internalized from neocolonial ideology) help maintain women in an inferior position to men. If male drinking runs the gamut of respectability from *macho* to "borracho, irresponsable, y degenerado" [drunken, irresponsible, and degenerate], drinking in any amount for women can topple them from the mythological position of Madonna to that of prostitute; that is, drinking for women is the outward sign of a loss of honor. The myth, all too familiar, runs as follows: a woman who drinks loses her defenses against men, who, because of their *machismo*, will therefore take sexual advantage of her. Dobles offers an example in the story of the rape of Natalia, the cook's daughter, by the *gringos* [Americans] who own the banana plantation where her mother works: "le habían dado ron a la chiquilla" (296) [they had given rum to the young girl]. Despite the explicit criticisms here of the abuse of colonial authority and the clear innocence of the victim, the results of women drinking are always the same and must remain so if the cultural fabric of society, that is the status quo, is to be upheld:

> Ahora Natalia se pinta los ojos y los labios, y vive con un *yankee* cuarentón que la alimenta con *brandy* y la enseña a decir *yes* a los otros norteños que la rodean en las veladas como los mosquitos de la costa. (297)

> [Now Natalia paints her eyes and lips and lives with a forty-year-old American guy who gives her brandy and teaches her to say "yes" to the other Yankees who flit around her in the candlelight like mosquitoes from the coast.]

The Yankee imposition of his language "yes" goes hand in hand with the concomitant imposition of his alcohol "brandy." The North American imperialists, of course, do not drink the local brew *guaro*.

Colonial society's control of its colonized, both men and women, in turn provides the pattern for patriarchal society to control its women. The technique is again *sí pero no*. First, phallocentric discourse appears to permit women to drink in moderation: "le susurra que no era mal visto tomar una cerveza" (402) [he whispered to her that it would not look bad to have one beer], but in actuality, the results are the same. The woman ends up a prostitute, "la flor de la virginidad cayó—, como un angelillo de mármol quebrado" (403) [the flower of her virginity toppled—, like a broken marble angel]. Drinking for a woman signifies that she is either a prostitute, a *bruja* [witch], or a bad mother: one female character "se olvidó de que tenía un hijo . . . untado su cuerpo de alcohol" (304) [forgot she had a child . . . her body so soaked in alcohol]. To explain such behavior that challenges the very foundations of patriarchal values, society calls on the supernatural: "la había tentado el pisuicas" (305) [the devil had tempted her]. Thus, a man who drinks in excess is simply "un borracho de todos los días" (361) [an everyday drunk], but a woman who drinks has joined forces with the devil himself. This clear double standard underlies a pattern of injustice that Dobles represents throughout the novel with his various stories of political, social, regional, and sexual victimization.

Dobles' deployment of alcohol as a rhetorical strategy is a careful creative choice. Speaking through his persona, the narrator, Dobles explains that the act of drinking permits the drinkers to reflect on the very behavior in which they are engaged: "Cuando se bebe alcohol, se habla y se llora. Surge lo blanco del alma, y lo negro también; surgen lo gris, la mescolanza, *la vida hecha palabras*" (398; emphasis mine) [When one drinks alcohol, one talks and cries. The whiteness of the soul emerges and the blackness, also; the gray emerges, the mixtures, *life transformed into words*]. Drinking, thus, helps subvert the binary oppositions with which official language controls its speakers (black/white) by interjecting gray, mixtures, *mestizaje*, that is, hybridizations, combinations, and varieties that defy monologic control. Life (reality) is a social construct, a linguistic composition, "la vida hecha palabras," which, Dobles asserts, is continually open to change, subversion and recreation.

3

The Controversial Novels

Una burbuja en el limbo. San José: Editorial L'Atelier, 1946; second edition, San José: Editorial Costa Rica, 1971. Reprints in 1978, 1995 include an introduction by Osvaldo Sauma.

Los leños vivientes. San José: Imprenta Elena, 1962; second edition, San José: Editorial Costa Rica, 1979; third edition, Heredia: Editorial de la Universidad Nacional, 1996.

UNA BURBUJA EN EL LIMBO

DOBLES' THIRD NOVEL, *UNA BURBUJA EN EL LIMBO* [A BUBBLE IN LIMBO], dedicated to his father Miguel,[1] is very different from his previous work. Instead of the broad social indictment to which he had accustomed his public, Dobles narrows his focus to explore the psychology of human subjectivity and individual difference. His sister Margarita calls this novel an autobiographical poem and claims that in terms of subject matter, specifically the problems of adolescence, it was ahead of its time by as much as almost half a century.[2] Dobles' language is also different from his earlier work, less vernacular, less oral, less regional, and for the first time Dobles does not add a glossary of Costa Rican terms at the end of the narrative.

Reviews were mixed and much more restrained in their praise than with the earlier novels.[3] Alberto Cañas, who has reviewed everything Dobles ever wrote, looks back on Dobles' *Obras completas* and states point blank that he felt "descontento" [unhappy] with *Una burbuja en el limbo.*[4] In an earlier review he had faulted the novel precisely for its language and claimed that it suffered from being a transitional piece between his earlier and later work: "Debió ser leve, vivaracha y traviesa, y no lo es: es más bien lenta, prolija, y analítica"[5] [It should have been light, lively, daring, and it's not: instead, it's slow, tedious, and analytical]. While Chase, from his vantage point of fifty years after the publication of the first edition, extols its "vigencia del tema y su alta categoría literaria" [relevance of theme and high literary quality], he admits it is "Novela extraña, es cierto"[6] [Certainly a strange novel]. What little critical study has been made of this book agrees with Chase that the main character, Ignacio Ríos Galarza, is the "símbolo y realidad de la adolescencia"[7] [symbol and reality of adolescence], the "rebel without a cause," the teenager who constantly challenges the authority of the adult world for the sake of challenge alone, "ese ancestral espíritu insurrecto en cada hombre"[8] [that ancestral rebel spirit in every man]. Contemporary recognition of the novel's value in delineating the problems of adolescence in Costa Rica resulted in 1995 in the Ministry of Education's recommendation that seventh graders read this narrative.[9] Autobiographical resonances are manifest from Dobles' own adolescent rebellion (explored more fully in his last novel)[10] as well as an implicit parallel between Dobles and the main character, dissident artists both in a society unable to appreciate art.[11] Certainly, the psychological aspects of this "novela de personaje" or character novel as Chase labels it, merit further exploration. My argument here, however, takes a different route.

The story of Ignacio Ríos, his family, and his *pueblo* [town] (significantly the colonial town of Heredia) may be read as an allegory of the challenges and limitations imposed by colonial ideology and discourse on the native artist. The term "colonial," however, needs some special clarification in the case of Costa Rica and in the specific case of this novel. Costa Rica's colonial history differs dramatically from the rest of Central America's in that the autochthonous indigenous populations were comparatively small and easily marginalized when not eliminated altogether. Furthermore, there was little homogeneity among the few extant Indian groups in the region when compared with the massive Mayan and Aztec populations to the north and the Inca to the south. Costa Rica functioned as a geographical land bridge, an intermediate zone and border territory that saw diminished indigenous populations drifting south and breaking away from northern groups and other peoples wandering north from the South American continent. The phenomenon of Spanish racial mixing with the Indians, *el mestizaje*, therefore, occurred in proportionally less degree. Even today Costa Ricans are predominantly Caucasian and of European descent, more Creole than *mestizo*. The postcolonial notion of *mestizaje*, therefore, must be qualified in the Costa Rican context to mean a social rather than a purely racial mixing.

The Spanish domination of Costa Rica (an ecological conquest over land more so than people) established its language, its religion, its values, its colonial architecture, its institutions, and its worldview with minimal difficulty and virtually no opposition. Costa Rica's independence from Spain in 1821 was never fought for or even particularly desired; it came as a by-product of the independence movement in Guatemala and was foisted gratuitously onto a population that was not at all sure it wanted to be decolonized.[12] In fact, what amounted to the Costa Rican aristocracy was largely in favor of being annexed by Mexico's Emperor Agustín de Iturbide (1783–1824)—a move from one imperial power to another.[13] There was some brief fighting; the aristocrats lost to a nascent populism and nationalism, only to find out (and news traveled slowly) that Iturbide had fallen in Mexico before the fighting in Costa Rica had even begun. Ironically, Costa Rica could not have been annexed by Mexico even if the aristocrats had won.[14]

This is the historical background to which one of the characters in the novel, significantly not a Costa Rican, alludes when he describes Costa Rica as a country in limbo:

Carece del sentido de tragedia. Lo único que hubiera podido mantenerlo, por muy oscuramente que hubiese sido, ya casi no existe aquí: el indio . . . Entiendo que la historia de este país es también una sucesión de tranquilidades ligeramente empañadas de vez en cuando por uno que otro sacudimiento superficial . . . Cada cual siente el deseo de convertirse en un burgués tranquilo, y a eso van, lenta, pero seguramente, los que tengan fortuna, sin nada vital, sin nada trascendental. He allí lo verdaderamente trágico: que por falta de tragedia no podrán crear.[15]

[It lacks a sense of tragedy. The only thing that could have maintained one, however obscurely, no longer exists here: the Indian . . . I understand that the history of this country is a succession of tranquil times sandwiched every so often between some superficial shock . . . Everybody wants to become a complaisant member of the bourgeoisie, and toward this end those fortunate enough march slowly but surely, undisturbed by anything vital, anything transcendental. Here is the real tragedy: that for lack of tragedy they cannot create.]

The colonial mentality in Costa Rica effectively silences native art. Given this historical context, it is revealing to review the reactions to colonialism and independence that Alfred Arteaga outlines in his essay "An Other Tongue."[16] Using Arteaga's terminology, "autocolonialism" (that is, the colonial mentality supported from within) and "nationalism" (that is, the complete rejection of colonial impo-sition) compete for supremacy and control in the political fighting that takes place throughout the novel between conservatives and lib-erals in nineteenth-century Costa Rica, each faction attempting to place its discourse in an authoritative position while discrediting and suppressing any other voice. Ignacio's family, for example, is divided between its conservative and liberal members, each trying to shout down the other, each monologue deaf to its opposition: "lo que sucedía en la calle, lo que se gritaba y hacía en los periódicos y las tribunas públicas, repercutía callada y mordazmente en aquel hogar hasta hacía poco ajeno a tales discordias" (144) [what hap-pened in the street, what was shouted and done in the newspapers and public forums, was reproduced quietly and bitterly in that home that up until recently had not suffered such discord]. Ignacio, the rebellious adolescent, refuses to take part in these mostly verbal, but sometimes physical, power struggles that he rightly sees as authori-tarian discourses both. Instead, his character functions as an attempt to negotiate the discourse of hybridization, which, in the specific case of Costa Rica, may be understood to be social rather than bio-logical *mestizaje.* That is, he is at once a part of his family and society and yet different from them: "Te has rebelado contra Dios, pero no estás tampoco con Satanás" (124) [You have rebelled against God, but you're not on Satan's side either]. He searches for an alternative discourse that can stand in opposition to, but is willing to dialogue with, all authoritarian discourses whether colonialist, autocolonia-list, or nationalist. He is a product of all and none (*sí pero no*).[17] His very identity, therefore, is in question.

¿Por qué yo he de ser Ignacio Ríos y no Juan Porras, o equis equis, o sencillamente no llamarme de ningún modo? Desgraciado el hombre, que no puede vivir de otra manera que siendo fulano o zutano, el hijo de don Pablo, o el sobrino de doña Jacinta, o el nieto de don Pedro. ¿Es que no se puede ser, a secas, sin tener que ser esto o lo otro? . . . Porque los atributos a través de los cuales la gente lo piensa a uno no son de uno. Son suyos. Ella es quien los inventa y luego se los cuelga al fulano para hacerlo ser necesariamente Ignacio Ríos, el hijo de don Pablo el alcalde. (52)

[Why do I have to be Ignacio Ríos and not Juan Porras, or XX, or just not have a name at all? People are so unlucky that they can live no other way but by being Mr. So and So, or Pablo's son, or Jacinta's niece, or Pedro's grandson. Can't a body just simply be, without having to be this

or that? . . . Because the attributes that people give you aren't yours.
They're theirs. People are the ones who invent them and then hang
them around your neck to make you be Ignacio Rios, the son of Pablo,
the mayor.]

Ignacio refers in this quotation to the act of naming as a function
of the dominant discourse. A great deal of energy must be expended
to name, to differentiate *A* from everything that is not *A*, and to enforce those classifications. Adam begins the process in his "colonization" of Eden, turning a natural environment into a social and
linguistic construct by way of language, which, by force, limits, orders, and gives value (or marginalizes) all that is named or denied a
name. Ignacio intuitively understands this power: "Pero que estú-
pido soy. Si yo le pusiera un nombre, la perdería. No, ella ni yo de-
biéramos llamarnos con un nombre" (127) [But I'm so stupid. If I
were to give her a name, I would lose her. No, neither she nor I
should be called by a name]. Naming inscribes the named within
the official discourse. To refuse a name paradoxically asserts independence but ensures marginalization. In effect, one unavoidably
adopts the name of Other (a non-name) and puts oneself in a virtually untenable position within neocolonial script.[18] Once Adam in-
vades Eden and deploys language to conquer and control his
environment, nothing can escape the naming process. The unnamed becomes a negative name and suffers the negative representations of the marginalized Other.

Significantly, Dobles posits Costa Rica in its formative national
stages as a kind of Eden, at least in terms of memory and nostalgia
though such a paradise certainly would hardly correspond to official
historical rendering. Ignacio's grandfather recalls:

No había divisiones de partidos, ni rencores de familias. No existían los
intereses antagónicos. Todos nos ayudábamos los unos a los otros, nos
dolíamos de nuestros enfermos, sentíamos a nuestros muertos . . . Las
gentes se confundían con las gentes, a través de los matrimonios, los
hijos, los nietos. (138–39)

[There were neither party divisions nor resentments among families.
Opposing interests did not exist. We all helped one another; we suffered
with our sick; we grieved for our dead . . . People mixed with other people through marriages, children, and grandchildren.]

Clearly, this privileging of social *mestizaje*, "las gentes se confundían," equates a harmonious mixing with a utopian ideal anterior

and in opposition to the current state of affairs: "Las divisiones empezaron más o menos del setenta en adelante . . . En el ochenta y nueve, nos hallábamos en el reinado del rencor" (139) [The divisions began more or less in the seventies . . . By eighty-nine, we found ourselves in the kingdom of hatred], a situation that has continued, according to Ignacio's grandfather (and most history books) to the present time of the novel, the 1940s.

The metaphor Dobles employs to represent this construct of harmonious mixing or felicitous social *mestizaje* is water. The narrative explains that in the Edenic past the population took its water supply from the various brooks that ran through the city: "de donde los vecinos tomaban lo necesario, sin ensuciar, sin mancillar, dejando para los otros. En las acequias estaba el reflejo de lo que éramos: una sola y grande corriente de agua clara" (139) [from where neighbors took what was necessary, without contaminating, without staining, leaving enough for others. In the streams we saw the reflection of what we were: one great current of clear water]—a precolonial image[19] of nature in its uncorrupted original state, harmonious mixing to the point that difference loses its meaning within the clear water. It is no accident, of course, that Ignacio's last name is Ríos [River] or that his "angels" first appear in water. Neocolonialism and the system of "cañería para el agua" [water pipes] effectively puts an end to Eden in an effort to modernize it. Everything thereafter in postmodern, postcolonial Costa Rica becomes a search for this lost innocence, this time/space that exists only in myth and in the national imaginary. Dobles explains in a review that came out after the first edition in 1946 how his novel corresponds to this search for those precolonial narratives:

> . . . en la anécdota de familia, en la tradición, en el libro de historia. Apenas se ha hecho un escarabajeo ligero por encontrar su sentido. Y una literatura del presente debe buscar sus raíces en el pasado; para entroncarlas con lo actual, y hacerse fuerte. Es el caso general de toda nuestra cultura, empezando por el fenómeno político.
>
> *Una burbuja en el limbo*, de cuyos méritos no soy el llamado a opinar, significa un esfuerzo dirigido a esa exploración legendaria, fabulesca, en los dominios de lo viejo.[20]

> [. . . in family anecdotes, tradition, and history books. The surface has only been scratched to find their meaning. And a literature of the present should look for its roots in the past; to join them with the present

to make them strong. In the general case of our culture, starting with
politics.
    Una burbuja en el limbo, about whose merits I am not qualified to speak,
signifies an effort directed toward this exploration into the legendary,
the fabulous, and the dominions of old.]

Ignacio's presence in the novel becomes a trace of this precolonial innocence at the same time that it offers new possibilities for
mixing with difference; after all, he is the "burbuja" [bubble] in
limbo[21]—unable to exist as a bubble outside his environment, but
clearly different from limbo itself. Psychologically, he symbolizes the
problem of adolescence that strives to express and define itself in an
adult world that discourages originality; politically, he refuses to be
appropriated by dominant autocolonial discourse or its nationalistic
antithesis; artistically, he threatens the official narratives of his culture. Even as a child he subverts the religious binary opposition
Heaven/Hell by claiming that his grandfather visited hell once and
it was a delightful place. The threat of the devil and consequent pun-
ishment in hell used by adult/dominant discourse to control its chil-
dren/colonized holds no sway over Ignacio; he has successfully
challenged this story and its authoritarian neocolonial control. Ignacio then proceeds to subvert the much more intransigent and
foundational binary opposition within scientific discourse, specifically, human biology, the antithesis between life and death. His refusal to accept his grandfather's death provokes an unusual form of
resistance, i.e., psychological (artistic) recreation:

> Nunca pudo olvidarlo. Cuando hubo saboreado hasta el fondo del cáliz
> su ausencia, volvió a recrearlo. El tiempo transcurrido de sus siete a
> doce, catorce, quizá más años, constituyó una constante resurrección del
> abuelo. Y el abuelo era de nuevo real. Lo acompañaba en sus correrías
> por las estrellas. El y él—uno solo—(57)

> [He could never forget him. When he had tasted his absence at the bot-
> tom of the chalice, he recreated him. The time that passed from when
> he was seven until he was twelve, fourteen, perhaps older, constituted a
> continual resurrection of his grandfather. And his grandfather was once
> again real. He accompanied him on his trips through the stars. He and
> he—one person—]

Ignacio's ability to subvert official "truth" is surpassed only by Dobles himself. In fact, Dobles may have missed his true calling as a

comic writer by minimizing in this novel his subversion of official
scripts through humorous recreations. The few examples where he
gives free reign to the rhetorical device of comic subversion are genuine masterpieces. His version of the fall of Lucifer, for example, is
a long quotation and impossible to translate faithfully but well worth
the effort:

> Una vez, antes de que fuera creado el hombre, solo [*sic*] habitaban en
> el Cielo Tatica Dios y los ángeles . . . Dios se pasaba los días sentado en
> su trono, en el centro del Cielo, rodeado por los ángeles y los serafines
> más lindos. Todo transcurría en paz. Pero Luzbella era orgulloso. Sentía
> envidia del Señor. Un día empezó a creer que él podría llegar a ser más
> poderoso que el mismo Dios . . . Dio la casualidad que cierta vez el Todo-
> poderoso tuvo que hacer algo en otra parte del Cielo, y llamando a Luz-
> bella, le ordenó:
> "Cuídame el trono mientras regreso."
> Ya el maldito ángel tenía convencidos por entonces a casi todos los
> demás habitantes del Cielo de que él debía ser su nuevo Señor. "Miren
> ustedes, les había dicho, yo soy fuerte, soy hermoso, y mucho más joven
> que ese tal Tatica Dios, que está ya tan viejo y achacoso. Se va poniendo
> de muy mal genio y va perdiendo iniciativa y popularidad. Debe susti-
> tuirlo sangre joven, gente nueva" . . . Pues bien; se sentó el arcángel
> revolucionario en el trono de Dios y, cuando más tarde este volvió y le
> pidió su lugar, se hizo el tonto y . . . si te oí, no me acuerdo. Por lo que
> Tatica Dios, con una cara que daba miedo de agria y amenazadora le
> dijo: . . . "Quítate de ahí, Luzbel . . . Vete a los infiernos . . ." El Señor
> continuó:
> "Síganle todos aquellos que hayan querido traicionarme."
> Sucedió entonces algo tremendo. Empezaron a salir del Cielo, dispa-
> rados por la ira del Todopoderoso, todos, pero todos los ángeles . . . Con
> lo que, muy asustado Tatica Dios ante tal desbandada que lo iba a dejar
> solo en su Gloria, levantó presurosamente el dedo y exclamó:
> "Ya no más, ya no más. Que cado uno se quede donde está." (23–24)

[Once, before man was created, only Our Father and the angels lived
in Heaven . . . God spent His days sitting on His throne in the center of
Heaven, surrounded by the loveliest of the angels and seraphim. All was
peace. But Lucifer was proud. He envied the Lord. One day he began to
believe that he could be as powerful as God Himself . . . It just so happened that one day the Almighty had to do something in another part
of Heaven, and calling Lucifer, he ordered:
"Watch my throne until I return."
By then the damned angel had convinced almost all the other inhabitants of Heaven that he should be their new Lord. "Look here," he had
told them, "I'm strong, I'm handsome, and I'm a lot younger than Our

Father, who is old now and sickly. He's becoming bad tempered and losing his initiative and popularity. He should be substituted by young
blood, new folks . . ." So there he was, the revolutionary archangel sitting
on the throne of God. Later when God returned and asked for His
throne back, Lucifer pretended not to see Him . . . as if maybe I heard
you, but I don't remember. So Our Father said, with a look that made
you scared it was so bitter and threatening: . . . "Get out of there Lucifer
. . . Go to hell . . ." The Lord continued:
    "Follow him all of you who intended to betray me."
    Something really surprising happened then. Each and every one of
the angels started to leap out of Heaven, as fast as they could, when they
saw the anger of the Almighty. That's when Our Father, frightened in
the wake of such an exodus that was about to leave him all alone in His
Glory, raised His finger quickly and exclaimed:
    "OK, that's it, no more. Everyone stay right where you are."]

Such a recreation of official script provides the background and
context for Ignacio's later artistic subversions, the angels he sculpts
out of wood. His figures are unorthodox, grotesque, comic—clear
representations of the angels in the aforementioned rendition of
the fall of Lucifer. Needless to say, his art is not considered valuable
or authentic by his society. He is at first marginalized, "me condena
mi padre, y abomina de mí la ciudad, y me maldice la iglesia" (126)
[my father condemns me, the city hates me, and the church damns
me] and ultimately silenced—he disappears totally from the novel:
"Nadie, hasta hoy, supo nada más del loco de los papalotes y los
ángeles" (159) [No one, to this day, ever found out anything else
about the crazy man with the kites and the angels]. His figures are
broken and lost:

Cierto día, revolviendo objetos viejos en la casa de una tía abuela mía, vi
una esculturilla en un desván abandonado. No conservaba las alas; el
tiempo se las había robado. Pero quedaban el tronco y el semblante.
Nadie logró darme razón de su origen. Allí había estado por años.
¿Cómo había llegado allí? ¿Quién la había hecho? Pensé en Ignacio. A
pesar de estar maltrecha, la figura desconcertaba. La guardé con cariño
. . . No sé cómo, alguien me la robó después y no he sabido más de ella
. . . Quien la tenga, posee un pedazo de Ignacio Ríos y es venturoso. (17)

[One day, as I was going through some old things in my great aunt's
house, I saw a little sculpture in an abandoned loft. It no longer had
wings; time had stolen them. But the trunk and the face remained. Nobody could tell me where it came from. It had been there for years. How

had it gotten there? Who had made it? I thought of Ignacio. Despite its bad condition, the figure disturbed me. I put it away lovingly . . . I don't know how but somebody stole it later, and I never saw it again . . . Whoever has it possesses a piece of Ignacio Rios and is a lucky person.]

The unidentified narrative voice here that corresponds to Dobles' own submits an alternative value judgment of Ignacio's art, one at odds with that of his society. This narrative voice that later in the novel seems to disappear depicts Ignacio as a sympathetic character, the eternal innocent, "the artist as a young man," who is victimized for his difference both by those who do not love him as well as by those who do.[22]

The apparent success of neocolonial ideology in the virtual erasure of Ignacio from the text: "no existe ya ni como un recuerdo" (164) [he no longer exists even as a memory] is at last subverted by the novel itself, the permanent inscription of Ignacio into narrative. Within the boundaries of the text there are also indications that total erasure has been subverted: a former friend recognizes the effects of his presence, "Creo que iba muy adelante de nosotros" (164) [I think he was way ahead of us]; his brother discovers that Ignacio has fathered a child, implicit faith that more Ignacios will be born: "es la semilla" (163) [he's the seed], but most significantly his brother now sees himself as Ignacio's shadow, an idea he voices in the powerful last line of the novel, "Quizá yo sea una sombra de Ignacio . . ." (164) [Perhaps I am Ignacio's shadow].

The notion of shadow in postcolonial discourse is significant;[23] its presence implies all that colonialism or its antithesis, nationalism, cannot fully erase or exclude. It is more vibrant than a trace, more noticeable than a lack, and more threatening than an absence. Shadows hover; they frighten and mock, and they indicate a presence somewhere beyond the field of vision that blocks the dominant light, whether it is the glow from heaven or "las llamas del infierno" [the flames of hell]. The shadow also exists as a presence in itself even as it presupposes another presence (light), which is even more powerful. No matter how hard colonialism works to erase the Other, how much energy it expends, it must ultimately remain unsuccessful in the totalizing effects of its hegemony.[24] The colonized Other is a slippery shadow that melts into darkness, hides within palimpsestic layers, and darkens the brightest of colonial successes. As the foreigner in the novel who dubs Costa Rica a "limbo" and Ignacio a "bubble" in it explains:

. . . me ha sorprendido que un muchacho como usted haga esculturas
que no se asemejan para nada a las imágenes de santos, pobres en todo
sentido, que fueron lo único que hallé en el interior de la meseta . . .
Demuestra que a pesar de la quietud e intranscendencia de su pueblo,
debajo de él una oscura fuerza se esconde. (123)

[I am surprised that a boy like you makes sculptures that don't look anything like the saints, artistically poor in every sense, that were the only
things I found in the interior of the Central Plain . . . It shows that despite the calmness and intranscendence of your people, underneath
there is a dark force hiding.]

This shadowy obscure force, though "débil ahora . . . ha de crecer y
reventar" (123) [weak now . . . must grow and explode], that is
"burst" like the title's bubble to produce the revolutionary and subversive energy that will "buscar el arma de lo hermoso para luchar
contra las llamas de infierno" (124) [find the weapon of beauty to
fight the flames of hell]. Thus in a narrative that is ostensibly a psychological discourse on adolescence, Dobles firmly positions himself, both politically and artistically, at the very center of Costa Rica's
ongoing postcolonial struggle.

At the heart of this struggle is the explicitly conscious attempt to
create a cultural identity within the national imaginary, that is, to
inscribe and impose a construct of who and what Costa Ricans are
and perhaps more importantly, who and what they are not. Such a
task, of course, beset all the new Latin American republics from the
time independence was first considered, and literature throughout
the continent played a key role in the creation and dissemination of
ideas about national identity. In this sense, Costa Rica was no different; its intellectuals attempted to define and describe Costa Rica in
all its aspects from politics and geography to society and morality. At
this formative period in Costa Rican history the nation's oligarchs
began to create their "cuadros de costumbres" [local color
sketches], literature that clearly marginalized the *campesino* and limited national identity to the Central Plateau region. Cracks in this
national picture begin to emerge between the two world wars as
major economic changes and construction of the railroads brought
other national territories (the banana plantations of the coasts, the
Guanacaste region) into the public focus. After the Costa Rican Civil
War of 1948, these cracks became crevices as the nation's oligarchs
lost both economic and political power and competing liberal and

conservative discourses vied for control over the management of a national identity.

Here is where Dobles' work plays a key role. Dobles insists on problematizing the image of the Costa Rican *campesino* by assigning him a number of attributes with which the Costa Rican people can identify. The image of "el labriego sencillo" [the plain worker] that he borrows from the Costa Rican national anthem (similar to José Martí's "el hombre natural"), that is, the simple but heroic *campesino* in national folkloric costume in front of his "casa típica"[25] is what took hold of Costa Rica's national imaginary and, it can be argued, still maintains a firm grip today. Dobles' own take on this image is emblematic. He actually belongs to the old oligarchy; his mother's side of the family in particular was composed of wealthy landholders. Yet Dobles promoted, throughout his long career, the myth of the Costa Rican *campesinos* as the representatives of not only who Costa Ricans are but also who they should be. Despite his family status and upper-class training and education, he thought of himself as a *campesino* and his public routinely identified him with one of his most famous fictional creations, Tata Mundo, the irascible peasant protagonist/narrator of two sets of popular short stories.[26]

Particularly apparent in *Una burbuja en el limbo* is Dobles' dilemma over the role of the artist in the national imaginary, and Dobles' own biography once again provides a case in point. His training and education are Eurocentric, but he is firmly Costa Rican in terms of national and cultural identity. He is upper class but strongly supports the proletariat. He wants modernity but eschews the loss of tradition. Like Ignacio, he wants to rebel, to speak out against the status quo, to give free reign to his artistic imagination, but like Ignacio he yearns for the harmony of a mythically lost moment in time and fears that his artistic efforts are to no avail. Dobles has not yet found in Ignacio an example of the hybridity he needs to forge a new role for the Costa Rican artist and the concomitant discourse for a revised national and cultural identity, but he is certainly moving in the right direction. Once he finally creates Tata Mundo, the *campesino* artist, the oral storyteller, he finally has his man. Tata Mundo is a survivor; Ignacio is not. Tata Mundo holds a firm grip on the national imaginary to the point that the most elite Costa Rican openly identifies with the national image of the *campesino*. *Una burbuja en el limbo*, then, is truly a novel about adolescence, but specifically a book about national adolescence, of identity still in formation, and of a national discourse that in 1946 had only just begun.

LOS LEÑOS VIVIENTES

Los leños vivientes [the live firewood], Dobles' fifth novel, from its rocky publication history alone, survives as clear testimony to Dobles' controversial personality, both as writer and political activist. The novel, begun shortly after the Costa Rican Civil War of 1948, is based on Dobles' own experiences in jail as a direct consequence of his political involvement with the losing side.[27] An early manuscript of the book titled *Una araña verde* [a green spider] was reviewed by José Garnier in 1950[28] before the novel had actually been published, a rather unusual phenomenon. Based on Garnier's comments, the manuscript at this point only encompassed what later became the first section of the novel. It would appear that the second section and the jail scenes that provide the overall frame and structure for the finished novel were added sometime later. The early title, a green spider, refers literally to the pet of one of the main characters, a boy Chepe, who has moved with his mother and five brothers and sisters from the countryside to the city. The spider not only serves as a reminder of home, but functions symbolically, according to Garnier, as a weaver of illusions.

By 1954, Dobles had found a publisher, the Imprenta Trejos Hnos, and had changed the title to *Hombres de tres tiempos* [men of three times]. While it is unclear from the records, the title seems to indicate that the manuscript had taken its final form by this time covering three distinct time periods: pre–civil war, civil war, and post–civil war. The novel, however, was stopped in mid-printing when the director of the editorial decided that it was too politically controversial.[29] After all, the Costa Rican Civil War was still a recent event, and Dobles was clearly criticizing the winners. At this point, Dobles began his Tata Mundo stories, apparently inoffensive folksy narratives told from a realist perspective. He had no trouble publishing them.[30]

Los leños vivientes lay dormant until 1962 when Dobles finally was able to find another publisher, more than ten years after it was originally written. The change in the title is clear indication that Dobles had not given up his unpopular political views. His side may have lost the Costa Rican Civil War, but his political passions still burned; the *leños* [firewood] of the title are still *vivientes* [alive]. At least one reviewer, José Piedra, saw the novel as a direct response to contemporary U.S. meddling in Central America. Furthermore, Piedra claimed that Dobles, who had recently been fired from his teaching post at a local high school for his visit to Cuba and his outspoken socialist views, had been victimized by "la tendencia inquisitorial que trata de arrollar con todo en Costa Rica, a impulsos de los consejos, órdenes y sobornos de la embajada de los Estados Unidos"[31] [the inquisition-like tendency that is attempting to take over Costa Rica in response to the advice, orders, and bribes from the U.S. Embassy]. Other than this review, the novel received very little attention, in part, as Dobles himself recognizes later in a short introduction included in his *Obras completas*,[32] because of the sociopolitical climate of the times and in part because of the poor quality of its printing, "tan pobre que no estimulaba para nada a su lectura" (9) [so bad that it in no way stimulated its reading]. The novel was not edited again until 1979 when the Editorial Costa Rica took very little risk publishing it since Dobles had a well-established reputation by then as a foundational national writer.[33] In addition, some thirty years had elapsed since the historical events that form the basis for the novel. Even then, Alberto Cañas, Dobles' faithful friend and honest critic, remembers feeling skeptical about this novel, certainly not one of his favorites.[34] It was not until 1996, when the Editorial de la Universidad Nacional edited both *Los leños vivientes* and Dobles' 1967 novel, *En el San Juan hay tiburón* [in the San Juan river there are sharks], that reviewers, now separated by almost five decades from the events themselves, speak glowingly of Dobles' narrative capability.[35] Clearly, nationalist forces, as repressive as any colonial or neocolonial regime, held the upper hand for almost half a century in suppressing this novel that speaks clearly to the political and ideological issues of its day and eerily foreshadows the political and cultural consequences of the continued alliance (or dependence) between Costa Rican nationalism and United States first-world capitalism.

Dobles, in fact, was imprisoned twice after the Civil War of 1948, the first time for reading his revolutionary poetry over the radio to boost governmental troop morale and the second time for supposedly hiding weapons in his yard (what turned out to be a compost heap). His sister Margarita was instrumental in securing his release. It is no coincidence that the unnamed prisoner with the delicate hands, arrested at the beginning of *Los leños vivientes,* is a writer. Neither is it insignificant that the weight of the second section of the novel revolves around Don Belisa (Belisario), a failed novelist. Dobles has split himself into two characters here as he explores the possibilities and limitations of dissident art under a repressive nationalist regime.

The structure of this novel is palimpsestic. The frame story constitutes the surface layer in the present tense and centers on three political prisoners: a Spaniard (Pedro Canalías), a Negro (Ustos Robinson), and the unnamed Costa Rican writer with the delicate hands. All are political comrades; all know each other from before, and as they talk and find out about other acquaintances, the successive layers of the text are peeled back. One story uncovers another. Memories uncover dreams; dreams uncover memories. Stories from the "Mornings" section, pre–Civil War narratives, converge with the multiple stories of the "Nights" section, events during the Civil War, with each section bordered on either side by a prison episode (post–Civil War), fractioning the "Day" into multiple voices and multiple times that ultimately merge in a dialogic challenge to the dominant master discourse.

The course of colonialism in Central America changes radically with the Spanish Civil War and World War II. Spain no longer writes the dominant script; the Republicans lose to Franco's fascism and the United States emerges as the dominant world force. Dobles' three prisoners represent this political and economic change. Pedro, the Asturian, is no longer a colonizer in Costa Rica but a new settler, an antifascist Republican refugee. The Negro Robinson, from the banana plantations on the Costa Rican Atlantic Coast, a descendent of English-speaking slaves from Jamaica, is the new subaltern in Costa Rica, victimized by United States corporate capitalism in cahoots with Costa Rica's antigovernment nationalist forces. The writer, the self-appointed spokesman for the Costa Rican Other (the "pueblo"), is part of the dissident Marxist left that has formed an unholy alliance with governmental forces.[36] Unconvinced by the government, the Communists still support it as the lesser of two evils: "Ah gobiernito . . . En lugar de contrarrestar la jodarria por donde se la han planteado, con rápidas contramedidas económicas, los saca a ustedes (los militares) a relucir" (98) [Oh dear government . . . Instead of counteracting the problem where it arises, with quick economic countermeasures, it hauls out you guys (the military) to show off]. These three men, then, the Spanish refugee, the displaced Negro, and the Marxist writer, form the fundamental hybrid resistance to a new colonialist mentality in the guise of nationalism and democracy but clearly dictated to by United States economic and military interests in the region.

The agenda of the United States in Costa Rica's Civil War is overt: "¿Quién impidió que el gobierno consiguiera armas en el extranjero? ¿Quién hacía posible en cambio que a la oposición le llegaran por aire desde Guatemala hombres y material de guerra?" (21) [Who prevented the government from getting arms abroad? Who made it possible, on the other hand, for the opposition to get men and war materials by air from Guatemala?] There is no question that President Calderón's governmental forces have succumbed, not just to nationalist rebel troops, but also to a superior (foreign) military capability: "ya roncaban en Panamá los aviones yanquis y . . . la Guardia Nacional de Nicaragua nos había invadido por Villa Quesada." (22) [U.S. planes were already snoring in Panama and the Nicaraguan National Guard had already invaded us through Villa Quesada]. Costa Rica is effectively sandwiched between United States controlled Nicaragua to the North (through the Somoza dynasty) and the North American military bases in Panama to the South. United States political and military opposition to Calderón's government for its pact with the Communists opens the door to direct and indirect intervention backed by the Monroe Doctrine that continues to the present day. Once the antigovernment forces are in power, they round up the dissidents; the legal system is deployed to concentrate land and power in the hands of the new ruling group: "Entre abogados y jueces qué sé yo cómo lo hicieron" (109) [Between lawyers and judges, I don't know how they did it]. The dominant script speaks of democracy while committing the same atrocities as other totalitarian regimes: "Total . . . que andamos haciendo las mismas barbaridades del portorriqueño Morales en Dominical" (90) [In the end . . . we commit the same barbarous acts as the Puerto Rican Morales in Dominical]. Furthermore, oppositional voices are effectively silenced or erased: "nos ha borrado constitucionalmente de la ciudadanía" (23)[37] [we have been constitutionally erased from the citizenry].

In the midst of this historical context, the failed writer, Don Belisa, tries to make sense of his life and his art, but his confusion over language prevents him; he mixes words and sounds in an incoherent and virtually untranslatable succession: "yo imagiro, miragino . . . Remuero, !remuerdo! ¿Pienso, siento siquiera? Pensar, censar, !cesar! ¿Seso? o ¿ceso? . . . ¿Por qué insisto en palabrejas? Ella me decía que mi enemigo eran las palabras. 'Por ellas te desvivís'" (125) [I imagyrate, I mirage . . . I redie, I rebite. Do I even think or feel? Think, censor, cease! Brain? Cessation? . . . Why do I insist on broken words? She used to tell me that words were my enemy. "You would give anything for them"]. He cannot make the words mean what he wants; they are not his to deploy; they do not allow him to construct an authentic subjectivity. Caught within the master discourse, he becomes negative subjectivity, Other, "un-living." He is haunted by the past, by the events and ultimately the language that have constructed him: "el hombre tiene su parla. Quizá una imperfección más. Como no ha alcanzado el lenguaje de la abeja, por allí se consuela" (133) [Man has his speech. Maybe just one more imperfection. Since he has not mastered the bee's language, he consoles himself with his own]. In addition, his efforts to go backward in time, to peel away the layers of the past in palimpsestic fashion as prerequisites for writing, ultimately silence him, "hay que desnacer, desvivir" (94) [one must be unborn, one must unlive]:

> bueno, eso que llaman hacer, no empieza por desrehacerse a sí mismo y desrecrearse su propio mundo . . . y cuando su mundo no encaja y resulta que estaba fuera de toda probabilidad real, y además le ronda el problema de los reales,[38] entonces . . . irrealidad . . . entonces . . . oblicúa . . . desvalija los recuerdos . . . fabrica con ellos una carta sin dirección. (126; Dobles' ellipses)

> [Well, what they call doing, doesn't that begin by unredoing oneself and unrecreating your own world . . . and when your world doesn't fit and turns out to be outside the realm of all realistic probability, and, what is more, the problem of reality surrounds you, then . . . irreality . . . then . . . obstructs . . . invalidates memories . . . creates from them a letter without an address.]

His death in the Civil War, a symbolic suicide, merely erases from the text a voice that has already been silenced through his psychological stasis and self-censorship.

Don Belisa is an example of what Spivak[39] calls epistemic violence: "yo tenía el cómo, pero no sabía qué" [I had the know-how, but I didn't know what]. Between overt repression and the internalization and naturalization of the dominant ideology by the masses, the writer's "hands/language" are effectively tied: "¡Qué mi cerebro carecía de manos, manos!" (126) [My brain lacked hands, hands!]. Dobles' multiple references to "hands" throughout the novel, therefore, become heavily nuanced. Like the silenced voice of the subaltern, Dobles creates a trope of the writer's (worker's) hands, wounded, bound, insufficient, and lacking (in one instance cut off by a machete: "la mano cortada . . . Es como símbolo de todo este ancho y largo emporio; entrega estéril de lo más valioso, de la capacidad de coger, de hacer, de la riqueza esencial" [137]) [the cut hand . . . It's like a symbol of this entire enterprise; the sterile relinquishing of what is most valuable, of the capability to choose, to create from the essential richness]. The implicit parallel between the workers, "el pueblo," and its writers—both living from the labor of their hands—underpins Dobles' rhetorical strategy for countering the master discourse. The novel becomes the locus for the multiplicity of voices within the working class and reverses the monologic We/They (superior/inferior) binary opposition of dominant script to a dialogic We, the voices of the people, versus They, the oppressors, both foreign and national.

Dobles seems at odds with himself here, however, literally a split subjectivity: on the one hand, the hopeful writer with the delicate hands and, on the other, the failed writer who lacks hands, lost in a mire of dominant discourse: "la maldición escrita" (132) [inscribed damnation]. Of the two, however, the imprisoned writer survives, and it is he who insists at the end of the novel that faith be maintained in a viable resistance. He insists that despite the setbacks, the lives lost, the "duros aletazos" [hard knocks], they have learned to "hablar lenguaje propio" (163) [speak their own language] and that ultimately they will emerge stronger than "todas las palabras, que todos los engaños y todas las cancillerías" (163) [all the words, all the tricks, and all the government offices]. He admits, however, that the future will not be painless: "Nos lo seguirán cobrando por años" (163) [They will keep blaming us for years], but in the end (symbolically the end of capitalism or the end of history but literally the end of the growing season) "germinará el maíz[40] . . . Y en el fogón del tiempo manos abundarán para sazonar la tortilla que apenas si pudimos comenzar a palmear" (163) [corn will grow . . . and on the hearth of time, there will be plenty of hands to season the tortilla that we just barely started to shape]. Once again Dobles' emphasis is on the working presence of the hands, an autochthonous cultural metaphor.

The optimism, at least in part, seems justified. The prisoners have maintained a high morale. Even in jail, they continue debating, talking, joking, and laughing. In fact, as the novel begins, the prisoners stage a mock bull fight with two comrades under a blanket as the bull, another prisoner dressed as the matador, and the radio announcer "vociferando al mango de paraguas que le sirve de micrófono: TI-PENI, en 1225 presos políticos, anunciándoles que la formidable corrida ha terminado" (28) [speaking into an umbrella handle that serves as his microphone: TI-PENI, at 1225 political prisoners, announcing that the formidable bullfight is over]. Talk continues even though the prisoners are the only ones listening, and one wonders if they have not misdirected their sub(di)version; after all, the wrong imperial force (Spain rather than the United States) is being targeted in the parody of the bullfight.

Dobles, however, clearly intends to portray a hopeful ending. One of the comrades thought dead turns up alive at the end of the novel, and a great deal of time is spent recreating the heroism of the workers who cross the Cerro de la Muerte [Death Ridge] to form part of a labor manifestation opposing the political right. Indeed, the fight for socioeconomic equality has its heroic moments in Costa Rican history as well as a long list of achievements, but the optimism of the prisoners ultimately seems contrived and is undermined by the very date of the workers' march, 1947. By 1948 the government has capitulated and the remaining comrades are either dead or in prison. The banana plantations of the east coast have depleted the land and have been moved by U.S. companies to the west coast where they proceed to repeat the same ecological violence.

The prisoners have all been wounded, shot or beaten, and left with scars, and it is this scarring that takes on a rhetorical, ambivalent, double voice: the "cicatriz" [scar] is both evidence of physical oppression and violence as well as a mark of resistance. It is testimony to the repressive measures used to control a population (whether by a nationalist or a neocolonialist project) and the concomitant efforts to resist, subvert, and counter that control. Like the shadows left by the subaltern, the silenced, and the erased, the scar becomes a visible trace of opposition and resistance. The repressive forces are called to task to maintain their continually challenged and tenuous control. Juan Bautista,[41] the comrade thought dead who turns up as another political prisoner, represents the resilience of the oppressed: "ven, algunos hay que así no más no se acaban" (164) [come now, there are some of us who can't be gotten rid of so easily]. Nevertheless, the optimism is ultimately undercut by the powerful last line in the novel: "[Ustos] corre a abrazar a Juan Bautista mientras en la frente, sobre la negra yesca de los húmedos ojos, *las cicatrices de los culatazos parecen multiplicársele*" (164; emphasis mine) [(Ustos) runs to embrace Juan Bautista, while on his forehead, over the black tinder of his damp eyes, *his scars from the beating of a rifle butt seem to multiply*]. The scarring is an ambivalent trope; it implies resistance, but not victory. The scars seem to multiply and will, no doubt, continue to do so. Indeed, they have continued to do so. Dobles could not have known, for example, that his rebel Nicaraguan character, a follower of Sandino, who lives "como las raticas, al margen" (111) [like little rats, on the margin] would ultimately become a victorious force ousting Somoza, curiously enough, in the same year *Los leños vivientes* was reedited, 1979. Yet as this novel anticipates, victory (in this case the Sandinista take over) only produces renewed fighting, more oppression and a new resistance as Marx's synthesis becomes a new thesis and the confrontation between thesis and antithesis continues in a never-ending struggle. The neocolonial-nationalist debate is a continual dialectic that demands continual reevaluation. Belisario, despite his ultimate failure, is on the right track as he splits his own subjectivity (like Dobles himself) into two parts:

> Paréceme que ya no estoy solo. Me acompaña un segundo Belisario que brota de las sombras y entre las sombras se encuentra, y me conversa de recuerdos que no tienen relación con lo que se ha sido sino con lo que se ha deseado ser. (140)

> [It seems to me that I am no longer alone. A second Belisario is with me who pops up out of the shadows and hovers among the shadows, and he talks to me of memories that have no relationship with what has been, but rather with what one wishes would have been.]

It is from this continual dialogue, that a hybrid resistance is born and maintained. And it is only from the defeats, the suppressions, and the scars that its presence is ultimately perceived out of the "shadows." The *pueblo*, Costa Rica's equivalent to Africa's or India's "native," is like the fig trees (the subtitle in the novel for the jail scenes). These trees grow back time and again even though they are cut down: "Pero el pueblo no puede ser derrotado, hombres.—Retoña siempre.—Como los higuerones" (22) [But the people cannot be defeated, men.—They always come back—Like the fig trees]. The very definition of resistance, therefore, centers on its wound, its martyrdom, as well as its capacity for endurance and renovation: "Esos leños vivientes me han hecho sentirme renovado" (23) [This green firewood has made me feel like a new man].

The novel's title underlines this paradox while it speaks to the ambivalent and vexed enterprise of hybridity and resistance. The "leña" [firewood] of this novel (that is, the prisoners) are branches that have been chopped off from their source of life, the trees and the "pueblo" they represent. Thus, the wood is technically dead, or if green, as in the title, is still mortally wounded and will eventually die. Yet even in (and because of) this state, the wood burns. The green firewood is the hybrid combination of life and death, a refusal to participate in the "either/or" mentality of binary oppositions. It is another version of Costa Rica's *si pero no* approach to colonial resistance; that is, the wood is dead but not altogether. The result of this hybrid resistance is that the *leña* will burn longer and perhaps brighter than might be expected. As long as more firewood is continually collected, green or otherwise, the fires of social revolution and resistance will, therefore, continue to burn and be reborn.

4

The Novel of Short Stories

Historias de Tata Mundo. San José: Editorial Trejos Hnos, 1955.
El Maijú y otras historias de Tata Mundo. San José: Editorial Trejos Hnos, 1957.[1]
Historias de Tata Mundo (integrating the two previous volumes); second edition, San José: Editorial Costa Rica, 1966; third edition, 1971; fourth edition, 1975; fifth edition, San José: Librería Lehmann S.A., 1976; sixth through twelfth editions, San José: Editorial Costa Rica, 1977–1988. Special edition, illustrated with watercolors by Luis Daell, San José: EUNED, 1993. Fourteenth edition, San José: Al Día, 1995; fifteenth edition, edited and illustrated by Carlos Barboza, Pamplona: EUNATE, 2000. Translated into English by Joan Henry as *The Stories of Tata Mundo*. San José: Editorial de la Universidad de Costa Rica, 1998.[2]

UNDOUBTEDLY HIS BEST WORK AND CERTAINLY HIS MOST POPULAR, *Historias de Tata Mundo* (1955), followed by *El Maijú y otras historias de Tata Mundo* (1957), has undergone fifteen editions from 1966 to 2000 integrating the two collections of twenty-four stories in total.[3] In addition, a special edition (part of the EUNED's gift books collection) was published in 1993; the leather cover is embossed in gold ink with Dobles' signature, and the edition includes watercolor illustrations by Luis Daell.[4] The late Costa Rican artists, César Valverde and Francisco Amighetti, illustrated earlier editions. The version included in the *Obras completas* (1993) is accompanied by sophisticated line drawings by Costa Rican psychologist Ricardo Ulloa Garay. Individual stories, originally published as periodic submissions to the *Diario de Costa Rica* and other local papers, have been included in a variety of anthologies and translated into German, Italian, Russian, Czech, French, and Portuguese as well as English. A translation of the entire collection into Russian was published in 1986, one into Italian for the Universal Library of UNESCO, and one into English

by Joan Henry, *The Stories of Tata Mundo,* in 1998. Two short films
have been made based on his stories: one directed by Juan Bautista
Castro called "Historias de Tata Mundo" (1984), which interweaves
two stories from the collection, "El detalle" [The Detail] and
"Mamita Maura" [Grandma Maura], the other directed by Victor
Vega, titled "El hombre de la pierna cruzada" [The Man With His
Legs Crossed] based on the story "Adelante" [Forward March!].

Initial reviews hailed the work as "la obra más acabada en su gé-
nero desde los cuentos vernáculos de Magón"[5] [the most polished
work in its genre since the vernacular stories by Magón], compared
it to *Don Segundo Sombra,*[6] and celebrated its inclusion in the list of
the best books of 1956 by the *Encyclopedia Britanica.*[7] Later editions
of the book were equally well received. According to Ronald Solano's study of the criticism on Tata Mundo: "a pesar de que abun-
dan los comentarios y las 'críticas,' los fundamentos 'teóricos' que
los sustentan parecen repetirse invariablemente"[8] [despite the fact
that commentaries and "criticisms" abound, the "theoretical" assumptions that underpin them seem to repeat invariably]. Specifically, Dobles' critics and reviewers agree that "la literatura refleja la
realidad tal y como es percibida por un sujeto, especialmente do-
tado, y que permite a otros sujetos reconocer lo que él dice como
verdadero"[9] [literature reflects reality as it is perceived by an especially gifted subject, who permits other subjects to recognize what he
says as truthful]. The stories have been labeled "truthful," "realistic," even "delicious." Solano points out all the gastronomic metaphors used to describe Tata Mundo. In addition, he indicates that
Tata Mundo is also seen, not only as a character but also as a function, that is, the art of storytelling.[10] Based on these assumptions,
Dobles is for his critics a first-rate writer, and his popularity remains
undiminished as evidenced by reviews[11] of his latest collection of
short stories[12] published posthumously.

Deferring the controversial issue of "realism, reflection, or mime-
sis" in literature for the moment, the more enduring secret of the
success of *Historias de Tata Mundo* can be traced to Dobles' able manipulation of humor and language, a combination that his earlier
novels often lack. Dobles' true genius lies in his ability to produce
comic episodes in the country vernacular. The humor is culturally
contextualized, never gratuitous, and the stories have an authentic
ring, not only because of the familiar Costa Rican settings Dobles
describes, but also because of the first-person narrative point of view.
Each of Tata Mundo's stories is framed by a first-person narrator

who listens to Mundo, comments on the surroundings, the story, and the storyteller. Thus, as Ronald Solano observes: "las *Historias* incluyen tanto la dimensión de la narración como la de los efectos de lectura"[13] [the *Historias* not only include the dimension of the narration but also the effects of the reading]. This complexity creates a space for observing how a story works, what it does, and how it touches and affects the listener/reader. Each story, therefore, has at least two storytellers, an unnamed, mostly admiring, first person narrator, probably a family relation to Mundo, obviously younger than he, perhaps a nephew or grandson, implied by Mundo's appelative "Tata," Costa Rican slang for father, and at least two stories: the story Tata Mundo tells and the story of his telling it.

Mundo's name, a shortened form of Raimundo but also a word in its own right meaning *world,* indicates his wealth of experience and knowledge even though his "world" is limited to Costa Rica, particularly the Northern frontier with Nicaragua, the banana plantations of the Atlantic coasts, the Pacific coast islands, and the central plains. In some stories, Mundo is simply the transmitter of another person's story putting the reader at three removes from the supposed "source"; some of the stories he claims are invented, "imaginadas y mentidas" [imagined and made up] but in most he plays an integral part in the action itself and claims to have personal knowledge of the veracity of the events he narrates. Not only does he tell his stories for the enjoyment of "los muchachos" [the fellows] in the evening, on the porch, in the bar, in the fields, but he also seems fully aware that his stories are being recorded, written down by an author that Solano calls "el narrador-oyente-transcriptor" (83) [the narrador-listener-transcriber].

Por ahí me ha soplado el viento que el autor de unas historias mías, que anda poniendo en letras, está en aprietos para ajustar la número nueve.

La verdad es que son tantas las que de esta redonda mal torneada me han ido saliendo a través de los años, unas vistas y oídas con otras quizá imaginadas y mentidas, que me admiro de verlo ya jadeando apenas en la octava. Ya ven; para que aprendan, yo sin fuerte ser de pluma pues la mano me tiembla y tengo oscura la letra, me animo a ayudarle en algo y ahí les mando esta, a ver si con retoques y mejoras el autor la viste de apóstol y la saca en andas con las otras.[14]

[I've heard tell that the author of some of my stories, the one who is writing them down, needs a ninth story for his collection.

The truth is that there are so many stories that this old man has told over the years, some seen or heard, others imagined or made up, that I'm surprised to see him already panting over the eighth. You see, while I'm not a good writer (my hand trembles and I can't spell), I thought I would help him out a little and so I've sent this, to see if with some touch ups and improvements, the author can dress it up to parade with the others.]

Tata Mundo clearly makes a tongue-in-cheek distinction between his oral storytelling practices and the sophisticated editing, "colonizing," that must take place before his stories can see print for elite readers. While he seems to acknowledge the superior learning of the "autor" [author] or "cronista" [chronicler] as Isaac Felipe Azofeifa calls him in his prologue to the 1971 edition (84), who must make "retoques y mejoras" [touch ups and improvements], the comic irony of the author "jadeando" [panting like a dog] over a story he has not even created himself but is merely transcribing, reinforces the description of Tata Mundo as the master storyteller who subtly resists "official" inscription.

Mundo, who tells his stories according to Azofeifa "en forma autobiográfica" (83) [in autobiographical form], is an interesting figure in himself, apart from the stories he tells. He has experienced life in the first half of the twentieth century when mining and banana plantations served as Costa Rica's economic base, a period prior to the liberalized laws protecting workers that came into existence toward the end of Tata Mundo's working life (1940s). A common man with strong affiliations to his community of peers, he experiences both sides of the work/management conflict and ultimately sides with the workers, landing in prison many times for his participation in unauthorized strikes and pickets. He is poor and irascible and not beyond the petty stealing of corn from the large landowners' crops or a little ore from the foreign-owned mines. His sympathies invariably lie with the country folk, the downtrodden, and his admiration for anyone who can fool others is unabated.[15] He is a hard drinker, definitely a *macho* man who admires a strong woman and an even stronger man, who has the gift of narrative, the ability to tell a yarn, create mood, and maintain suspense. He has an eye for detail, the timing of a comedian, and an ability to create metaphors from common objects and everyday occurrences. Azofeifa sums him up based on details from all the stories:

buen bebedor, bigotudo, sentencioso, reflexivo, lleno de refranes, socarrón, de ojillos burlones; ha cruzado el país en todas direcciones traba-

jando de carretero, palero en los cafetales, minero, liniero; con algunos
rasgos de pícaro, lleno siempre de malicia y bondad; empresario de aca-
rreos, huelguista, mandador en las fincas de banano, raicillero por afi-
ción de aventura, y hasta militar a la fuerza. (85)

[a hard drinker, with a big mustache, pithy, full of sayings, cunning, with
little teasing eyes; he has crossed the country in every direction working
as an ox cart driver, a coffee plantation worker, a miner, a banana plantation worker; with some of the traits of a picaro, always full of deviltry and
kindness; he has been a transportation entrepreneur, striker, banana
plantation foreman, collector of wild roots for adventure, and even a sol-
dier by force.]

Mundo is the kind of man and storyteller that Dobles most certainly aims to be. Dobles' own intellectual background and cosmo-
politanism, however, force him to speak through the persona of
Mundo, who is the epitome of the rude, uncultured country spinner
of yarns. The frame narrator, on the other hand, a popular comic
device used by Mark Twain, a North American writer with whom Dobles was undoubtedly familiar, suggests Tata Mundo's younger self,
the learner, who would seem to represent Dobles' more authentic
personality, the youth who loves the experience of country life (we
must remember Dobles grew up in the country, the son of a rural
doctor) but who clearly does not belong there, who loves the stories,
the adventures, the closeness of family ties but who most certainly
will leave when vacation is over to go back to school in the city. Thus,
the two narrators of *Historias de Tata Mundo* form the dual potential
of Dobles himself, and in this sense his own last name is coinciden-
tally symbolic: *dobles* [doubles]. The narrator is both himself and
other, ego and alter-ego,[16] past and future, listener and speaker, in-
ventor and recorder, apprentice and consummate storyteller. What
impresses Azofeifa most, however, is Dobles' ability to create narrative that sounds spoken in the manner of Costa Rican speech at the
turn of the century:

La lengua de Tata Mundo no es la del campesino, sin dejar de serlo
[read *sí pero no*] . . . el autor pone cierto arcaísmo de expresión cuando
estiliza típicos modos sintácticos de nuestra habla campesina y apro-
vecha los arcaísmos más característicos del vocabulario rural de princi-
pios de siglo. (88)

[The language of Tata Mundo is not that of the country farmer, and yet
it is . . . the author uses certain archaic expressions while he stylizes the

typical syntactic manner of our country farmer's speech and takes advantage of the archaisms that are most characteristic of rural vocabulary at
the beginning of the century.]

Historias de Tata Mundo, for Azofeifa, represent "la gracia y la anda-
dura del mejor estilo oral: porque es como si se oyera hablar" (88)
[the grace and flow of the best oral style: because it is as if one could
hear the speech].

The issue of language in the stories underlines a crucial theoretical point. As Dobles explains almost forty years later: "Decíme con
cuál idioma hablás y te diré quién sos"[17] [Tell me what language you
use, and I'll tell you who you are]. His choice of the familiar you
form, the *voseo* in this comment, is not gratuitous. One of the clearest linguistic markers of Costa Rican speech is the use of *vos* instead
of *tú*. Thus, the implication of Dobles' comment is more nuanced
than the literal meaning would seem to indicate. He implies that
Costa Rican Spanish is tantamount to another language, perhaps
not as linguistically different as French or English, but just as culturally defining. His contention, which interfaces well with postcolonial
theory, is that language and cultural identity cannot be separated.
Each affects the other; each creates and constructs the other.
Through a person's speech, we become aware, not only of who the
person is, but of who he is not.

Tata Mundo's language, despite the critics who classify Dobles'
work as realistic and who see his language as transparent, revealing
an outside, objectively verifiable "real" world, actually constructs
the semblance of reality. As Azofeifa notices in typically Costa Rican
sí pero no style, it both *is* and *is not* the language of the *campesino*; that
is, it is not "realistic" but rather a literary creation that poses as real.
Alberto Cañas once remarked, "uno no sabe si es que los campesinos autóctonos hablaban así, o es que todos aprendieron a hablar
con el lenguaje que les enseñó Fabián Dobles"[18] [it is not clear if
the Costa Rican peasants talked like that, or if all of them learned to
talk from the language that Fabián Dobles taught them]. As reviewer
Lorenzo Vives notes, even as he misses the irony of his own statement dominated as it is by the Spanish "Vosotros,"[19] "Contad lo
mismo con el decir culto, y la relación será hueca"[20] [Tell the same
thing with cultured language, and the story will be hollow]. Here
again, as with Dobles' earlier comment, the use of the *vosotros* form
in "contad" immediately situates the speaker as either being from
Spain (colonialist) or imitating Castilian Spanish (neocolonialist).

The language of the commentator, therefore, ultimately reveals more about the values of the reviewer than of the story he is reviewing.

The story, of course, *is* the language, and the language, because it derives from the Costa Rican vernacular, is in *clave* [code], as Dobles himself claims, so that the dominant class has only the illusion of understanding. Dobles even offers a glossary of Costa Rican terms at the end of the collection, which works as a kind of translation from subaltern Costa Rican speech to standard Spanish. Dobles' refusal, through his Mundo persona, to tell his stories in "el decir culto," however, is a form of post-colonial resistance to the "culturación, aculturación o deformación cultural"²¹ [transculturation, aculturation or cultural deformation] of regional identity through the imposition of official language: "los deslenguan para lenguarlos a su gusto y sabor"²² [they detongue them in order to tongue them according to their likes and tastes]. Whether Dobles' language realistically reflects the language of the *campesino* or merely gives the illusion that it does, all Costa Ricans understand it. It becomes, therefore, a private language that permits communication between subaltern writer and reader. The joke, ultimately, is on the colonial intruders, the dominant class, and the falsely erudite.

The first story in the collection, "El responso" [Prayer for the Dead] recounts a personal experience from Tata Mundo's adolescence when he was an alter boy, a "monaguillo," as Dobles himself once was. Dobles displays at the outset his ability to interweave and layer images, themes, and threads of narration in order to move seamlessly from present to past. Literally, the title refers not only to Tata Mundo's turn to tell a story "el cuento del responso" [the response story], but also to the statement and response prayers of Catholic ceremony, as well as to the human response to a good deed. The Catholic priest takes Mundo to the graveyard on a night that "se había vestido . . . de luto rígido" (90) [had dressed . . . in strict mourning]²³ (appropriate attire for an evening in a cemetery) similar to the dark night of the present evening that serves as the catalyst for Tata Mundo to recount this experience: "Asina como esta fue la noche cuando . . ." [The night was just like this when . . . (15)]. The priest intends to perform a ceremony to expiate his own guilt for having wrongly judged another human being. His anger at a landowner who refuses to donate some of his land for a soccer field prevents him from praying sincerely for the man's soul upon his death, "ese día tata cura no rezó con devoción el responso" (96) [that day the priest did not say the prayer with true devotion][24]. Ironically, however, "ñor Evaristo" [*ñor* is short for *señor* or Mister] leaves both land and money to the town, throwing the priest into a paroxysm of guilt and repentance that leads him to redo the ceremonial prayers over Evaristo's grave with the help of young Mundo.

More ironic still is the way Evaristo dies, hitting his head on a rock in a confrontation with the same boys who continued to play soccer on his land. The priest remarks on his own inability to understand such events, "Qué sé yo; hay casualidades raras, como por dedo de Dios" (95) [How do I know? Rare accidents do happen as though they're caused by the hand of God (20)]. He pledges Mundo to silence for fear that "algún feligrés malicioso vaya a imaginar que andábamos vos y yo haciendo alguna barbaridad en el cementerio" (97) [I don't want any malicious parishioner to go and imagine that you and I went to do anything wicked in the graveyard (22)], that is, for fear his actions might be misinterpreted. This inability of the characters as well as the narrators to "interpret," that is to understand the meaning or significance of an event/experience/story underlies all the tales in *Historias de Tata Mundo*. Like an ancient version of an innocent Huck Finn, who never really understands the importance of his own decisions, Tata Mundo claims a fundamental ingenuousness with regard to the significance of the very stories he chooses to tell. The difference is, he is not a young innocent, and neither are we innocent or ingenuous readers. His disclaimers (and those of his protagonists) merely serve to make the coded communication between Dobles and his audience more acute.

Several stories fall into the trickster category: "El detalle" [The Detail] where a *contrabandista* fools the police; "El rezador" [The Man Who Led the Prayers] where the man hired by a husband to pray and cry at his wife's funeral does so with unusual sincerity, making us guess that he probably had a romantic relationship with the woman unbeknown to her husband; "El trueque" [The Exchange] where two brothers switch identities to avoid persecution by the police; "El reloj" [The Watch] in which we are left with many doubts as to whether a watch supposedly owned by Porfirio Díaz is authentic or not and whether it is ultimately melted down or not; "La nuca tiesa" [Stiff Neck] where we are left to wonder whether or not the female protagonist is really abused by her husband; "La toboba"[25] [The Snake] in which a man kills another for stealing from him but is able to claim that he was trying to kill a snake on the man's hat; "El bejuco" [The Vine][26] in which a younger brother revenges himself in a sort of one-upmanship on his older brother, and "Mamita Maura" where Tata Mundo's grandmother fools everyone into believing that she is dying only to be able to watch her own funeral and then have everyone present fix up her house. The two most famous trickster stories, however, are undoubtedly "Matatigres" [Tiger-hunter], who eludes the police even as he stands in their midst and "El Maijú"[27][The Yoo-Hoo], a monster invented by Alvaricia Ordóñez to keep others out of a particularly fertile area of *raicilla* [a wild root].

Several of the stories fall into the category of unusually loyal animals: the dog that finds Tata Mundo again in "El pálpito" [Premonition] after he has gone away, the parrot who saves Pascuala from being buried alive in "La lapa" [The Macaw] and the vulture who revenges himself on the murderer of his beloved master in "Eulalio." Almost all the stories have a surprise ending, particularly: "La bruja" [The Witch], where a wife kills her husband before her son can kill him leaving no one for him to kill but her; "La viga" [The Beam], where a father has hidden gold that his son can only find as he is about to hang himself; "El angelito" [The Dead Child], the switch of two sick babies in the hospital, one of whom dies, and the ensuing confusion at the funeral; "Mano Pedro" [Brother Pedro],[28] who believes his wishes come true and therefore blames himself for events around him, only to be liberated from such suffocating guilt at the end of the story with the realization that he never had such power to begin with; and finally three autobiographical stories: "El préstamo" [The Loan], dedicated to Dobles' nephew Ignacio Dobles Oropeza[29] in which Tata Mundo loans a friend some money, not out of goodness or sympathy, but so as to look good in front of his old girlfriend, now the wife of his friend; "La última de Tata Mundo" [Tata Mundo's Last Story], where Tata Mundo has to figure out what to do with an elaborately carved coffin left to him by a friend, and "El gato con zapatos" [Too Big for his Boots],[30] a takeoff on "El gato con botas" [Puss in Boots] in which Tata Mundo ultimately discovers that his loyalties lie not with the banana company as foreman but with the workers as striker.

If Tata Mundo is not the protagonist of his own tale, he often plays a supporting role or is at least present as an eyewitness. These stories, of course, have realistic settings and describe actions that, even if surprising, are at least plausible. There are two stories, however, that do not fit this pattern: "Adelante" [Forward March!], a legend about a man who represents the epitome of laziness and "Caballos

y venado" [The Islands of Caballos and Venado], a fable in which
the animals tell the story. Mundo prefaces his story "Adelante" with
a disclaimer: "La historia que voy a referirles . . . no es cosa que me
conste por verdadera" (196) [The story I am going to tell you isn't
true (127)]. In fact, it has all the trappings of oral folklore: a story
passed down from generation to generation, (Tata Mundo's mother,
who used to tell it to him, says that her father used to tell it to her),
and a formulaic, Quijote-like beginning—once upon a time in an
unspecified place: "una vez, en no sé que lugar de nuestro mundo,
hubo un pueblo muy bonito . . ." (196) [once in a certain place
in our region, there was a pretty little village (127)]. From the very
beginning of this tale, Mundo encourages us to doubt its veracity
and listen to it for the entertainment (actually, the language)
alone—"caigo en pensar que no sucedió ni en los tiempos de naide
. . . Yo qué sé. A mí el cuento me gustaba" (196) [So I realize it
didn't happen in anyone's lifetime at all . . . Anyway I liked the story
(127)]— although he admits that his mother used to tell it to him
for didactic purposes, since he tended to be a lazy child.

The other clearly fantastic story is the fable, "Caballos y venado,"
although the setting once again is in Costa Rica and the historical
background is accurate. The ostensible purpose of the tale is to explain the reason that two Costa Rican islands located in the Gulf of
Nicoya off the Pacific coast are named Caballos [Horses] and Venado [Deer]. As background the narrative refers to the defeat of William Walker in 1856, and to two important historical figures, Juanito
Mora, Costa Rican president at the time, and Juan Santamaría, Costa
Rican martyr/hero, credited with instigating the final defeat of
Walker.[31] Against this background, the fable's two old warhorses,
who supposedly once belonged to Juanito Mora and Juan Santamaría, have now been put to pasture, much to their chagrin. The
story has the sound of humorous oral folklore, but apparently the
plot is Dobles' invention, according to his widow,[32] and not a reconstruction of local tales, despite Mundo's claim to the contrary: "Pero
esta segunda historia es tan revieja, que yo estaba creyendo que
ustedes se la sabían, por revenida que la tiene ya la humedad de los
tiempos" (281) [But this second story is so very old I thought you
knew it, because people still tell it (215)].

INTERTEXTUALITY

Despite the fact that Dobles titles this collection "Historias" and
Costa Rican critics have accepted them as such, the argument can

legitimately be made that *Historias de Tata Mundo* is actually a novel, in the same way that Ernest Hemingway's Nick Adams stories in *In Our Time* (1924) or Sherwood Anderson's stories in *Winesburg, Ohio* (1919) actually form a comprehensive picture of a person, place, and time. Most of the stories, for example, cannot be read out of order since successive stories refer back to previous ones. In "La de arena" [The Carrot or the Stick][33] the ending would be unintelligible without having first read "El pálpito" [Premonition]. Both stories revolve around a bridge that suddenly collapses, and both tales share a central character, Flaco Arroyo,[34] the villain who almost kills Mundo in "El pálpito" by weakening the bridge supports as well as the father of the young man who saves the mule driver from a mortal fall in "La de arena." The force of the latter story depends not only on the comparison between the two bridges but also on the comparison between father and son, one bad, the other good, in an implicit refutation of the biblical curse that the sins of the fathers will be visited on the sons. Many of the stories share characters; for example, la negra Pascuala, the central character of "La lapa" appears in "El gato con zapatos" and later in "La luz en la oscurana" [Light in Darkness]. In addition, a chronological sequencing among the stories is identifiable. "El gato con zapatos" takes place three years after "La lapa," based on the age of Pascuala's daughter, and "La luz en la oscurana" takes place sometime after the strike that occurs in "El gato con zapatos." Another repeating character is Mundo's cousin Eulogia, who saves him from death in "El Pálpito" and later saves him from poverty in his old age ("El gato con zapatos") by leaving Mundo a solid inheritance of land and coffee crops. Somewhere inbetween, Tata Mundo's grandmother talks to her in "Mamita Maura" and asks her to keep a special eye on Mundito [Little Mundo]. Likewise, the main character of "Luz en la oscurana," Honduran Tiburcio Andrade, reappears in a supporting role in "La toboba."

Not only do a variety of characters resurface but also events that occur in one story are referred to again in others. More than one mention is made of the banana strike and Tata Mundo's stint as foreman on an Atlantic coast plantation. Mundo tells one story from bed as he convalesces from pneumonia and a later story refers to his previous illness. Not only do we end up with a fairly comprehensive picture of the biography of Tata Mundo (insofar as he wishes to tell it), but we also witness the growth into manhood of the listener/chronicler. We see him take his first taste of contraband liquor, undergo the embarrassment of making a stupid remark and being laughed at by his peers, and discover, much to his surprise, that Mundo is not to be entirely trusted. The connections between and among stories as well as the overall picture we form of the two narrators indicate a narrative continuity far greater than a miscellaneous string of stories and is undoubtedly one of the factors that establishes this work as Dobles' best.

LANGUAGE

The other factor is certainly Dobles' masterful control over language. What appears to be the ease and informality of oral storytelling is actually a highly crafted and consciously artistic control of image and metaphor, as Azofeifa claims, "una creación estética, antes que todo" (88) [an esthetic creation above all]. "Local color" or the Costa Rican vernacular alone cannot account for either the wealth or the quality of Dobles' images. In particular, the image of water underlies the entire collection from start to finish: "Aguacero de burlas el que me cayó encima" (206) [A storm of teasing fell on me];"temporal de la huelga. Algunos nunca se mojan" (247) [the strike's (rainy) season. Some people never get wet].[35] This frequency of water images is more than Dobles' personal preference; it is an image with a multitude of possibilities in a tropical country where it rains some eight months out of the year. One striking passage and a good example of Dobles' technique is Tata Mundo's description of married life, entirely in terms of swimming and water images:

Y, *chupulín*, el gran tarantas *se tiró con todo y ropas de cabeza en la poza*, y en los primeros meses el matrimonio le pareció *una agüita tibia y retozona, y él a nadar a gusto, y todo suave* . . . Acá empezó Casimiro a ver cómo *el agua se le enfriaba* y la cosa se le ponía cuestuda . . . Y nuestro Casimiro más echaba los pujos montaña arriba y *más se nos mojaba* . . . Ah lluvia, ah *lluvia gruesa y pesada* la que se le vino encima. (135, 136, 139; emphasis mine)

[And, *splash*, the big idiot *dove into the water hole* with all his clothes on, and during the first months of matrimony *the water seemed warm and frisky* and *he swam* as he pleased, everything smooth . . . Then Casimiro began to see how *the water started cooling off* and things got harder . . . And our Casimiro plowed forward uphill and got *wetter and wetter* . . . Oh rain, *thick and heavy rain* that fell on him.][36]

In fact, the humor lies precisely in Mundo's use of this kind of language; that is, the humor is in the storytelling, not the tale told, which, if anything, is often tragic or at best pathetic. His representation of a family in agricultural terms, for example, is typical of this opposition between humorous tone and depressing social circumstances:

> Habiendo la madre del muchacho pasado a mejor vida, pasó Pedro a mejor mujer . . . de quien cosechó más familia poco a poco, mientras el zafalomos de su hijo mayor, sin dirección ni madre, crecía como quien dice pastando en orillas de calle. (134)

> [The boy's mother, having passed to a better life, Pedro passed to a better wife . . . who harvested more family little by little, while his lazy eldest son, without direction or mother, grew up, as they say, grazing by the side of the road.][37]

Tata Mundo's colorful images ("harvesting children" and "grazing" through life), not to mention his frequent puns (from "better life" to "better wife") maintain a constant sense of humor even in his stories of unfortunate events.

Often his images tie a story together thematically. For instance, in "El bejuco," which is also the nickname of the main character, all the images are long and thin and tall, like the "bejuco" [vine].

> Ayudado por *el saco de huesos fuertes* con su poco de cabeza lista que era su mujer, los dos continuaron *estirándose, estirándose* . . . Y en seguida fueron tres y cuatro y cinco y seis, hasta llegar a diez bejucos; el Bejuco y la Bejuca con ocho Bejuquitos, hombres y mujeres, y toditicos *delgados y larguiruchos*, como *anguilas de mar.* (279; emphasis mine)

> [Helped by *the sack of strong bones* with its not too intelligent head, which was his wife, the two kept on stretching and stretching . . . And soon there were three and four and five and six, until they got to ten vines; Mr. Vine and Mrs. Vine and eight little vines, boys and girls, and down to the last one, *thin and long like sea eels.*][38]

This underlying image of longness and thinness reappears throughout the story—"tan flaco y largotote como estaba" (275) [skinny and lanky as he was (211)]; "el larguirucho se había casado con una muchachona alta y delgada como él" (276) [the lanky fellow was marrying a tall girl, slender like him (211)]; "largas manos" (279)

[long hands]³⁹—and unifies the story as it refers backward and forward linguistically to different parts of itself.

As many critics have commented, Dobles is a master of the vernacular. He shifts easily between Costa Rican, Nicaraguan, and Honduran speech characteristics. Overall, however, his language is Costa
Rican. He employs the *vos*, which while not exclusive to Costa Rica,
is characteristic of Costa Rican speech. He also employs the diminu-
tive *tico*, which is so prevalent in Costa Rican speech that Costa Ricans have come to be known throughout Central America as
"Ticos." He even provides a glossary of Costa Ricanisms at the end
of the collection in order to make his stories more accessible to both
non–Costa Ricans and younger Costa Ricans who, with increasing
cultural imperialism and a popular desire for all things modern and
urban, may have distanced themselves from Tata Mundo's early
twentieth-century rural speech. Far from making his work sound
more provincial, however, the very local specificity of the language
increases the oral quality and humor of the stories and is ultimately
responsible for the legendary status of Tata Mundo, himself.

ANALYSIS OF SPECIFIC STORIES

Several of Dobles' stories from Tata Mundo that have often been
anthologized merit special attention, specifically "El angelito," "Matatigres," and "El gato con zapatos." "El angelito," translated for
inclusion in a West German anthology, is particularly interesting for
its frame narrative that provides us with information about Tata
Mundo's storytelling technique. First, as in many of the other stories, there is a clear connection between what is going on in the present in the frame with the past events in the story. In this case, Mundo
is at a wake for a child, "un angelito" [a little angel], which reminds
him of another wake for another child who had been mixed up in
the hospital and sent home with the wrong family. In surprisingly
bad taste Mundo asks his host:

> Hombre, Lesmes, ¿reparaste bien en el muertico? Véle con cuidado la
> cara, no sea que te pase a vos lo que una vez les cayó encima a dos amigos
> míos por asunto de unos críos enfermos que llevaron a San José. (141)

> [Well, Lesmes, did you examine the dead boy closely? Look carefully at
> his face. I hope that what happened once to two of my friends concern-
> ing sick children they took to San José won't happen to you. (67)]

His question is asked in a particularly loud voice that immediately stops the music and noise and turns people's attention from all over the room to hear "la misa al viejo" (142) [the old man's story[40] (68)]. The chronicler/apprentice is clearly paying attention to the old man's technique and comments, using the agricultural metaphors he has learned from the master, "pues sí que le gustaba limpiar primero el terreno de otras hierbas que la suya" (142) [he first liked to clear the ground of any other grass but his own].[41] As soon as Mundo has the crowd's attention, he begins the story.

Briefly, two families each take a sick infant to the hospital where one recovers and the other dies. The two children are mixed up and sent home with the wrong families. The family who receives the live child knows immediately that he is not theirs but decides to keep him anyway, to round off their full dozen. Mundo goes to the wake for the other child. The ceremony turns into a brawl when the family discovers the mix-up. Amidst all the drinking, celebrating, and carousing, the little coffin is bumped and the "angelito" falls out and rolls on the ground. Afterward, Mundo is sent as the messenger to the other family, also friends of his, to insist on the other child's return. The father admits that a mix-up has taken place but refuses to return the baby and shames Mundo in the process for even asking: "Yo no puedo aceptar como mío el angelito aquel después que lo ensuciaron como lo ensuciaron. Tal vez si me lo hubieran respetado . . . / Allí sí que me acabó de desarmar. Me llené de vergüenza" (149) ["I can't accept that dead child as mine after they defiled him as they did. Perhaps they should have shown him some respect."/ That's how he succeeded in convincing me. I was full of shame (75)].

Here Dobles states point blank his philosphy of child rearing, which he employs in several other stories: "Mirá, un hijo es hijo más porque uno lo quiere y lo cría que por el chorrillo de sangre que uno le ha dado" (148) [Look, a son is a son more because he is loved and brought up than because of blood relationship (75)]. This preference for nurture over nature is markedly different from the dominant cultural attitudes of the time; yet Dobles provides multiple examples in other stories of fathers who accept other men's children as their own.[42] Mundo is forced to return to the first family with a lie, "creo que los dejé medio convencidos de que, a saber si por la mucha bebedera, aquella noche de la vela ellos habían visto mal y habían tomado por ajeno al angelillo propio" (149) [I think I left them half convinced that because of so much drinking on the night of the vigil, they hadn't seen straight, and had taken their own dead child for somebody else's (76)]. Implicit in this story is Tata Mundo's need to justify his actions rather than merely entertain a crowd of listeners. Like Samuel Coleridge's Ancient Mariner, he must tell his story over and over to anyone who will listen in an attempt to expiate his guilt, not only his guilt for lying to the grieving family but also his deeper guilt for participating in a drunken brawl that ignored the central tragedy for both families, a dead child.

"Matatigres," one of the longest stories in the collection, was chosen along with several other Central American stories to be converted into film for an Italian movie directed by Federico Patellani (1955–56) as well as a Costa Rican production in 1983 directed by Juan Bautista Castro. The story is particularly intriguing because of the moral ambiguity surrounding the title character, Julián Ballestero, nicknamed Tigerkiller. The frame emphasizes Tata Mundo's preoccupation with moral issues. He claims to have met Matatigres when he was thirty-three years old, Christ's age at the crucifixion "los treinta y tres de Jesucristo y yo" (181) [I was thirty-three like Jesus Christ (109)], precisely because (Christlike) "por intento de igualármele en redimir humanidades" (181) [with the intention of doing as well as He did in redeeming mankind], he had been exiled to the remote region of San Carlos for having led a strike in the Minas de Abangares [Abangares Mines].

Mundo likes Matatigres right away and they become good friends; the entire story, in fact, is told in a tone of admiration for his friend's ability to elude the police. The moral ambiguity revolves around Matatigres' crime in the first place—the reason he also finds himself living in this remote region. In a fit of jealousy, Matatigres has killed his wife with a machete. Mundo tries to soften the crime: "Asina pasa, Julián. Macheteaste a Baldomera. Si lo hubieras pensado, quizá no lo hacés" (183) [That's how it was, Julian. You killed Baldomera with your machete. If you'd thought about it, perhaps you'd not have done it (110)]. Unrepentant, Matatigres claims to take responsibility for his action: "No me arrepiento. Porque un hombre debe alzar con lo que ha hecho, cargarlo toda su vida, y responder por el acto" (182) [I'm not sorry. Because a man has to hide what he's done and carry it around with him all his life and be responsible for it (111)]. The irony, of course, is that Matatigres runs, rather than turning himself into the police. He views the crime as a "tortón" [goof] rather than a serious lapse in moral judgment.

Everyone, from Matatigres, to his mother, to the crowd outside his house, to Mundo himself, admits the immorality of the murder; yet sympathy still lies with Julián rather than with the victim. His mother defends him because she is his mother; his friends remain loyal because they are his friends, and the neighbors ultimately support him as well rather than help the police: "la corriente que lo empezaba a favorecer seguía creciendo" (187) [the current which was beginning to favour him went on growing (115)]. This sympathy for the husband, a confessed murderer, rather than for the wife, who is the victim, results, in part, from the dominant patriarchal (*machista*) moral code that would tend to excuse Matatigres for a crime of passion. Moreover, the general antipathy toward the police as representative of neocolonial control might ultimately outweigh public condemnation for the crime. Matatigres is still a member of the community; the police are not. Most importantly, however, the sympathetic nature of Julián's personality wins him many loyal admirers. He becomes a symbol of postcolonial resistance, the underdog who ultimately wins in a game of one-upmanship, the ultimate trickster, and as Alberto Cañas calls him, a mythical hero.[43] As Matatigres leads the police on a wild goose chase, we (the listener/reader) soon find the crime forgotten amidst our enthusiastic rooting for the "hero":

¿Y Matatigres—dirán ustedes—qué se había hecho? Pero si Matatigres estaba allí, a mi lado. Y se reía cuando uno de chacalín se había jalado la mejor travesura de su vida. (195)

["What had become of Tiger-hunter?" you'll ask. But Tiger-hunter was there, at my side, laughing like a child who had pulled off the best prank of this life. (126)]

The laughter is pervasive (if not perverse)—not only Matatigres, but also Mundo the teller, as well as his listeners join in, thus ignoring the implicit moral dilemma that was first raised and permitting Mundo and the subaltern reader to participate in Julián's escape, free of moral (self)condemnation.

"El gato con zapatos" specifically alludes to the strike in the mines that Mundo mentions in "Matatigres." This time, however, Mundo finds himself on the management side of the conflict since "Mister Smith" made him foreman on a banana plantation. He admits from the outset, that is, from the story's frame, that he had

no business in that position, "¿Quién mete a los gatos con zapatos?"
(236) [Who makes cats wear shoes? (169)]; that is, a cat with shoes
is not an authentic cat and Mundo as a foreman is equally unauthen-
tic. Friends try to warn him of the impending dangers of taking what
is ultimately a neocolonial position, specifically, that he will not be
able to make individual choices but rather that the position will
choose for him. Mundo is no innocent adolescent in this story; his
hair is graying and he has the experience of another strike under
his belt; yet he acts strangely naive: "vos sabés muy bien que no soy
capaz de matar a naide. / — Usted no, don Mundo . . . Pero de la
Frutera no digo yo lo mesmo. Y usted ahora es la Frutera" (239) [you
know very well that I'm not capable of killing anybody. / Not you,
Don Mundo . . . But I don't say the same about the Fruit Company.
And you're the Fruit Company now (173)]. Mundo refuses at the
time to acknowledge this neocolonial identity ("Usted ahora es la
Frutera") and the *sí pero no* situation it puts him in. Nevertheless, he
warns his audience of young listeners now that his past error should
serve to teach them: "y apréndanselo ustedes que están jóvenes"
(239) [and learn from it you who are young].[44] Mundo straddles
both sides of the fence for as long as possible, but ultimately he realizes that he cannot be simultaneously colonizer and colonized. The
positions are mutually exclusive. His final choice to side with the
workers "como se han puesto las cosas yo vengo a jugármela junto
con ustedes" (247) [as things have turned out, I've come to take
sides with you (180)] reaffirms his cultural identity and his refusal
to be co-opted by a neocolonial institution: "También yo nací con la
pata en el suelo. !Qué se vaya al diablo la Companía!" (247) [I was
born with my feet on the ground too. To hell with the Company!
(180)]. Eight days later, after armed conflict, he finds himself in jail
with the other uninjured strikers, but he is satisfied that he has acted
authentically and honorably even though it has meant personal sacrifice: "Hay veces que uno no tiene más remedio que portarse bien.
Si no, después, ¿en dónde diantres escondería la conciencia?" (248)
[There are times when we have no other remedy but to do the right
thing. If not, where the devil would conscience be later on? (181)].

TATA MUNDO AS ARCHETYPE

In the same way José Hernández (1834–1886) created the archetypal figure of the Argentinean gaucho, Martín Fierro, in his narra-

tive poems *El gaucho Martín Fierro* (1872) and *La vuelta de Martín Fierro* (1879), Dobles has created the archetypal Costa Rican *campesino* in Tata Mundo. Clearly, he is a very different figure from the Argentinean idealized, tragic, and romantic gaucho, but the differences between the two archetypes only accentuate the fundamental differences in national and cultural identities between one Latin American state and another.

Tata Mundo is the figure that no one really is, but that every Costa Rican male wants to be, at least at the unconscious level of his ideal ego. Both at the individual as well as the national level, Costa Ricans see themselves, like Tata Mundo, as the underdog who manages to have the last laugh, a rural, third world, unsophisticated people who have an innate intelligence and common sense often lacking among the richer and more powerful nations of the first world. Tata Mundo is a jack of all trades, a rogue with a big heart and a soft spot for the weak and troubled, a hard drinker, a jokester, and an inveterate storyteller—all qualities that Costa Ricans, particularly Costa Rican men, aim to possess. In other words, Tata Mundo is the Costa Rican Everyman, something along the lines of an adult Huckleberry Finn.

Through Tata Mundo, Dobles provides an image for what Costa Ricans look and sound like, for how they think, how they talk and how they act. He is, as Martín Fierro is to Argentineans or Huckleberry Finn to North Americans, a cultural icon, a name all Costa Ricans know and grow up with, everyone's narrative grandfather, the figure who both reflects them and mocks them, and who, they will argue, is not merely a fictional construct. More than any other character from Dobles' novels, Tata Mundo is remembered and revered for all the qualities that Costa Ricans want to believe they possess.

The "authentic" Costa Rican *campesino*, if he ever existed as such, is a rapidly disappearing figure, no longer a legitimate focus of realistic narrative. As Seymour Menton explains:

> Ya no se podrá escribir sobre el gaucho argentino ni sobre el concho costarricense; en parte, porque el prototipo se ha ido desapareciendo a causa de los adelantos de la civilización y, por otra parte, a causa de estas obras maestras que idealizando al último de la especie, serían difíciles de superar.[45]

> [Authors can no longer write about the Argentinean gaucho or the Costa Rican peasant; partly because the prototype is quickly disappearing with advancements in civilization and partly because these masterful

works, which idealize the last of the species, would be difficult to super-
sede.]

Nevertheless, as a reflection of myth and a projection of the self,
both personal and national, the imagined *campesino* remains a vital
part of the national identity. As Alcida Ramos explains about the
Brazilian Indian (and we could easily substitute Costa Rica for Brazil
and *campesino* for Indian) "Brazil needed the Indian but only the
fictionalized Indian, the redeeming ectoplasm of troublesome flesh-
and-blood Indians who needed to die in order to populate the con-
querors' imagination."[46]

Dobles' stories, while written for adults, are also read by children
throughout their public school years as representative of Costa
Rican literature. Since primary education in Costa Rica is free and
compulsory, it is the rare Costa Rican who has never heard of Tata
Mundo.[47] Furthermore, since five editions of the stories have been
illustrated by Costa Rican artists, there is also a visual image that Tata
Mundo conjures up with his huge mustache and wiry frame, much
like Huckleberry Finn with his straw hat and corncob pipe or Martín
Fierro and his typical gaucho gear. This image of Tata Mundo has
been inscribed in a variety of discourses from newspaper articles, to
pedagogical texts, to academic criticism. The fact that Tata Mundo
is so clearly grounded in the life and experience, even the looks, of
the aging Dobles, (although Dobles created him long before his
own hair turned gray and he began to sport the emblematic Tata
Mundo mustache), only reinforces the popular belief in his authenticity. Thus, within the national imaginary of Costa Rica, Tata
Mundo emerges as a foundational national symbol.

5

Other Stories and Collections

La Rescoldera. San José: Editorial L'Atelier, 1947.

LA RESCOLDERA [EMBERS], ALSO THE TITLE OF ONE OF THE ELEVEN STO-
ries in Dobles' first collection of short fiction, refers to smoldering
ashes, the burning sensation in the pit of the stomach that each of
these tales aims to produce in the reader. For such a young writer
(Dobles was not yet thirty when the collection was published and
several of the stories are dated as early as 1941, a year before the
publication of his first novel), the stories reflect a sophisticated control of the medium of short fiction. While each tale functions as an
isolated unit, the cumulative effect of the collection works as a political and social indictment of the powerful over the weak, the rich
over the poor, ideology over critical thought. Local setting, common
people, and first-person narration or third-person narrators well acquainted with events provide the stories with an air of authenticity
associated with the diminished distance between teller and listener
in oral tradition. Frustration is the dominant theme, a logical psychological response to colonialism that by definition asserts dominant and repressive social, political, and economic forces beyond
individual control. María Amoretti, in her structuralist study of Dobles' early short stories, calls these forces *obstaculadores* and divides
them into four groups: "Quienes ostentan el poder económico . . ."
[Those with economic power], "Quienes constituyen la
autoridad . . ." [Those in authority], "Quienes ostentan niveles sociales superiores . . ." [Those in the upper class], and "La naturaleza" [Nature], although she admits that this last group also finds
itself victimized "como el hombre"[1] [like man].

The language in these stories is different, however, from the Costa
Rican vernacular employed in the Tata Mundo stories. In this collection, Dobles has not quite found his "sí pero no" subversive response to the neocolonial enterprise, but he is clearly learning.

While his language reflects more standard Spanish (no need for a glossary of Costa Rican vocabulary at the end of the collection), he has begun to experiment with first-person narration in this collection and humorous descriptions of individual characters.

The first story is emblematic. "La última piedra" [The Last Stone] focuses on a man so frustrated that all he can do is to throw stones. He has fallen in love with the picture of a girl in the newspaper, an extreme example of dominant capitalist ideology that convinces us to want what we cannot have. No fundamental difference exists between goods and people; everything is marketable. The paradox of this situation is that even when people get what they think they want, still they are neither happy nor satisfied. This story, however, offers more than just its plot. The unidentified first-person narrator, while clearly not a Tata Mundo campesino, is still good at telling a story. His eye for detail and humerous descriptions undercuts the surface tragedy (an early form of "sí pero no") but the narrator cannot sustain this dual, tragically funny approach, and at the end, Dobles runs into both structural and linguistic problems. First, the narrator loses his humorous tone and becomes almost moralistic, and second, the narrator concludes the story with information he could not possibly have known. This piece, dated 1941, shows promise, but clearly, Dobles is just beginning.

The double-edged irony of the first story underpins a later story in the collection, "El musiquillo de la flauta" [The Little Musician with the Flute], dated 1943, in which a poor musician finds his artistic abilities frustrated rather than enhanced when he is patronized by well-meaning friends who set him up with a place to live, a record player, and a new flute. What the colonizer considers helpful, the colonized feels as an imposition. When the flute player finally flees his apartment to return to his old way of life, we may read his behavior as the allegory of flight from all that is not authentic in the struggle to value what is. The colonizer, of course, interprets the behavior as blatant ingratitude. The first-person narrator of this story, like Tata Mundo, clearly appreciates the humor of his descriptions: "Yo, simplemente, lo conocía por *el musiquillo de la flauta*, o *el orejudo*" [I knew him simply as *the little musician with the flute,* or *big ears*].[2] The difference between this narrator and Tata Mundo, however, is that this narrator is part of the opposition; that is, he allies himself with the rich and dominant class, the neocolonialists. His attitude toward the musician is condescending, and he only vaguely understands why the musician left his comfortable apartment to return to the street. His noncomprehension, however, is not an assumed simplicity as it is with Tata Mundo, but rather the inability of the neocolonialist to understand the people he "controls."

"Al fin se encontró a sí mismo" [At Last He Found Himself] is an important story about gaining consciousness of one's identity. It centers on the frustration of a man who believes he withstands all the problems in his life like a bull, only to discover that he has really been an ass, a fool, all along. Such is the insight that results from naming the unconscious or naturalized assumptions upon which we live, from finally seeing what has been made invisible by ideology.

"Antes que nada, tata" [Before Anything, Papa] emphasizes the frustration of a man caught between two loves, the love he feels for his daughter, on the one hand, and for his best friend, on the other. When the best friend rapes his daughter, the father kills the friend to preserve his own and his family's honor. While his pain at the funeral is genuine (he has killed a man he loves in order to obey the patriarchal dictates of society that require fathers to protect daughters or, at least, to avenge them), he is also grieving for his daughter. Here Dobles is beginning to see the possibilities of subverting the neocolonial hierarchy with a "sí pero no" response. The father here is, and at the same time, he is not, grieving for his friend. "La vela del lagarto" [The Crocodile's Wake] presents a similar situation of mourning the killer of the beloved. In this almost magically real tale, a man hunts down an enormous crocodile and holds a wake for him since he cannot hold the vigil for his wife who was eaten by the crocodile. The psychological needs revealed in this story are the same as those that underly a much later story by Elena Poniatowska, "Las lavanderas" (1979) of a similar case of misplaced frustration in which a town puts the church bell in prison for killing the bell ringer. Such deep frustration against superior forces, in this case death itself, requires inordinate behavior on the part of the living to create a semblance of justice in a world that has none. The husband's behavior is once again "sí pero no." Technically, he holds the wake for the crocodile, but clearly he is grieving for his wife's death, not the crocodile's.

Likewise, in "Despedida del viejo Beltrán" [Firing Old Beltran], a son attempts to explain to his father that the world has changed, that the paternalistic relations between *patrón* [employer] and worker have given way to the heartless relationship of management and labor under modern-day capitalism.

Esos hombres como don José ya no existen. Ahora son otros. Ellos, los
patrones, y también nosotros los asalariados, vivimos en circunstancias
muy distintas. Ellos no pueden darse el lujo de sentir por sus peones
ningún cariño, y nosotros tampoco por ellos. (72)

[Men like Mr. José don't exist any more. They're different now. They,
the employers, and also we, the workers, live in very different circumstances. They cannot afford to have feelings for their employees, nor can
we afford to have feelings for them.]

The father, however, represents the tragedy of internalizing or naturalizing the dominant values of the ruling class. He cannot understand his son's political activism against this new state of affairs and
can only accept fatalistically and passively the rationale he has been
given for being fired, "Pero yo estoy, de veras, tan viejo" (72) [But
I am, really, very old]. This particular story exemplifies the impact
Dobles' father, the country doctor, made on his son's work. Although not specifically autobiographical, Dobles includes a remark
his father made that haunted him all his life: "Fabiancito, se me
mueren de hambre"[3] [Fabián, my boy, they're dying on me of hun-
ger]. In this story, Dobles refers to the typhoid epidemic of the
1920s and to "un médico inteligente" [an intelligent doctor] who
claims *"Eso no mata a nadie. Esa gente se está muriendo de desnutrición"*
(70, Dobles' italics) *[That (typhoid) doesn't kill anybody. These people are
dying from malnutrition].*
    The final story in the collection, "La mujer negra del río" [The
Black Woman of the River], is a combination of legend and political
commentary, in which Dobles not only condemns the presence of
North American owned and operated banana plantations on the Atlantic coast but also aims a well-placed criticism at U.S. racism, unre-
pentantly segregationist and bigoted in 1946. In the English-
inflected Spanish of black speech typical of the Limón area of Costa
Rica's Atlantic coast, Dobles' Negro character explains: "al negro lo
tratan . . . como a un pierro, *my good friend,* como a un pierro" (80)
[they treat Negroes like dogs, *my good friend,* like dogs]. The fact that
the Negro of this story, the son of a Costa Rican black woman and a
white *Gringo* father, leaves the United States and returns to live in
Costa Rica suggests a number of interesting possibilities: one, that a
Costa Rican·black man may look like an American black man, but
his cultural identity is radically different, and two, that the postcolonial position of Negroes in Costa Rica is less vexed than the complex

race relations present in the United States. Dobles is also practicing in this story with the vernacular, in this case, the heavily accented Spanish of Negroes who had originally learned English in Jamaica before being brought to Costa Rica to work on the railroads.

The story that names the collection "La rescoldera" [Embers] treats one of Dobles' persistent themes, and one he develops in detail in his first novel, *Aguas turbias,* as well as in his *Historias de Tata Mundo* and in his narrative poetry: the plight of the *contrabandista.* Following the same story line from *Aguas turbias,* where the *contrabandista,* Juan Manuel, is sent to prison for two years during which time his girlfriend marries another man, the protagonist of "La rescoldera" also loses his girlfriend during a two-year stint he spends in prison for fabricating contraband liquor. Despite his frustration and resentment, he helps his former girlfriend have her baby while her husband ironically gets drunk and arrested when he goes to town in search of the doctor. The smoldering ashes of the title refer not only to part of the distillation process in making liquor but also to the feelings that Lucas, the *contrabandista,* has for his old girlfriend. Implicit in the fabric of the story is the injustice of criminalizing the practice of making alcohol. Dobles insists that there is no inherent evil or moral wrongdoing in the behavior. Nevertheless, since the government owns a monopoly on the production of alcohol, it has declared all competition illegitimate. Legal control merely facilitates the government's economic control. Thus, the example of the *contrabandista* is a clear case of subversive behavior that attempts to resist neocolonial imposition.

Perhaps the most significant story in the collection, certainly the most prophetic, is "El hombre que obedeció" [The Man Who Obeyed] about a writer who takes to heart the negative criticism about his first book. He becomes so critical of himself and so absorbed in his self-evaluation that he progressively loses his girlfriend, his job, and finally his life. The irony of his suicide over the failure of his book is, of course, that later his work becomes enormously popular and successful. It is as though Dobles is preparing himself to withstand the criticism that he knows will plague him because of his leftist political views. In fact, his burst of productivity in the 1940s is cut short by the Costa Rican Civil War of 1948, after which Dobles was imprisoned for a short time and reduced to menial jobs like street vendor and milkman. During the 1950s, he did, indeed, experience difficult times, not only economically but also artistically, as Costa Ricans refused to identify their own reality with what Dobles wrote; yet paradoxically refused to separate Dobles the man from his fiction.

> Luego de los sucesos de 48, su obra escrita, inseparable de su persona, entró por el camino de la sospecha: era demasiado buena para que fuera de un autor costarricense; demasiado real para que esas historias se dieran en la Costa Rica ensimismada en sí misma . . . Esas vidas enflaquecidas enfermas y palúdicas sólo eran realidad en los pueblos vecinos centroamericanos . . . Ante esta denuncia, el profeta de la palabra veraz quedaba desacreditado en sus libros, y sus ciegos detractores cargaban con la mentira libremente.[4]

> [After the events of 48, his written work, inseparable from his person, fell under suspicion: it was too good to have been written by a Costa Rican; too real for the stories to have occurred in a Costa Rica that was so content with itself . . . Those thin, sickly, malaria-afflicted lives were only real in neighboring Central American countries . . . With this denunciation, the prophet of the true word was discredited in his books, and his blind detractors continued unrestrained with their lies.]

The very fact that Costa Ricans, themselves, believed this self-deprecating criticism that Dobles' writing was too good to come from a Costa Rican demonstrates the extent to which Eurocentric ideas dominated in this decade. Dobles, of course, spent his life countering this kind of criticism and the inferiority complex associated with it. In contrast to his protagonist in "El hombre que obedeció," Dobles refused to obey, refused to conform, refused to become discouraged, and most significantly, refused to be silent. Instead, he went on to produce his most famous stories, *Historias de Tata Mundo*, despite his own personal economic problems as well as the antagonism toward his artistic work produced by the political conservatism and anticommunism of the 1950s.

LATER STORIES AND COLLECTIONS

El violín y la chatarra. San José: Editorial Pablo Presbere, 1966; second edition, San José: Editorial Universidad Estatal a Distancia (EUNED), 1992.

Cuentos de Fabián Dobles. San José: Editorial Universidad Centroamericana (EDUCA), 1971; second edition, 1982.

Cuentos escogidos (anthology). San José: Editorial Educativa Costarricense, 1992.

La pesadilla y otros cuentos (anthology). San José: Editorial Costa
   Rica, 1984.
Cuentos. San José: Editorial Universitaria Centroamericana
   (EDUCA), 1996; second edition, 1997.
Y otros cuentos. San José: Editorial Universidad Nacional, 1999.

Dobles continued to publish short stories after the success of the
Tata Mundo collections but never again tied his stories together in
any kind of structural and narrative continuity as he had with *Historias de Tata Mundo.* Instead, he began to experiment with the individual tale as a self-contained unit and often published isolated stories
in local newspapers before he gathered them together in various
collections and anthologies. His next major collection of new stories
came out in 1966, *El violín y la chatarra* [The Violin and Scrap Metal]
and was fairly well received although never as popular as *Historias de
Tata Mundo.* Alberto Cañas, for one, was particularly disappointed
in the collection, which he claimed, "lejos de constituir un avance
en la carrera prolífica de Dobles, es un retroceso"[5] [far from consti-
tuting an advance in Dobles' prolific career, it has moved him back-
ward]. He only liked three of the stories and felt the rest were
"unidimensional" [one-dimensional] and suffered unduly from Soviet influence; that is, they too clearly revealed Dobles' Marxist
views. The second edition, published in 1992,[6] received guarded
praise:

> Por momentos pareciera que el ámbito constructivo y las instancias dra-
> máticas, que enlazan este mundo, descansaran en una horizontalidad
> bastante previsible. No obstante, el largo trayecto del autor solventa so-
> bradamente esa línea subterránea que acecha el realismo expresionista.[7]

> [Sometimes it would seem that the constructive atmosphere and the dra-
> matic moments that tie together this (fictional) world were resting on a
> relatively foreseeable horizontal plane. Nevertheless, the author's long
> trajectory should more than dilute this underground vein of lurking ex-
> pressionist realism.]

Composed of eighteen stories, all but the last two are extremely
short, almost *mini-cuentos*, less than three pages. Cañas may have
been unduly harsh on the collection, since most of the stories suggest a multidimensionality that is not readily visible if they are read
only from a "realistic" stance. Though the collection lacks the linguistic continuity of the Tata Mundo stories, these tales have a cer-

tain thematic commonality, denouncing not only surface injustices (what Cañas sees), but also revealing an underlying pattern of colonial domination.

The first three stories are based on odd coincidences. In "El encuentro" [The Meeting], two amateur short-wave radio fanatics with a long-standing friendship over the air finally meet and discover that both have been crippled by polio since childhood. Significantly and ironically, this central fact in their lives has been omitted from their radio correspondence. Their refusal to talk about their disability parallels a similar phenomenon in postcolonial society. The native people, in Costa Rica's case the *mestizo*, has been crippled by dominant colonial forces even after independence; their identity has been erased or altered and their ability to function independently has been diminished. Everyone knows it, but no one talks about it. Dominant ideology is naturalized, internalized, and appropriated, and life goes on blind to its own paralysis. Ultimately, however, it is this commonly shared problem that ties together not only these two men from different countries, but also the imagined countries they represent.

In "La flor de itabo" [The Itabo Flower] a daughter waits for her estranged father, who ironically has been killed in an accident on his way to the rendezvous, and in "El gordo" [The Lottery] the number of the winning lottery ticket is erroneously reported over the radio leading a man to believe he has won the big prize and to celebrate accordingly. These coincidences underscore the precariousness and irrationality of life in the Third World. Fundamental to Costa Rican/Catholic culture is the ever-present belief that the individual is never in control of his or her destiny (the subject as object), contrary to U.S./Protestant ideology that affirms the centrality of the subject, free will, and the power to make choices (especially if the individual is white and male). This other-directedness, typical of the colonized mentality, is represented symbolically in the Costa Rican vernacular: any sentence in future tense is always prefaced with the qualifying phrase, *si Dios quiere* [God willing]. Understood and subsumed under *Dios* is the current dominant power (Spain, Europe, the United States, those who lend money, run the government, enforce the law, and so forth).

Eight of the stories, that is, almost half, are more explicitly political, reflecting Dobles' leftist views and his criticism of capitalism, its hypersensitive and extreme fear of communism, and its amorality, undoubtedly provoking Cañas' criticism about Soviet influence. The first of these, "El baúl" [The Trunk], which was translated into German for inclusion (ironically, given Dobles' ideological ties with the Soviet Union) in a West German anthology of short stories, is the brief and sardonic tale of a man arrested for political subversion. His offense, however, is merely his claim that the chains he has packed away in his trunk symbolize "las condenadas cadenas con que nos joden, si señor: la ignorancia, la miseria" (332) [the damned chains that weigh on us all, yes sir: ignorance and misery]. In "El dependiente" [The Saleslady] an ignorant woman is fired for having named her child Lumumba. Her offense is ignorance. She has heard this name and likes it but is unaware that it is the name of a famous African communist leader. The subtext of this story is clearly Dobles' disgust at how some authorities (whether it be the saleslady's boss or Dobles' critics) impose their political interpretations on the innocent actions of others, something he suffered frequently in his own life.[8] In "La huelga" [The Strike] a Nicaraguan must leave his children when he is deported from Costa Rica for participating in a strike, and in "El mercado común" [The Common Market] a man sacrifices his family for his business.

In opposition to these pathetic tales, "La vaca" [The Cow], "La baja" [The Resignation], "La coconingalinde"[9] and "El machete" all reflect the power of the underdog to stand up to the superior forces of capitalism. "La vaca," for example, is, on a superficial level, the story of a man imprisoned for four years for stealing his employer's cow. Since the reason for the theft was to pay for his dying wife's medical bills, the power of the story lies not in the tale itself, but the effect of the tale upon the teller. The narrator, who is not the man who stole the cow, but a friend who met him in prison, explains that once he heard the man's story: "desde entonces, me hice comunista" (350) [since then, I became a Communist]. In "La baja" a National Guardsman resigns his position in protest over the government's abuse of power that would have him kill his fellow countrymen, and in "La coconingalinde" a young, fired employee miraculously gets her job back by playing a game of one-upmanship against her boss and winning. Finally, in "El machete" despite the many obstacles to organizing a union meeting, a common man persists: "Había que hacer la reunión, y la harían, aunque fuera en el monte" (361) [The meeting had to be held, and it would be held, even if they had to convene in the woods]. In this same political vein, two of the stories criticize the Catholic Church, a vestige of Spanish colonialism: "El matrimonio" [The Wedding] and "El

mandamiento" [The Commandment], both of which show the in-
sensitivity of church doctrine when indiscriminately applied to the
country's poor.

Only one story in the collection is obviously autobiographical, "El
parto" [The Birth], based on Dobles' father's career as a country
doctor and written in clear admiration for his selflessness. Two of
the stories have existential themes, in which the main characters
react positively or negatively to the course of their lives: "El cum-
pleaños" [The Birthday] where the main character ironically laments, "Hoy cumplo sesenta años y nunca jamás en la vida me ha
sucedido nada que valga la pena" (348) [Today I turn sixty and
never in my life has anything worthwhile ever happened to me] and
"El chiclero,"[10] the story of a Christlike figure who sacrifices himself
for a friend.

All the stories but three are told by an objective third-person narrator and bear no resemblance to the oral storytelling techniques of
Tata Mundo. One, however, "El gordo," recalls Tata Mundo's style
by having a narrator begin the story as though he were someone
known to us, "¿Recuerdan ustedes a Lico Méndez, aquel barbero
de Golfito, gordo, colorado, parlanchín y terco jugador de lotería?"
(328) [Do you remember Lico Méndez, that barber from Golfito, a
fat guy, with a ruddy complexion, talkative, and a stubborn lottery
player?] Another story, "El chiclero," interweaves the first-person
thoughts of the main character with objective third-person narration, and finally, "El diario" [The Diary] has a frame story about two
men, historians or researchers perhaps, who read a journal kept by
two North Americans living in Puerto Limón from 1911 to 1919. The
frame story is narrated in first-person plural: "Y comenzamos a leer"
(371) [And we began to read], and the central story emerges from
the diary entries written by the two men, Sandiford and Forrester,
forming an irregular dialogue between them.

"El diario," which has been anthologized in a collection of Costa
Rican short stories published in the United States, is one of Dobles'
best tales in terms of structure and one of his most intriguing in
terms of its racial theme and irony. Both journal writers, one of
whom ironically is from the racist Southern United States, fall in
love with the same black woman. Set in the turbulent period of
North American investment in large banana plantations along the
Costa Rican Atlantic coast, Sandiford kills a black man in a labor
confrontation. Forrester, neither a U.S. Southerner nor a believer in
Sandiford's "prejuicios y tonterías sobre pigmentos" (374) [preju-

dices and stupidities over pigmentation], still horrifyingly relegates the killing to "bueno, un pequeño error, ya está" (374) [well, a small error, that's all]. Whether from guilt, imagination, or a touch of magical realism (an unusual experiment for a writer known for his realistic fidelity), Sandiford believes he is actually turning black himself. Dobles leaves the issue in such ambiguous terms that we are never sure whether or not the man suffers from paranoid delusions or whether or not he, in fact, is actually metamorphosing.

This question intrigues the frame story historians, who are quite taken aback by the black woman's son who has lent them the diary. In their effort to find out how the story ends "¿Qué sería finalmente de Sandiford y Forrester?" (378) [What finally became of Sandiford and Forrester?], they overlook the significance of the tale, its central point; the boy Lawrence, son of the black woman and either Forrester or Sandiford, claims neither father: "el mulato se encogió orgullosamente de hombros.—Tengo sólo el apellido de la madre" (379) [the mulato pulled his shoulders back proudly.—I only have my mother's last name]. He refuses to acknowledge any inheritance from the metropolis; even the diary itself belongs, not to its authors, but to his mother "la viejecita, sus papeles" (379) [the old woman, her papers].

The last story in the collection provides the book's title "El violín y la chatarra." Widely anthologized and translated into German, it is a complex tale of self-interest, without a hero or an admirable character. As Rodolfo Cerdeño explains, "la metáfora del antagonismo conceptual (violín contra chatarra) . . . privilegia **el haber** antes que **el ser**"[11] [the metaphor of the conceptual antagonism (violin versus scrap metal) . . . privileges **having** over **being**]. The irony of the story invests it with humor, but the overall shallowness and superficiality of the characters, their concerns limited to money and status, reflect a segment of neocolonial, high society that disgusts and offends, which may very well have been Dobles' intention.

UNCOLLECTED STORIES

Dobles' *Obras completas* collects in a section titled "Y otros cuentos" [And Other Stories] eighteen remaining stories written between 1956 and 1983, many of which, until the publication of *Obras completas,* were still in manuscript. Among these last stories are some of his strongest isolated works and most anthologized pieces as well

as his one excursion into science fiction depicting Costa Rica in the
year 3165. Dobles' title (in English in the original), "To Be and Not
to Be," plays on Hamlet's famous soliloquy by switching Shake-
speare's binary "or" to Dobles' hybrid "and," once again offering a
sí pero no[12] rendering of third world existence. Finally, two of the stories are versions of theater pieces set to narrative: "El barrilete"
[The Kite] and "La pesadilla" [The Nightmare].

It is hard to make any generalizations regarding the themes of all
these stories since they range from broad political indictments to
psychological studies of character. True to his established style, the
treatment of character and setting is fundamentally realistic; however, Dobles does allow himself a few experiments with magical realism, a literary space that permits the intrusion of non-ordinary
reality into narrative, a tendency that steadily gained popularity during the 1960s with Gabriel García Márquez and Alejo Carpentier
among others. One of these stories, although not specifically autobiographical, "El jaspe" [Jasper], stems from Dobles' stint as a car-
penter and sawmill administrator. The tale recounts the experience
of an independently minded black man, who both literally and figuratively becomes the heart of the zurá tree where he lives until banana company police assassinate him. As the tree is sawed up, his
likeness appears as part of the tree rings: "La naturaleza, a veces, le
roba el crayón al Greco" (431) [Sometimes nature steals the brush
from El Greco]. The man's cultural identity and, metaphorically, his
ecological identity are ultimately destroyed by neocolonial authority, but the story itself, handed down by oral tradition, serves to resist
those forces that would destroy the region's environment along with
its people and culture.

As in the Tata Mundo stories, our inability to explain certain natural events, to understand coincidences, or to puzzle out a design in
the chaotic flow of life underscores many of these last uncollected
stories. The difference, however, between more recent examples of
magical realism in Spanish American literature and what Dobles
does, however, is crucial. While Dobles recognizes the inexplicable,
the magical, and the supernatural within his realistic representation
of the world, he does not accept magic as a natural part of life, undif-
ferentiated from any other part of life. His magic is highlighted,
commented upon as something strange and out of the ordinary, and
even disclaimed as possibly a figment of the imagination. It is a part
of the "real world" only in that he must include it if he is to represent or construct that world in all of its verisimilitude; that is, magic

is a part of the folklore that cannot be ignored and should be recorded, inscribed, and remembered, but it is an aspect of his culture that he ultimately attributes to superstition, legend, or fantasy, and in this sense, Dobles succumbs to the imperialism of the scientific community and eighteenth-century rationalism, quite consistent with his Marxist perspective.

Perhaps the most horrifying story in terms of its political denunciation and its psychological profundity is "Defensa propia" [Self-Defense], widely anthologized in both Spanish and English collections. In his own voice, a hired killer tells of shooting a friend in the back and then claiming it was self-defense. His lack of remorse and his wholesale acceptance of the status quo as justification for his atrocities, "el que tiene y puede, puede y tiene" (444) [he who has and can, can and has], is a chilling rendition of cynicism, cruelty, and uncritical collaboration with and appropriation of colonial and neocolonial forces.

In opposition to the cynicism of this story, however, Dobles writes "El puente" [The Bridge], considered one of his strongest stories, widely anthologized and translated as Alberto Cañas correctly predicted: "Apareció anteayer un cuento nuevo, de Fabián Dobles, 'El Puente,' que o mucho nos equivocamos, o va de cabeza hacia las antologías"[13] [The day before yesterday a new story appeared by Fabián Dobles, "The Bridge," that either we are very mistaken or it is headed straight for the anthologies]. Dedicated to his sister Margarita, with whom he was always close, "El puente" celebrates the possibilities and achievements of the marginalized voice. It is a tribute to persistence and resistance, to the fight for survival and improvement of the community. The story (as oral testimony) functions as an alternative version to official (written) history: "Así como el protagonista se enfrenta a las autoridades, el relato, al presentarse como la visión verdadera, se opone a la historia oficial, que adjudica la construcción del puente al gobierno"[14] [Just as the protagonist confronts the authorities, this tale, by presenting itself as the true version of events, confronts official history, which attributes the construction of the bridge to the government]. Critics and translators, Flora Ovares and Margarita Rojas, point out Dobles' manipulation of classical mythology in the story, which vests the protagonist with a degree of heroism otherwise unavailable to him:

... para lograr la construcción del puente, Godínez, como los héroes de los antiguios cuentos, debe vencer a tres adversarios: el río, los vecinos y el gobierno. Igualmente son tres los intentos que lleva a cabo en su afán de mejorar las condiciones de vida de su comunidad.

Cuando finalmente los vecinos exigen a la comitiva gubermental el paso de su entierro, Godínez triunfa sobre sus tres oponentes: ya cumplida su misión en este mundo, el puente le permite acceder a la orilla de la muerte.[15]

[. . . to have the bridge built, Godínez, like the heroes of antiquity, must triumph over three adversaries: the river, the neighbors, and the government. Likewise, there are three trials he must complete in his aim to improve the conditions of life in his community.

When the neighbors finally demand from the governmental committee the right for the funeral procession to pass, Godinez triumphs over his three opponents: since his mission in this world is now complete, the bridge allows him to reach the shore of death.]

Dobles' strength in comic representation and the use of the vernacular is also evident in this last group of stories. One of his funniest tales is "Antes muerta" [Over My Dead Body] about a womanizer who is seemingly irresistible: "Pero qué rayos tendrá ese demonio" (452) [But what in heaven's name does this devil have]. Several other stories have ironic twists: "La conejera" [The Rabbit Hole], "La mata de familia" [The Family Plant], "De amoroso" [Lovingly], "El ayote" [The Squash], and "La tentación" [The Temptation], an incident told to Dobles by his mother-in-law, Alice Donaldson de Trejos, to whom he dedicates the story.

Two of his uncollected stories are autobiographical, "Los hombres no lloran" [Men Don't Cry], in which Dobles' father, the country doctor, and his mother, Carmen, play secondary roles and "Sin ninguna duda" [Without a Doubt], in which Fabián himself appears at age thirteen, accompanying his father, the doctor, on his rounds. This particular incident recreates a formative moment in his journey toward manhood and his increasing awareness of social injustice. The tone of the story is lighthearted, yet with serious underpinnings, producing a tension between humor and tragedy that recalls the composition of the Tata Mundo stories. As the doctor himself says, reminiscent of the experienced Mundo instructing the youth accompanying him, "Mi hijito, a la verdad a veces hay que sopapearla para que no se duerma. Así la enderezamos. Ya lo irá comprendiendo con el tiempo. Usted guardará el secreto. Es un hombrecito" (457) [Son, sometimes you have to give truth a good shaking so it doesn't fall asleep. That's how we straighten it out. You will understand with time. You will keep the secret. You're becoming a man now]. The young Fabián watches as the priest, the lawyer, and his father, the doctor (symbolic of the three political forces that combined under the leadership of President Calderón Guardia before the Civil War of 1948), who all disagree violently on religious and political issues, come together on a matter of social welfare—all agree to witness a will dictated by a dead man, without which his companion of years and his children would be left penniless. Fabián is in charge of holding the dead man's head and nodding it up and down in agreement to leaving his worldly goods to his common law wife and his children: "¿Les consta sin ninguna duda que dijo sí?—Nos consta. Y estamparon las firmas" (462) [You certify without a doubt that he said yes?—We certify. And they signed their names]. The story is told in admiration for the way these three professionals, the fundamental figures implicitly charged with the welfare of a poor country and generally at odds about how to achieve it, agree to twist the facts and bend the rules, for the ultimate good of a struggling family. The three function together as a trickster figure in disguise once again fooling the overriding colonial (now nationalist) legal system.

All of these stories reflect Dobles' increasing control over language, his ability to construct speech and dialogue, his sophisticated creation of images and metaphors, and his ability to delve into the psychological recesses of character. His fundamental interest, as always, lies with the social and individual situations of common people, with their existential struggles as well as their political challenges and social realities. The setting is always somewhere in Costa Rica and Dobles' determination to represent, recreate, and inscribe the land and people he knows and imagines is obvious. In so doing, as Alberto Cañas noted about his fellow writer and lifelong friend, it is no longer clear whether Dobles reflected the identity and speech of the Costa Rican *campesino* or whether the *campesino* adopted the personal and cultural identity that Dobles constructed for him in his fiction.

PARACUENTOS

Paracuentos[16] are an unusual group of stories that are among the first that Dobles ever wrote back in the 1940s. They remained unpublished until he collected them in 1993 for his complete works.

The term itself *paracuentos* is a made-up word with multiple possibilities. The second part of the word is clearly *cuento* [story]. The first
part, *para*, may come from the Spanish preposition *para* [for] or may
also refer to the Greek *pará*, meaning *against* or *beside*. These narratives, then, may represent material for stories, or on the contrary,
anti-stories—something that looks like a story (parallel to a story)
but is not. This collection, comprised of a total of nine narratives
dedicated to fellow writer and friend, Joaquín Gutiérrez, seems to
support the second view; that is, the material appears to be a grand
experiment in language resulting in absurdist, surreal tales, but not
what could or should be labeled stories. Each piece has the same
central character, el Descorazonador Madrigales [Madrigales, the
Heartbreaker], who reappears or is referred to in each narrative. On
the surface each piece has all the outward characteristics of short
fiction: a narrator, characters, dialogue, plot, setting, title; yet none
make any more sense than Lewis Carroll's nonsense poems. For Dobles, who as an adolescent set out to memorize the *Larousse Dictionary*, stopping at *G* because of increasing doubts as to the ultimate
benefits of such an exercise, the manipulation of the way words
function as opposed to their socially agreed upon meanings is para-
mount. Sentences look like sentences: there are nouns and verbs
and adjectives, all in the appropriate places, but the ultimate significance of these combinations of words eludes us: "El profesor de
Alfonsina Celajes jamás habría podido descifrar aquel bendito ori-
fraño de no ser por la cotorra, que estaba esa mañana endiablada-
mente extraña y transuránica" (11) [Alfonsina Celajes' professor
would never have been able to figure out that blessed orifran if it
hadn't been for the cotorra, who was feeling devilishly strange and
transuranic that morning.] The end result is the sensation of a looking glass world where people talk, get excited, and move about in
stories that are seriously narrated in objective third person point of
view in a language that paradoxically is and is not one we can understand (once again *sí pero no*). The effect is as though we are at some
distance from the teller, barely able to hear, understanding words
here and there but unable to make sense out of the whole.

Such an experiment might be expected from a man with Dobles'
sense of humor and erudite background, but ultimately the language, though altered, is not decolonized. It cannot function as a
medium of communication between subaltern writer and reader; in
fact, ironically only the elite reader will appreciate the joke. Ulti-

mately, the stories do not *do* anything or mean anything; they just are. For Dobles, who was so opposed to art for art's sake and art for entertainment, who in the 1950s in his essays argued specifically for art "con un contenido ético al mismo tiempo que estético"[17] [with an ethical as well as an aesthetic content], these stories apparently held little value for him beyond the practice and experimentation they provided. Only in hindsight could they be considered worthy of publication, along with his early poems, as a record of the development of an artist.

6

The Mature Novels

El sitio de las abras. Guatemala: Editorial del Ministerio de Educa-
lción Pública, 1950; second through tenth editions, San José:
Editorial Costa Rica, 1970–1999.

En el San Juan hay tiburón. San José: Editorial L'Atelier, 1967;
second edition, San José: Editorial Costa Rica, 1978; third
edition, Heredia: Editorial de la Universidad Nacional, 1996.

EL SITIO DE LAS ABRAS

UNQUESTIONABLY DOBLES' MOST POPULAR NOVEL AND ONE OF THE
foundational fictions of Costa Rica, *El sitio de las abras* has been the
subject of numerous theses, critical articles, and university lectures
both in Costa Rica and the United States.[1] The manuscript, finished
in 1946 and favorably mentioned in a local newspaper,[2] won the
gold medal and a publishing contract in the Guatemalan sponsored
"Certamen Centroamericano—15 de setiembre" in 1947. It took
three more years, however, for Guatemala's Ministry of Public Education to actually complete publication (1950). A Guatemalan newspaper *Ultima Hora* reviewed the winning novel in 1947 and described
it as "la primera novela agraria, netamente agraria, que se escribe
en Costa Rica, y, además, contiene la historia de los campesinos y de
la tierra, así, a secas, de aquí y de todas partes"[3] [the first agrarian
novel, really agrarian, written in Costa Rica, and, what is more, it
contains the history of the peasant farmers and the land, in short,
from here and from everywhere].[4]

Despite the novel's popularity, (a Spanish critic even mentioned
it favorably, which is quite unusual for a Central American work of
fiction),[5] a second edition did not appear in Costa Rica for twenty
years. Reviews for successive editions have all been favorable,[6] com-
menting on Dobles' ability to represent "social reality" and to

sound like the *campesinos* he depicts. Only Alberto Cañas has dared suggest that the novel is not flawless. Even though he chooses this work after Dobles' death as his all-time favorite,[7] he laments in 1971 that the ending seems hurried and that the epic tone is lost in the last third of the book.[8] The general consensus among the reviewers, however, agrees with Argentinean critic Carlos Catania that the novel "ayuda a comprender la realidad nacional, los orígenes de problemas que *subsisten*"[9] [helps understand national reality, the origin of problems that *continue*]. The Costa Rican Ministry of Education obviously agrees since it has at various times made the novel required high school reading for students throughout the country. Such a requirement is not without theoretical support assuming, as Doris Sommer explains, "that literature has the capacity to intervene in history, to help construct it," a belief that permeates Latin American literature where virtually all the foundational fictions suggest "the inextricability of politics from fiction in the history of nation-building."[10]

After independence from Spain in 1821, Costa Rica, like other Latin American countries, entered a period of national consolidation, "which featured programs to populate the empty and ungovernable spaces . . . the [independence] fighter was called home to be a father."[11] This pattern is precisely the one presented by Dobles' protagonist, ñor Espíritu Santo Vega, who is a veteran of the War of 1856. This war (an extension of the independence struggle) pitted Central Americans against the North American filibuster William Walker, who attempted to take over the region with his private army and set up his personal dominion. Vega and his son clear and cultivate a piece of land, "las abras" [the open spaces], in the wilderness frontiers of the nineteenth-century Costa Rican Central Plateau in order to move the family out of the capital city San José. This time "la guerra no iba contra hombres, sino contra la naturaleza. Otro modo de defender a la patria, sí, aunque ñor Espíritu Santo no lo pensara, porque tan sólo quería atrincherar bien a su familia"[12] [the war was not against men, but against nature. Another way of defending the country, yes, even though Mr. Espíritu Santo wouldn't think of it that way since he only wanted to settle his family well]. Though the challenge to domesticate nature is by no means inconsiderable, the work to clear *las abras* takes on an idyllic and utopian tone that places ñor Espíritu Santo [Mr. Holy Ghost], as his name implies, in the position of the Creator of an

Edenic national history. This idealized reconstruction of the voiceless past posits an innocent, monologic group of seven[13] families
who share fundamental beliefs and values and who work coopera-
tively, dividing unalienated labor more or less equitably between
the sexes. Vega and his neighbors are the Creoles, the new colo-
nists, transplanted Europeans with a new American identity and
the utopian project of beginning again in a new world, a new
space—this time without Spain's oversight.

It is this foundational period that Dobles implies has been
erased from the national memory with the passage of time and
the unthinking drive toward modernity. National consolidation is
equated with the fortification of the family, a frequent analogy in
political philosophy: "no hay que pensarlo mucho. Hay que ha-
cerla, por la familia" (192) [a person shouldn't think about it
much. He just has to do it, for the family]. Dobles' imagery reminds us that Costa Rica (both nation and family) is founded on
agriculture, on the land, and that the impulse toward industrialization and development perilously divorces the country from its
origins: "Ha molido el tiempo tanta harina de hombres y de días,
que los que hoy viven allí y los que llegamos de paso, alguna vez,
lo ignoramos casi todo" (183) [The mills of time have ground up
so much flour in the form of men and days that those living today
and those just passing through are ignorant of almost everything].
The nation's beginnings are inscribed in the land itself: "escrito
en medio de la montaña" (183) [written in the midst of the
mountain] and any knowledge of this past that has not faded into
oblivion is passed down almost entirely through oral tradition. As
in his other works, Dobles suggests this orality in his language.
The narrator literally talks to his reader: "Parecía impresionante,
sí, señor, parecía impresionante" (185) [It seemed impressive,
yes, sir, it seemed impressive].

This first period in the creation of *las abras* is characterized by an
unspoken, inarticulate drive and compulsion to dominate the wilderness in order to build:

[N]o lo decían, ni lo pensaban. Trabajaban. Edificaban. Abrían . . .
Abrir, romper, botar para levantar, como todo lo verdadero. Estaban
edificando las abras, *nuestras antepasadas las abras, madres de todos nosotros
y de nuestros hijos*, esas que están olvidadas bajo las sementeras de hoy
y cubiertas por el hojarascal de los tiempos. (p. 185; emphasis mine)

[They didn't talk about it or think about it. They worked. They built. They cleared. Clear, break, tear down in order to build, like everything authentic. They were building the open spaces, *our heritage the open spaces, mothers of us all* and of our children, those that are forgotten under today's seedbeds and covered by the rotting leaves of time.]

The violent conquering (a metaphorical rape) of the motherland[14] by the patriarch Vega secures the foundational national family, literally producing (giving birth to) a national space. Vega's wife and the other women involved in the colonial project participate in fundamentally equal conditions alongside their men to conquer the land: "la ruda femineidad de sus mujeres de furibundas manos" (183) [the rough femininity of their busy hands]. Bourgeois gender distinctions, the product of alienation in a market economy that denies women a vital role in the construction of history, have not yet come into existence. This integration of gender allows the "abras" men and women to function together as human beings in a symbolic masculine subjugation of the mother (feminine) land: "Dolores de Vega . . . más hombre que nadie" (222) [Dolores de Vega . . . more of a man than anybody]. Dobles' insistence on the equality between the sexes during this formative period in the nation, "mujeres y hombres jugaban un papel de conjunto en las pequeñas fincas que se agarraban a la montaña" (214) [women and men worked together on the small farms that clung to the mountain] actually depends upon this erasure of difference between genders under a symbolic masculinity and the concomitant projection of female gender onto the land. In the battle of "humanity/man" against "nature/woman," man ultimately triumphs, of course, and from this victory and hierarchical union comes the symbolic birth of the nation.

Dolores Vega, ñor Espíritu Santo's wife, sets the standards and boundaries of female power during this idyllic national past. Her tactics and strategies in this foundational work have become embedded in the cultural fabric of the nation and serve as a model for a kind of nonconfrontational feminism. According to this model men and women wield equal decision-making power but women act behind the scenes, never directly or openly challenging the male self-image:

De un modo habilidoso, sin hacer nunca oposición directa a ñor Espíritu Santo, pero con firmeza que se insinuaba sin manifestarse por entero, muy a menudo ella tomaba las decisiones importantes y lo hacía de tal manera que el bueno de su esposo creía a pie juntillas que eran suyas. (194)

[Very effectively, without ever directly opposing Mr. Holy Ghost, but with a firmness that she insinuated without actually showing, she frequently made the important decisions, and she did so in a way that her good husband believed without a doubt that the decisions were entirely his.]

Whether such a pattern reflects actual female behavior of the nineteenth century (or today), or whether it is a model that Dobles fundamentally likes and imposes on Costa Rica's past is, of course, unclear. Apparently, however, it is a fairly common model in postcolonial fiction, according to Michael Cooke, who argues that:

A lot of female submission, though we take it as the mark of victimization, really reflects a kind of inexorable contempt for men . . . The effect is a seesaw in the following arrangement, with men on top in apparent strength but women on top in real strength.

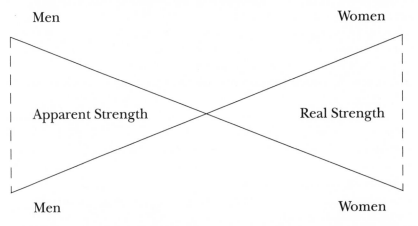

Men   Women

Apparent Strength   Real Strength

Men   Women

Masculine vulnerability breeds in the gap between apparent (social) and real (spiritual) strength, but it is also in that gap that women cultivate apparent submission.[15]

Actually Cooke's diagram is somewhat unclear and might better be understood by labeling the lines A = apparent strength and B = real strength as follows. Thus, men control the left side of the diagram (apparent strength) while women control the right side of the diagram (real strength:

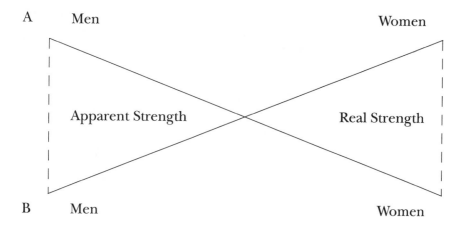

The Costa Rican version of this model must be drawn in slightly different terms, however, with men at the top of the seesaw in the public sphere (line A) and women at the top in the private sphere (line B). The following diagram is actually more descriptive of Dolores' behavior where women control the right side of the diagram (the private sphere) and men control the left side (the public sphere).

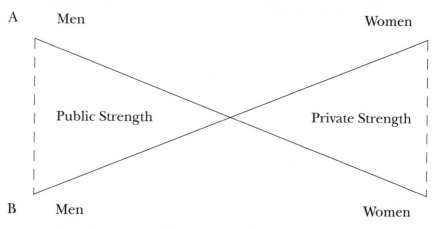

Cultural belief and acceptance of this model is still very strong. Indeed, such a system of designating different social spaces for the exercise of power may actually have worked in a premodern society; (Dobles obviously thinks so), but it presents some obvious drawbacks for women today and may now simply serve as male justification for a fundamentally inequitable distribution of power. Nevertheless, it is this carefully designated space for the apparent

exercise of "equal" power (another version of *sí pero no*) that justi-
fies the common cultural belief in Costa Rica that such a model not
only exists but also that it should exist. The model itself, however,
silences any possible protest or criticism by women since such protest would take place in a public forum where decorum and truly
feminine behavior would not permit women a voice. Certainly, Dobles is a product of his time and culture (and his gender) in propos-
ing Dolores (and implicitly this system) as worthy of female
emulation.[16] Nevertheless, Dobles' point is well taken—the relationship between the sexes, even under this model during the formative
period of *las abras*, is healthier and more egalitarian than in the ensuing period where class and gender distinctions increase once the
land is no longer the female object of desire but a commodity to be
acquired and exchanged in a market economy.

Structurally, the novel closes the idealized Edenic period of *las
abras* with the symbolic birth of nationhood. The continuing story
of the land and its foundational families (national consolidation) is
represented in terms of a human life span (infancy, youth, maturity,
death). With the sale of a parcel of *las abras* to an outsider, Ambrosio
Castro "oriundo de la capital" (210) [native of the capital], the vices
of urbanity and modernity invade. Castro, the speaker for an unfet-
tered and amoral pursuit of wealth, wants more land and is determined to get it. The war of man against nature, thus, begins to slip
into "la peor pelea: la del hombre contra el hombre" (210) [the
worst fight: that of man against man].

With the introduction of economic and military power wielded by
a dominant minority, class distinctions become ingrained—"Castro
no se daba jamás por vencido fácilmente. Conocedor de la fuerza de
su dinero y de su puntería con la pistola, se creía hombre valiente"
(231) [Castro didn't give up easily. Aware of the power of his money
and his marksmanship with a pistol, he believed himself to be a
brave man]. Along with class distinctions, equally powerful gender
distinctions emerge: "Aparte de sus humos de señora encumbrada
[la mujer de Castro] no era sino una inofensiva ama de casa con
muy poco de la vigorosa capacidad de las mujeres de las abras"
(213–14) [Without her airs of a superior woman (Castro's wife) was
nothing more than an inoffensive housewife with little of the vigor-
ous capacity of the women of the open spaces]. Bourgeois women,
with the emergence of a market economy, lose their vital role in the
mode of production and must occupy a plastic and superfluous femininity that devalues and directly opposes the strength and "rough

femininity" of the *campesina*. Martín Villalta, the renegade neighbor who is willing to call Castro's hand—"¿Acepta la paz, Ambrosio Castro, o prefiere usted la guerra?" (245) [Accept peace, Ambrosio Castro, or do you prefer war?]—saves the community but sacrifices the women. In fighting fire with fire, he falls victim to bourgeois gender definitions. Thus, he denigrates the community's previous attempts to counter Castro's avarice by invalidating the *abras* women: "Ese es juego de mujeres" (245) [That's a game for women]. The community, through Villalta, temporarily wins the right to keep its land, but at the price of its innocence and the value of its women: ". . . Y así terminó la infancia de las abras" (245) [. . . And so ended the infancy of the open spaces].

The *abras* women are not the only victims in this narrative of national history. Dobles is one of the few Costa Rican writers who consider the plight of the scarce autochthonous Indian population. In the formative stages of the *abras* (and nationhood) they appear as double victims, both of the landed Castro and of the founding families who colonize the area without regard to local indigenous inhabitants. Castro hires the Indians to help him enlarge his piece of land and recommends that his neighbors do the same with the ulterior motive of lending them money to do so. His arrogant and condescending description of the voiceless Indians from Talamanca reinforces our perception of his greed and lack of ethics:

> Contráte unos cuantos inditos de estos y agrandás lo tuyo. No es difícil, vos podés pagarles con guaro, les gusta. Salen desde Talamanca, ahí para el sur. Es cosa de mandar un recado con alguno de ellos y después vienen apareciendo los otros. Son tratables. Bueno, desconfiados y mudos que nadie les saca ni un gesto, pero se les paga cualquier pendejada. Ni siquiera conocen el castellano, lo que es otra ventaja para uno. (215)

> [Hire a few of these Indians and clear more land for yourself. It's not hard, you can pay them with liquor, they like it. They come from Talamanca and move south. It's just a matter of sending a message with one of them and then the others will appear. They're easy to work with. Well, suspicious and tight-lipped, you can't get a word out of them, but you can pay them whatever. They don't even speak Spanish, which is another advantage for us.]

The neighbor's reluctance to borrow money from Castro does not stem from a more ethical position with regard to the Indians, but rather from the fear of losing his land. In fact, one of Villalta's strategies for opposing Castro is first to eliminate his cheap labor supply. Thus, in his attempt to preserve the *abras* for the white families who colonized them, he, too, exploits the ignorance and fear of the Indians:

> Villalta les advirtió que él era una "autoridad" del Gobierno y estaba encargado de enlistar a hombres para una guerra en la que se necesitaba a todos los individuos aptos para tomar armas . . . El no hubiera querido tener que ser grosero con aquellos indefensos hombrecillos de rostro taciturno y había buscado esa mañosa manera de hacerlos alejarse. (243–44)

> [Villalta told them that he was a Government "authority" and that he was in charge of enlisting men for a war that needed every available man to bear arms . . . He didn't want to be nasty to those defenseless little men with the taciturn faces and so he had found this surreptitious means for making them leave.]

Once the Indians disappear into the mountains, they are erased as human beings both from Dobles' narrative as well as from national memory. All that remains are the palimpsestic erasure marks, the smudges and traces in Costa Rican legend that merely reinforce local prejudice and do nothing to vindicate the indigenous position. Furthermore, the Indians continue to be blamed even in their absence for natural phenomena:

> [C]orre la voz de que son los indios de la montaña quienes viendo que les envenenan su *peje*, hacen conjuros en las fuentes de los ríos para llamar en su ayuda al dios del agua y de la lluvia, que hincha enfurecido las aguas. Aunque donde nacen los manantiales desde hace tiempos no existen indígenas, la leyenda se resiste a perecer. (350)

> [Rumor has it that the Indians from the mountain, who saw that their *peje* had been poisoned, cast spells on the rivers' sources, calling on the god of water and rain to help them make the water swell furiously. Although where the springs are located, there haven't been Indians for a long time; still, the legend refuses to die out.]

Their very absence, thus, becomes a magically real presence in the folklore of the nation.

The next section of the novel narrates the growth and decline (youth, maturity, and old age) of the *abras*. Martin Villalta builds a sawmill that brings temporary prosperity to the community. While from today's vantage point we recognize this period as the inauguration of massive deforestation, at the time, the sawmill permits the foundational families of the *abras* to begin to accumulate capital. While they have won a temporary respite from the greed of Ambrosio Castro, his son Laureano, takes advantage of Villalta's departure from the area to pursue his father's goals of consolidating, not the nation, but his individual wealth. He reroutes the water from the stream that powers the sawmill, leaving it unable to function and bankrupting the families who own it. Espíritu Santo's death at this point in the novel signals the symbolic demise of the *abras*. The colonial situation, then, is turned on its head. The colonizers lose their land to the rich landholder, who creates an enormous *latifundio* [plantation] and hires the former owners to work the land that is now no longer theirs. The colonizers have become the colonized victims of a feudal system and an internal form of neocolonialism (the city versus country conflict).

Alberto Cañas is probably right that after Espíritu Santo's death the narrative loses its propelling force. The *campesino* struggle to regain the land is a losing battle all around, both in Dobles' narrative and in national history, and is only further complicated by the increasing pressure of North American interests, a topic that Dobles treats more fully in *Los leños vivientes*. The presidency of Calderón Guardia, however, mentioned only indirectly in this novel, does take some initial steps at countering the growth of the *latifundio* in Costa Rica. His administration passes a Labor Code designed to protect the worker from employer abuses. In addition, his administration is responsible for the "Ley de los Parásitos" [Parasite Law], (pejoratively named by the landholders), which allows the *campesino* to claim unused land that he clears and works as his own, despite its registered ownership by the large landholder. This law served a double purpose, on the one hand protecting the *campesino*, and on the other hand encouraging people to leave the overpopulated capital: "es irónico que por esa época Costa Rica sólo aprovechaba un 10 por ciento de las tierras labrantías. El resto eran prados o bosques sin limpiar"[17] [it is ironic that during this period Costa Rica only utilized 10 percent of its farmable lands. The rest were fields or woods that had not been cleared]. Given that Calderón had managed to pass a significant corpus of virtually irreversible social reforms,[18] the main problem, then, became educating the masses about their rights so that they could take advantage of them, a very different proposition from the history of land struggle elsewhere in Latin America.[19]

The last third of the novel involves the conflict between the heirs of the Castro family and the heirs of the initial families who opened *las abras*. The main character, Martín Vega Ledezma, is significantly heir to both Martín Villalta, the renegade hero of the *abras*, and the founding Vega family. An important part of this section is devoted to memories of Martín's childhood. Raised on the González-Leflair plantation (land that used to belong to the Vega family) where his mother is a cook, Martín has unusual access to upper-class education and commodities. He also befriends the daughter of the González-Leflair family, Concha, a relationship that ultimately slips into romance. These romantic entanglements between members of different social classes or groups are a hallmark of foundational fictions throughout Latin America as literature struggles with the emerging concepts of national and cultural identities:

> Whether the plots end happily or not, the romances are invariably about desire in young, chaste heroes for equally young and chaste heroines in order to establish conjugal and productive unions which represent national unification and which can be frustrated only by illegitimate social obstacles. Overcoming those obstacles produces the desired end.[20]

Where Dobles differs from this pattern of foundational romances throughout Latin America is his unwillingness to diminish or overcome the social obstacles that ultimately intervene in the Martín/Concha romance. He is, after all, a realist, not a romantic. The family sends Concha to Europe, and she eventually marries someone of her own class. Martín joins the Communist Party and becomes an organizer for the farmers' union. Even though the couple meet again and speak in the last chapter and despite Concha's claim that Martín's politics need not prevent their renewed friendship, "Eso no impide que podamos ser otra vez buenos amigos" (359) [That's no reason why we cannot be good friends again], Martín is no longer interested in a romantic consolidation of the nation. He has no desire to become Cinderella. "Las buenas relaciones entre patronos y obreros" (321) [Good relations between employers and employees] are a figment of the neocolonial imagination. What Dobles projects is low intensity war—repeated and continual resistances to a full range of neocolonial aspirations. The specific incidents in this last section are a matter of details, engagements lost, engagements won.

Whatever the course of events in the history of the nation, the battle lines have been irrevocably drawn: "Están situados en campos opuestos y tienen puntos de vista por entero divergentes" (322) [They are seated in opposite camps and have totally divergent points of view]. Ironically, the gender lines have also been drawn. Martín Vega, the hero of the last third of the novel, comes from an exclusively male line. His name derives from his grandfather (*Martín* Villalta) and great-grandfather (Espíritu Santo *Vega*). His own father, estranged from him during his youth, is reencountered and reengaged in the last chapter when Martín symbolically walks away from Concha (the feminine Other) and invites his father to "un par de tragos" (360) [a couple of drinks], the manly activity among Costa Rican males. In this novel once again, the male bonding through alcohol indicates an acceptance of existing social and political constructs. As they leave together, father and son, Dobles' narrator comments significantly in the novel's last line: "Ellos no lo saben; mas, se parecen tanto sus andados" (360) [They don't know it, but they look so much alike in the way they walk]. The future, it would seem, is squarely within the domain of Costa Rica's men. There are no women here, no mothers, sisters, wives, or girlfriends. Clearly, the gender issue has been deferred to class conflict, and the period of prehistory in *las abras* ironically becomes the mythical goal for the future, an impossible return to the past to escape the inevitable tragedy of modernity.

EN EL SAN JUAN HAY TIBURÓN

After the lukewarm reception of *Los leños vivientes* in 1962, Dobles did not offer his readers anything new for five years. Then, in 1967, his novel *En el San Juan hay tiburón* [There's a Shark in the San Juan River] won national critical acclaim and the esteemed Aquileo J. Echeverría prize for fiction. One year later in 1968 Dobles was awarded the Premio Magón for a lifetime of achievement in the arts. According to Alberto Cañas, Dobles' longtime friend and critic, *En el San Juan hay tiburón* may not be Dobles' best novel, but it is certainly his most mature and displays the linguistic and descriptive control of a seasoned writer.[21] While the novel has obviously not been as popular as *El sitio de las abras* (1950), reviewers have been uniformly positive and have remained so for all three editions. Dobles' English translator, Joan Henry, claims that this novel is the next work by Dobles that she would like to translate because of its social, political, and historical interest.[22]

Set in the San Carlos area, the northern frontier between Costa Rica and Nicaragua, the novel revolves around the contemporary revolutionary activities in the region, which, twelve years after its publication, culminate in the Sandinista triumph and the ousting of the Somoza regime from Nicaragua in June 1979. Still over a decade away from military victory, the resistance in the 1960s is intent on acquiring and accumulating weapons and ammunition for the Sandinista guerrillas in the mountains. One of the main supply routes, through the northern Costa Rican border, entails crossing the San Juan River. The title of the novel refers to the code phrase used to warn smugglers and revolutionaries that Somoza's military police were close by patrolling the waterway that runs between the two countries and, ironically, is still a source of tension and disagreement between the two nations.

Dobles' representation of this political moment (which resulted in his novel's being banned in Nicaragua when it was first published) entails a three-pronged rhetorical strategy that combines to produce a forceful piece of resistance writing. Fundamentally, there are three stories that intertwine, each adding a significant piece to the resistance discourse. The central story is a highly charged intrigue involving a contraband arms shipment, the discovery of a traitor and informer within the revolutionary group of smugglers, the group's ambush of a Nicaraguan patrol, and the competition between two members of the group, who are united in politics but divided over a woman. The surface action, worthy of a Hollywood adventure film, takes place in the present.

The sub-story delves into the past through memories and musings explaining how each of the revolutionaries—both Nicaraguan and Costa Rican—arrived at this juncture in history. These memories recall personal and individual struggles within an increasingly oppressive Nicaragua and an attempt to determine at what point each revolutionary gains consciousness of himself as objectified Other, refuses this role, and assumes responsibility for his own subjectivity through a direct challenge to the dominant script. These thoughts and memories involving descriptions of Nicaraguan jails, torture, and assassinations by Somoza's military police reinforce the guiding ideological position of the novel as resistance discourse. Interwoven in the text is an allegory of the revolution itself, in some ways, an allegory of the principal actors of all revolutions.

In this sense, Dobles' novel recalls Frederic Jameson's (in)famous directive that "all third-world texts are necessarily . . . *national allegories*" (Jameson's emphasis).[23] Allegories, which are rather straightforward, one to one equivalencies between narrative participants and symbolic referents, often function as thinly disguised resistance discourse. While Jameson's terminology "third world" and "national"[24] is problematic, it is probably safe to say that Dobles' text[25] may be read productively as allegory, if not as Jameson suggests, a *national* allegory, then at least, as a *regional* allegory.

The Sandinista Revolution, more than anything else since the Cuban Revolution in 1959, served to unify Central America as a "collectivity," that is, a dialogic hybridization—a mixture that is neither a blending nor erasing of difference but instead a strategic grouping of differences, as Spivak says, a "bonding in difference."[26] This collectivity shares a number of characteristics in common (language, geography, environment, postcolonial status, and most importantly, opposition to the Somoza regime) while retaining and recognizing national and regional differences, personal, separate and unique identities. The struggle to overthrow Somoza in the history of Central America mushroomed into much more than a national effort to oust a dictatorial dynasty; it accrued regional force and allegorical justification as a struggle of Good against the forces of Evil, Injustice, and Oppression. Most importantly, it opened up dialogue, not between tyranny and revolutionaries, but among the often very different members of the resistance. Costa Rica, which had abolished its standing army under the 1949 Constitution, tried to maintain an official position of neutrality with regard to the conflict, while unofficially encouraging the revolutionaries and often looking the other way at weapons trafficking across its northern border, a clear case of *sí pero no* or its inverse *no pero sí.* The historical situation, itself inherently allegorical (Sandinistas = forces of Good; Somozistas = forces of Evil), foregrounds Dobles' narrative—an allegory of the historical conflict; that is, an allegory of an allegory, or an allegory once removed.

Dobles' opening page introduces the principal players who represent the main actors in the Nicaraguan political conflict (Somoza, Nicaragua, her people, the resistance, Costa Rica):

El mudo ha salido del boscaje y se interna en el pastizal. Trae al hombro un cabro recién nacido y en la mano un grueso bejuco. Camina por entre las macollas del repasto hacia donde presiente las vacas. Cuando se les acerca . . . escoge la que le parece más mansa y trata de explicarle a punta de gruñidos y visajes lo que ha sucedido:

Este cabrito se quedó huérfano. Algún cazador le mató a la madre y si no lo alimentamos se va a morir. Te vas a portar bien conmigo y me le vas a regalar de esa agua blanca que le das a tu ternero.

A saber si la vaca lo comprende . . .

Cuando más tarde el sordomudo se va con él otra vez al hombro, el animalito ya viene lleno y levanta contento las orejas . . .

Piensa pedirle a su amigo del aserradero que le permita guardarlo en el galerón de los terneros, no vaya a ser que si lo deja en los pastizales lo devore el tigre. [27]

[The mute has left the woods and gone into the pasture. He has a newborn goat slung over his shoulder and a thick vine in his hand. He walks between the heaps of grass until he sees the cows. As he walks nearer . . . he picks the cow that seems the most docile and tries to explain to her in grunts and gestures what has happened:

This little goat has been left an orphan. Some hunter killed his mother and if we don't feed him, he's going to die. Now you be good and give me some of that white water you give your calf.

Who knows if the cow understands . . .

Later when the deaf mute leaves with the little animal over his shoulder again, the goat is full and lifts his ears contentedly . . .

He plans to ask his friend at the sawmill if he will let him keep the goat in amongst the calves, because if he leaves him out in the pasture, a tiger might devour him.]

This parable-like story of the deaf mute's efforts to save the orphaned goat reinscribes the Nicaraguan conflict. The hunter (human or tiger in this passage, a snake in a later passage) is the Somoza regime/Evil. The orphaned goat represents the Nicaraguan people who have had their country (the motherland, the goat's mother) killed or destroyed—that is, taken from them. The deaf mute is the embodiment of the resistance, which is good, silenced, marginalized, unable to hear or communicate, but acutely aware of the goat's plight.[28] The cow (who functions as the goat's surrogate mother) and everyone else who helps the deaf mute (the friend at the sawmill) become the multiple ways that Costa Rica and her people help the Sandinista cause. Throughout the narrative the deaf mute, Gugú, appears and disappears, almost tangential to the action of the failed arms shipment and the love triangle. Yet his continual reappearances suggest the strength of the resistance, despite setbacks and failures and absence from view. At the very end of the novel he appears one last time: "Va simplemente con sus pies, su frente, un cabro, su corazón y su escopeta" (261) [He goes simply with his feet, his forehead, a goat, his heart, and his rifle]. From the first page when his only weapon is a thick branch or vine, he now carries a shotgun. The challenge to Somoza is clearly moving from symbolic resistances to armed struggle. More significantly, Gugú's overriding concern, the goat, *el pueblo*, is still with him.

Gugú, like all resistance discourse, is a creature of the border, an outcast, relegated to the periphery of dominant script. Both literally and figuratively silenced, he is also deaf to the master text, and in this sense more immune to its persuasive ideological and epistemological power though not completely protected. In an early scene in the local grocery store/bar, we learn several important things about Gugú and, consequently, about the resistance. First, one of the men in the bar offers to buy the goat, but Gugú "visajea un no rotundo" (170) [signs a resounding "no"]; that is, the resistance is not to be bought off or sold out. Second, another man, significantly a Costa Rican, wonders aloud: "¿Este mudo es tontico?" (170) [Is this mute stupid?]. Popular Costa Rican belief, a thinly disguised ethnocentric condescension toward the Nicaraguan Other, has always held that Nicaraguans are not intelligent, certainly not capable enough to fight their own Revolution alone; they had to have help (even leadership and direction) from Costa Rica. This negative Nicaraguan stereotype inscribed in jokes and popular stories invariably depicts an uneducated, stupid *Nica* who speaks almost in grunts. Costa Ricans are famous for imitating the Nicaraguan accent and making the *Nica* the butt of the joke. The fact that the deaf mute is anything but *tontico* and that two of the principal characters in the novel are bright, admirable Nicaraguans is clearly Dobles' attempt to deconstruct and rewrite the negative representation by Costa Ricans of the Nicaraguan people.

Third, the deaf mute buys a soft drink at the bar, but the owner refuses his money: "Aquí este bandido mudo tiene cuenta corriente mientras no se lleve toda la pulpería" (170) [This darn mute has an open account here as long as he doesn't make off with the whole store]. In other words, Costa Ricans, like the bar owner, are willing to help the Sandinista cause (give it a free soda) as long as they do not have to sacrifice too much. Later, when the bar owner makes some insulting comments about the town's schoolteacher, a young pretty Nicaraguan woman, the deaf mute "le revienta la moneda sobre el mostrador y se aleja con su cabro" (172) [throws his money

back on the bar and leaves with his goat]. Thus, the resistance maintains clear ethical principles and disavows those who belittle the very
people it is fighting for: "[Gugú] no se lleva con los que cree malos
y se entiende muy bien con los buenos, nadie sabe por qué" (189)
[(Gugú) doesn't get along with those he thinks are bad and he gets
along well with good people, nobody knows why].

Dobles, already famous for his ability to recreate Costa Rican
speech and give his narratives an oral quality, does not shy away
from representing the Nicaraguan accent. The difference is that he
does not make fun of it. Here on the border the two accents interplay but never merge. National identities are clearly defined linguistically and phonetically, but the project of resistance is collective.
The dual presence of both accents emphasizes a dialogic resistance
to cultured Castilian speech, which, in turn, symbolizes a deeper
challenge to the dominant neocolonial (in this case tyrannical) master script.

The story itself, apart from the latticework frame of the deaf mute,
involves the attempt to smuggle arms across the Nicaraguan border.
Underlying this narrative is a multitude of hybridizations, that is,
unions that preserve difference emphasizing the collective nature of
the revolutionary enterprise. The clearest example is the coopera-
tion between don Jovel Carrillo, a Costa Rican businessman (owner
of a sawmill in the region) and Sebastián Molinos, exiled Nicaraguan and former schoolteacher. Both men are involved in smug-
gling weapons despite their divergent backgrounds and their
differing approaches to the armed struggle. Working for don Jovel
is another hybridized union: Don Jovel's right-hand man, Fermín
Pastora, a Costa Rican, married to Cayetana, don Jovel's cook, a Nicaraguan. Both preserve their distinct identity evidenced by their
speech and references to their native soil. Fermín Pastora's adopted
daughter, Graciela, also Nicaraguan, is the town's schoolteacher,
raised in Costa Rica yet closely identified with her Nicaraguan origin. She is the object of affection for both don Jovel (the Costa
Rican) and Sebastián (the Nicaraguan). Despite their competition
to win the love of this woman (Dobles is clearly not interested in
gender issues here), the political situation demands unity and coop-
eration and binds the men together, deferring love for another moment. Sebastián argues, "*Primero mi deber y después este sentimiento. El
compromiso con mi pueblo ante todo, mas no renunciaré a Graciela*" (214;
Dobles' italics) [*first my duty and then this sentiment. Solidarity with my
people above all, but I won't renounce Graciela*]. Don Jovel, older, more

mature, a pacifist, emblematic of Costa Rica itself, defers to Sebastián, renounces his pretensions for Graciela, and ultimately dies for the resistance. Many of Dobles' characters are martyrs, but here don Jovel's initials (J.C.) emphasize his Christlike sacrifice.

Don Jovel's father, drawn from the life of Dobles' own father, is a fiery debater over religious and political issues. He is not above a good fight but is a firm pacifist in terms of his beliefs regarding the inviolability of human life: "*Hombre no debe matar a hombre*—me dijo aquella vez solemnemente mi tata—. *Me vas a jurar que nunca martillarás un gatillo contra un semejante, ni aun en defensa propia. Y se lo juré*" (197; Dobles' italics) [*Man should not kill man*—my father solemnly told me that day—*You must swear you will never pull the trigger against another man, not even in self-defense.* And I swore it]. This ethical principal instilled in don Jovel by his father becomes the focal point for the moral tension in the narrative. How does Costa Rica, a pacifist nation without an army, ethically and practically justify involvement in an armed struggle, even a morally righteous one? As don Jovel's father explains, "*La vida es inviolable en el territorio de Costa Rica . . . tenemos que creer en eso, o somos extranjeros en nuestra propia tierra. Este es el mandamiento*" (203; Dobles' italics) [*Life is inviolable in Costa Rican territory . . . We have to believe in this, or else we are foreigners in our own land. This is the commandment*]. Dobles, however, is in a bind over the ethics of killing and seems unable or unwilling to resolve the issue. Costa Rica, along with its principles of nonviolence and passive resistance, finds itself at a moral impasse with regard to the Nicaraguan situation. The commandment that don Jovel's father insists on keeping ("La vida es inviolable en el territorio de Costa Rica") only works within a Costa Rican framework; it literally falls apart, however, in the face of a ruthless tyrant like Somoza. The choices of the resistance, therefore, are limited to binary oppositions: violence or victimization, assassination or martyrdom, liberation or death.[29] The typical Costa Rican approach of *sí pero no*, the ability to choose without seeming to choose, breaks down under such violent conditions.

These binary oppositions underpin a serious moral conflict between violent and nonviolent resistance in which the Nicaraguan situation functions as a biblical test of Costa Rica's pacifist principles. The moral tension is experienced internally: rhetorically within the novel, psychologically within don Jovel, and sociologically within the nation. When Sebastián discovers the deaf mute eating an uncooked dove he has just killed, it is clear that the resistance is long past the verbal and the symbolic challenge (Costa Rica's *sí pero no*); the dove of peace is dead. Choices will have to be made, eventually. But in the meantime these crucial decisions are deferred: "Creo que en esta cuestión cada uno de ustedes [don Jovel y Sebastián] está en lo bueno, a según por donde se la agarre. Pero para qué se van a aca-lorar; no vale la pena. Mejor dejen ya eso" (210) [I believe that on this question each of you (don Jovel and Sebastián) is right depend-ing on how you look at it. But why get all heated up; it's not worth it. Let's just drop it]. Thus, the collectivity is preserved; members engage in debate; they disagree, but they do not fight amongst themselves. There is a more immediate enemy. The resistance at this stage has achieved solidarity with difference.

As don Jovel's father realizes, however, the voice of resistance must challenge a triple wave of colonialism in Central America: first the Spaniards, then the North Americans, and always the neocolo-nial nationalists. Not only has Nicaragua fallen victim to an internal neocolonial dictator, but also it suffers from U.S. political and mili-tary meddling. North American intervention, however, is couched in thinly disguised religious terms. The overt and extreme anticom-munism of U.S. Evangelical proselytizing ultimately benefits the So-moza dictatorship. Don Jovel's father's arguments against the Evangelicals, therefore, imply a political, more so than a religious, position:

> Augusto César Sandino tenía que ver con aquello. Mi padre era sandi-nista de corazón y la gente relacionaba la intensa campaña de catequiza-ción evangelista con la penetración yanqui.
> —Ah vaya, ya se ve—interviene Sebastián—; biblias a la par de rifles. (199)

> [Augusto César Sandino had something to do with that. My father was a sandinista sympathizer and the people related the intense Evangelical campaign with Yankee penetration.
> —Oh yes, I see now—intervened Sebastian—; Bibles alongside rifles.]

This two-pronged method of colonial control is clear even to the uneducated: dominant discourse, the Bible (ideology) combined with physical oppression, rifles (force). The entire missionary enter-prise, in fact, is framed in terms of war: (e.g., Onward Christian Sol-diers); conversion to Protestantism symbolizes the soul's victory in the fight against evil. The success of the North American Evangelical project is, in fact, measured in terms of how many Bibles in the native language are carried under native "arms."[30]

The direct challenge to colonialist tyranny seems caught in these very same terms. Despite the pacifism and code of honor that don Jovel's father follows and imposes on his son, the Revolutionaries can see no other alternative to armed resistance. Their strategy is also two-pronged, rhetorical and physical. They are clearly aware that part of their job is to prepare the terrain, that is, win the support of the people: "*preparar la cosa dentro de la propia patria para organizar y hacer antes que todo el semillero, la conciencia . . . sin cuajo popular no hay revolución posible*" (242; Dobles' italics) [*prepare things within their own country in order to organize and form, above all, the seedbed, consciousness . . . without popular support, there is no possibility of revolution*]. This is a rhetorical enterprise, a challenge to the dominant episteme, and a function in which Dobles' novel may be said to participate. Only if the rhetorical challenge is successful can the armed struggle hope for success. The paradox, of course, is that the resistance has no voice, but as in the case of Gugú, "tuvo que entregar el habla . . . pero no su inteligencia. Por eso Gugú se defiende tan a gusto entre los montes . . . No más miren cómo, sin saber nada, sabe más que muchos de nosotros" (238) [he had to give up his ability to speak . . . but not his intelligence. That's why Gugú does so well in the mountains. Just look at how, without knowing anything, he knows more than many of us]. It is this "subjugated knowledge," as Foucault terms it, outside the bounds of language and official discourse "disqualified as inadequate to their task or insufficiently elaborated: naïve knowledges, located low down on the hierarchy, beneath the required level of cognition or scientificity"[31] that gives Gugú and the resistance such strength.

Ultimately, the Costa Ricans in the novel are compelled to choose between killing and being killed, between betraying their national tradition of pacifism and adding their names to the growing list of martyred victims of the Somoza regime. Don Jovel dies as a result of his choice in the explosion from a bomb he, himself, has created and dropped on the Nicaraguan patrol. His ambiguous last words "había que ser . . . uno . . . *y* su gente . . ." (254; emphasis mine) [One had to be . . . one . . . *and* his people] imply his faith in the revolutionary cause at the same time that he maintains his individuality and difference. That is, one must represent one's self as well as one's people. The key word here is *y* [and]; conspicuously absent is *con* [with]; he is one *and* his people, not one *with* his people). In a broad sense, of course, his people are the oppressed masses of the region, but he is, after all, Costa Rican, not Nicaraguan, and his national and personal ethics, which he has violated, support pacifism. Ultimately, his ethical hierarchy becomes clear. His people (the goal) are above his pacifism (the means), but such a hierarchy is not without conflict because of his firmly held value in the inviolability of human life.

Fermín's Costa Rican son from a previous marriage also chooses to sacrifice the national ethos and fatally shoots the man who has betrayed the group and who attacks him with a knife. From the point of view of the armed struggle, this killing "ha sido la mano de la justicia" (256) [has been the hand of justice] and is certainly justifiable as self-defense, but from the Costa Rican ethical standpoint of the inviolability of human life, this justification is neither compelling nor satisfying: "Mi hijo ya debe porque mató . . . ¡Malhaya sean los fierros estos! Y Fermín avienta la carbina a mitad del río" (256) [My son now owes because he killed . . . ! Damned these barbarians! And Fermín throws his carbine into the middle of the river]. The two positions (armed resistance and pacifism) are mutually exclusive: "Lástima; era una magnífica arma. ¡La necesitábamos!" (256) [Too bad; it was a magnificent weapon. We needed it!], but not necessarily antagonistic: "Oigan, huevones . . . no se van ahora a pelear como cipotes. No faltaba más" (259) [Listen, guys[32] . . . you're not going to start fighting now like children. That's all we need].

Once again the collectivity of the resistance defers internal disagreements to the larger issue facing the Revolution, liberating Nicaragua from the Somoza dictatorship, "y se abrazan sudorosamente" (260) [and they clasp each other in a sweaty embrace]. The suggestion of internal conflict, however, becomes an eerie foreshadowing of the eventual breakdown of this bond with difference in the continued fighting in Nicaragua even after the Sandinista victory, a triumph that solved one problem but fell victim to others, generating a new set of resistances. What seems to be a hopeful last line read solely within the context of the novel ("[Gugú] va simplemente con sus pies, su frente, un cabro, su corazón y su escopeta") takes on tragic proportions when read within the context of the narrative of history. The ethical debates over the sanctity of human life become moot/mute points, continually deferred to more immediate conflicts. Dobles is torn, no doubt, between the noble possibilities of nonviolence and rhetorical resistance, on the one hand, and his recognition, on the other, that rhetorical strategies alone are insufficient to the task in Nicaragua. If, in allegorical terms Gugú is equated with the resistance, and the resistance, in turn, is equated with the Good, then the Revolutionaries wield the sword of righteousness, indeed. But what, then, becomes of God's commandment to Moses, "Thou shalt not kill"? The answer clearly depends on who carries the rifle.

7

The Last Novel

Los años, pequeños días. San José: Editorial Costa Rica, 1989; second edition, San José: Editorial Costa Rica, 1991; third edition, San José: Farben Grupo Editorial Norma, 1993. Translated into English by Joan Henry as *Years Like Brief Days.* London: Peter Owen, 1996.

DOBLES SURPRISED EVERYONE WHEN HE PUBLISHED *LOS AÑOS, PEQUEÑOS días* in 1989 after more than twenty years of narrative silence. He was not literally silent, of course; rather, he had become a respected voice in the cultural life of his country, regularly working on new editions of his books, giving interviews, and participating in a multitude of cultural activities. No one, however, really thought he was writing. As he explained in an interview, he spent two decades collecting experiences, maturing ideas, and organizing thoughts. Despite his literary silence, he claims, "Soy un eterno escritor"[1] [I'm an eternal writer].

Not only was the publication itself surprising, but the kind of narrative it was left no doubt in anyone's mind that the distinguished old gentleman of Costa Rican letters had left the best for last.[2] The novel received excellent reviews[3] and won the Premio Ancora for literature (1989–1990), initiating a critical reevaluation of Dobles' work on the national level as well as attracting international attention through the publication of its English translation, *Years Like Brief Days* (1996) by Joan Henry.[4]

Dobles drew on contemporary narrative strategies and over seventy years of living to produce a novel that is and is not autobiography, is and is not history, is and is not fiction. This *sí pero no* strategy, the refusal to be limited by Eurocentric binomials, has been a favorite with Dobles throughout his career. Clearly the text is based on Dobles' life and the history of his family, which national reviewers saw immediately,[5] but as Alfonso Chase warns, "debe recharzarse la visión reductiva de que es una obra de contenido autobiográfico evidente, y establecer el distanciamiento real entre una obra de ficción y un presunto texto de memorias"[6] [the reductive vision that this is a work with obvious biographical content should be rejected in order to establish the real distance between a work of fiction and a presumed text of memories]. Chaverri sees the novel in terms of a mythical journey into the past, an attempt to recover a lost paradise[7] and Chase reads it more as a social allegory, following Jameson:[8]

> esa historia de un hombre que se levanta en la mañana—no es más que la historia de los otros hombres de su tiempo, del nuestro, y quizás del futuro, que apremiados por su propia existencia, construyen, en verdad, la historia de nuestro conglomerado social.[9]

> [that story of a man who gets up in the morning—is nothing less than the story of the other men of his time, of our time, and perhaps of future times, who, rewarded by their own existence, actually construct the history of our social conglomerate.]

The use of the term autobiography, however, does not arbitrarily lessen the literary value of the work nor deny its social, fictional, or mythical ramifications. Rather, it opens up a different critical space for understanding the process of subject formation in a postmodern,[10] postcolonial context. In this sense James Olney's claim about the autobiographical nature of all texts is fundamental:

> all writing that aspires to be literature is autobiography and nothing else . . . for behind every work of literature there is an "I" informing the whole and making its presence felt at every critical point, and without this "I," stated or implied, the work would collapse into mere insignificance.[11]

Hayden White's classic argument,[12] in turn, concludes that historical discourse is actually another form of literary narrative. He claims that historical sequences can be codified as narrative elements (the process of what he calls "emplotment"). Thus, history and autobiography, like fiction, are told through a process of narration by a subject whose perception is inevitably limited and whose mere presence, even as an observer, alters the "reality" he claims to objectify. This inevitable mediation of the external historical fact through the subject's perception produces alternatives for interpretation and the imputation of meaning. If we add to this problematic, those events that are based, not on historical facts, but on individual memories, the situation becomes even more vexed.

This Foucauldian or postmodern blurring of traditional boundaries between fact and fiction, history and narrative, memory and imagination is precisely the point of Dobles' last novel. His strategy is to disturb these binary oppositions that imply superiority to the first term, thereby decentering foundational concepts. Dobles' challenge to the dominant script, however, becomes, ironically, a challenge to himself since it was he, who, with his groundbreaking work of fifty years ago, rewrote the Costa Rican canon. This postcolonial subversion of his own script and of his own identity as a founding father of Costa Rican letters, patriarch, and master writer is emblematic of the divided subjectivity and denial of univocal personal identity that has always been present in Dobles' work and underpins the postmodern world.

Los años, pequeños días, from the title to the co-text, is obviously concerned with the passage of time and with what Foucault might call the "genealogy" of subjectivity, that is, those elements of experience, culture, history, and personality (gender, class, race, sexual orientation, economic possibilities, and so forth) that converge to describe identity in the present.[13] The frame story, told by an unnamed third-person narrator, describes a seventy-year-old man (Dobles' persona) in the process of remembering and reliving his youth, of retelling those formative existential experiences that made him a man, and of recreating those crucial moments that forged his political ideology and worldview. The structure for these memories is complex. The old man, speaking in the first person, takes the position of analytical observer, watching himself as a youth, as "Other," talking sometimes in second person to the boy, who is at the same time himself, as though he exists as a separate person. Consequently, in his remembering, reliving, and recounting of the past, the Dobles' persona acts simultaneously as both subject and object of his narrative. The complication of subject/object becomes more vexed as the frame narrator watches the old man who in turn watches the youth. It is clear that neither the narrator nor the old man watches from a point of neutrality or objectivity; all have a vested interest in this narrative of the past.

As Dobles explores the maze of relationships among multiple presents and multiple pasts, he exposes the various psychological exigencies of remembering: the need to reconcile one's present with the recollection of the past; the need to speak the past, to tell what has been buried in memory, to inscribe the dialogy of self; the need to negotiate the past, to corroborate memory, to review, to re-re-member, to relive; the need to complete or fulfill the past, to finish what was left undone, unsaid, unwritten and to respond to memory on an emotional and psychological level. Overall, Dobles' narrator underlines the need to decenter official history and view one's multiple and fractured selves over the diachrony of time. The memories of the main character—a fictional persona for Dobles himself, or as Chase claims, for all Costa Ricans—are clearly drawn from Dobles' life and experience, although he contemplates them from the point of view of the "Other." While the characters are unnamed, their discernible historical referents indicate the ambiguity of delineating between novel and autobiography, between history and fiction, and between objective fact and subjective memory. The present, Dobles suggests, is not mediated by any objective sense of the past nor by static, univocal, monologic memories of it, but rather by the complex and continual psychological process of recalling.

Dobles' story begins with an old man's need to revisit his childhood both literally and symbolically by traveling to the town where he grew up, Atenas, "el valle más lindo y resueño"[14] [the most beautiful and wonderful valley]. His journey takes him first to a landmark of his youth, an actual place in Costa Rica, the Custom's House built by Don Braulio Carrillo, one of the Republic's former presidents. As the narrator describes it in the novel, the site still exists near a hundred-year-old stone bridge and arch. The river that the old man remembers, however, has been drained, "lo sabía, pero no le importó"[15] ["he knew that, but it didn't matter to him" (14)]. His memory of it, "del tiempo inatajable" ["unassailable by time"], co-exists in the present alongside the actual "cauce, ahora casi sin agua" (39) ["river bed, now almost without water, small and dirty" (14)]. His obsessed visit acts as a catalyst for inducing memories so that present and past exist simultaneously in the same space: "estaba acariciando las piedras como si fueran carne y no granito, con fruición de adolescente, y de veras el río fue llenándosele de torrente y espumas, como en los años treinta" (39–40) ["there he was with the enjoyment of youth caressing the stones as if they were flesh and not granite. The river was really filling up with torrents and foam as it did in the thirties" (14)]. This dual vision of present and past, this unavoidable interplay of memory and actuality, constitutes the fundamental complexity of the divided "self," which paradoxically exists from present moment to present moment while also

maintaining a diachronic life, that is, an existence over the continuity of chronological time: "Pero este niño vive lo que también estoy
viviendo y no sé si soy o es o somos los dos quien ahora se levanta,
sale al zaguán y camina hasta la calle" (58) [But this lad is alive as I
am alive, and I don't know if I or he or we both are the ones who
get up now, go out to the entrance hall and walk to the street" (37)].

It is never enough, Dobles' narrator suggests, to remember si-
lently and alone. The mental image, in order to reveal itself fully to
the subject, must be spoken, must be consciously remembered and
told. The isolated incident in the past must be linked by the subject/
narrator to the overall life/story, so that the lived experience, in-
completely understood at the moment it occurs, takes a formative
place in the growth and development, the "genealogy" of the self
over time. In order to speak the past, to inscribe it, and attempt to
fix the fluidity of memory, Dobles' narrator writes a fictional letter
to his mother, now long dead, in which he reveals to her what he
never could have told her while she was alive. The cumulative effect
of the multitude of stories and memories included in this epistle
helps to explain and justify the narrator's present state of mind. He
(as subject of the action) essentially writes the letter to himself (as
object). Not only we the readers, then, but he himself can trace the
beginnings of his loss of faith in the Catholic Church, his question-
ing of authority, both parental and religious, and his disillusionment
with what he sees as a hypocritical society. The tone of the letter,
despite his mother's obvious ignorance regarding the major events
that affected him as a youth, is neither resentful nor bitter. Instead,
he reveals a sympathetic understanding of her and writes in a gentle,
evocative tone: "¿Lo recuerda, mamá?" (64) [Do you remember
that, Mama?" (44)], as Dobles reveals "la historia secreta entonces
de todo niño más o menos normal" (65) [the secret story of every
more or less normal lad" (45)], and as he recounts the multiple
tales of youthful lusts and disillusionments, of the hypocrisy of the
priest who attempts to seduce him, of his anxiety when he believes
his father is dying of cancer, and as he learns the lessons of adult-
hood: "Vas a sentirte de hoy en adelante un iniciado" (111) ["From
now on you're going to feel initiated" (100)].

Speaking the past, however, assumes a monologic continuum that
can be spoken, a univocal consistency of memory, an objectified representation of what once was. The issue, of course, is much more
complicated, as the old narrator comes to realize when he shows his
elder brother the letter he has written to his mother. The letter be-

comes the point of departure for the two old men to reminisce, but as they do so they are forced to see the past from the perspective of each other's unique memories. The brothers disagree and are surprised at how the other remembers their collective history, "¿Me entendés, hermano mío? No, claro que aún no." (84) [Do you understand me, brother? No, of course not" (69)]. Thus, the negotiation of the past begins, "¿por qué, por qué no recurristes a mí?" (85) ["but why, why didn't you consult me?" (70)]. Each brother defends his memories in order to maintain the integrity of his own "self": "—!Pero yo cantaba, hermano, cantaba! . . .—Pero yo soñaba también, qué te has creído" (88) ["but I sang, brother, I sang . . . I used to dream, too. Do you think I didn't?" (74)]. From this conversation in the present, we understand the fluidity of the past, the instability of memory, and the ambiguity inherent in the narrative of history. The retelling of history, rather than an objective recounting, becomes a negotiated recreation: "¿Te acordás? . . . Se te olvida . . .—Mirá, lo había olvidado por completo, qué barbaridad" (89, 92, 93) ["Do you remember? . . . Have you forgotten . . . Look, I'd completely forgotten that, how awful of me" (79)].

As the two old men corroborate and revise each other's memories (histories) of their youth, as they review and relive their stories and re-remember their different lives that occupied the same historical space, they add details from the memory of one to complement and complete the memory of the other. As they do so, both experience a concomitant affective response in the present to the experiences they have evoked from the past. They discuss, they laugh, they sing old songs, and they come to know each other more intimately than ever before. In the process they also come to know themselves at a deeper and more sympathetic level. Later, as the old man goes through a similar process of remembering with his wife, he allows himself the affective outlet he has denied himself in front of his brother when he "aguantó las ganas de sollozar y las anudó en su garganta" (108) ["overcame [his] desire to sob, though [he] had a lump in [his] throat" (97)]. Instead, "el hombre que se lo cuenta a su esposa aquí a su lado no puede contenerlas cuando ella enternecida le acaricia los recuerdos" (108) ["the man who is relating this to his wife sitting beside him cannot now refrain from sobs when she is moved to tenderness and cherishes his memories" (97). This affective completion of the past in the present as one shares one's past with another and asks for forgiveness, "Perdonáme, viejo, perdonáme aunque sea tarde.—No, no, perdonáme vos a mí" (112)

["For goodness' sake forgive me, old boy, even though it's a long time ago.—No, no. You must forgive me" (102)] allows the self to regenerate, to understand its multiplicity, to move forward as it sheds resentment, bitterness, and pride. Speaking the past acts as a catharsis for a subject who must live in the present even while he comes to terms with the memories of himself. In the words of Atahualpa Yupanqui,[16] whose song is simultaneously played and remembered in Dobles' text, "*Que no se quede callado quien quiera vivir feliz*" (112; Dobles' italics) ["He who wants to live a happy life must not remain silent" (102; no emphasis in Henry's translation)].

Many of the old narrator's memories center on the strong and influential figure of his father, a medical doctor who was trained in the University of New York and who dedicated himself to rural medicine. He recalls his father's quick and emotional temper, his rectitude, his rigorous Catholic devotion, and his unquestioned position as patriarchal authority of a large (ten children) family. It is this man, spiritually strong, rigid in his convictions, and indignant at social injustice, who ignites his son's passions and spurs his class consciousness. Thus, the narrator credits his father not only with encouraging his own political and social awareness but also and ironically, with his conversion to Marxism, a political ideology wholly incongruent with his father's fervent Catholic beliefs but certainly a logical secular response to social injustice. The narrator vividly remembers his father's fury at being unable to save the children in his community who died, not from disease, but from hunger. Initially, the father feeds the narrator's early misanthropy:

> Padecía de unas agruras que me querían abrasar la boca del estómago y desconfiaba, sí, me costaba creer en los demás. Quién decía verdad, quién mentía, cuál era sincero, cuál hipócrita, dónde él que siendo sincero te engañaba y te mentía y dónde él que no siéndolo te enseñaba verdad. (115)

> [I felt deeply bitter and this made me lose faith in other people. Who was telling the truth? Who was lying? Who was sincere? Who was a hypocrite when the one you trusted was being deceitful and lying to you and the insincere one was telling you the truth (106)].

Through the process of remembering, cross-checking those memories against the memories of others, and emotionally responding to the spoken image, the narrator eventually comes to terms with the distant father he never really understood: "Si en realidad fue él quien gracias a sus atrabiliarias imposiciones me vacunó para la vida" (115) ["It was really he who, thanks to his bad-tempered constraints, prepared me for life" (106)].

This (re)vision and subsequent reevaluation of the significance of the past deconstructs any pretense of objective history. Memory is clouded in confusion and ambiguity, inaccuracies, and forgetfulness. Moreover, the significance of the past must necessarily unfold in the present. As the present changes, so does its concomitant relationship to the past, making reevaluation and recreation a continual and renewable enterprise. Likewise, the sense of a univocal, fixed, and coherent self that moves unchangingly through time collapses as the narrator discovers "que uno no es solamente uno, sino multitudes en el tiempo y el espacio" (115) ["that one is not only one, but multitudes in time and space" (106)]. Thus, the old man's task in the narrative, as it is in life itself, is to reconstruct himself:

A mí me tocaba rearmar el mío para intentar amar y comprender y fue así como empecé a buscarle la otra cara, la invisible e ignorada, a mi cercana tribu familiar, y a auscultarles al mundo y a la historia las sonoridades escondidas como mi tata cuando ponía el cuenco de una mano en la cáscara del cuerpo y golpeaba con los dedos de la otra sobre el dorso del cuenco para sentir respuestas desde dentro del paciente. (116)

[It was my responsibility to reconstruct my being, to try to love and understand, and so I began to look for the other side, invisible and unknown, of my close family tribe, and to listen for sonorities hidden from the world and history, as my Papa did when he placed the hollow of one hand on the skin of a patient's body and tapped with the other on the back of the hollow to feel reactions from inside.] (107)

One of the characteristics of autobiography is that it is by nature open-ended. The story not only does not finish, since the "I" (both subject and object, teller and told) is still alive at the end of his tale, but the narrative must also by force delineate a context for the "I" that acquires a life (lives) of its own and continues even after an author's death. The "I" of this narrative has a place, Atenas, "Este sí que es mi valle, el rincón que no olvido" (114) ["This is certainly my valley, the place I can never forget" (105)] and a family, the Dobles clan, which for the duration of the novel stretches backward for two generations to Dobles' maternal grandparents, forward to his nieces and nephews, and sideways to his wife, who understands that "era desde hacía largo rato el jovencillo de los años treinta quien le iba repitiendo episodios de los que tantas veces habían platicado y a ella le traían al recuerdo pasajes de su propia vida y de los suyos" (120) ["it was a long time since [her husband] had been the young man of the thirties and who now went on repeating episodes that he had talked about so many times and that reminded her of parts of her own life and her family" (112)]. The wife, and nieces and nephews, in turn, have places and families of their own, some of them important agents in Dobles' narrative, and some who spill over outside the confines of the text itself.

From the varied memories and retellings of significant past events, Dobles evokes a mosaic of his life and the lives of the people close to him. Historical accuracy, however, is never his intention. The ephemeral past can only partially and inadequately be recreated through language. The past itself can never be fully known, only the telling of it; that is, the events themselves are unimportant; what matters is the story. Our actions and feelings in the present are predicated, not on the past itself, but on the stories we tell about the past. The old man explains as much to his brother: "si así no sucedió, de este modo te lo cuento" (99) ["If what happened to me . . . didn't happen like that, I'm now telling you how it did" (86)]. It is our present perception of the past through language, then, that really matters. For Dobles and his narrative persona, a life can only be represented by "innumerables historias . . . en un cuento de nunca acabar" (118) ["innumerable tales . . . in one endless story" (109)].

POSTSCRIPT

The suspicion, voiced by James Olney, that "the student and reader of autobiographies . . . is a vicarious or a closet autobiographer"[17] is particularly relevant in this case. It is neither unimportant nor insignificant that the "I" of this analytical study, the "literary critic," is also a niece by marriage of the "I" in *Los años, pequeños días.* As a daughter-in-law of the "hermana la que cantaba como alondra" (83) ["sister who sang like a lark" (67)], I, too, have a relationship to the story. As a North American, a *gringa,* I, too, share collective memories with Dobles' father, the doctor trained in New York. His recollections of the deplorable conditions and racist practices in the hospitals of New York at the turn of the century form part of my negative national heritage and background. The doctor's memories, which then become part of his son's memories, represent a time from my national history and converge with a piece of my collective past. Some of the stories that Dobles' narrator tells, I have already heard from my mother-in-law, from her perspective, or from my husband's aunt,[18] from her perspective, or from other family members. As all of our stories in their multivariate versions intersect at various points on the continuum of history, Dobles' narrative comes full circle. His novel, initially written perhaps like the narrator's letter to his mother, as an attempt at personal clarification, "si todo esto era y ya no es, y yo soy otro" (38) ["all this is and was no more, and I've changed" (13)], transcends the limitations of the author's unknowable purposes and extends to the reader, in this case to me, who cannot read divorced from my own present, my own context, and my own memories, both personal and collective. In this way, I (as reader, critic, and family member) become an integral part of the story itself, of the continuous narrative that overflows the boundaries of the pages of *Los años, pequeños días* and awaits the next story to be artificially and momentarily fixed, inscribed, remembered, and objectified in the pages of literary history.

8

Conclusion

As THE MOST PROLIFIC WRITER FROM THE GENERATION OF 1940, FABIÁN Dobles epitomizes the regionalist and realistic tendencies of the period, so fundamental to the process of national self-definition and the formation of a broader, more inclusive understanding of "patria" [fatherland]. Certainly, his work is foundational, not only for its role in the creation of a national literature, but also for its place in the psychic consciousness of a people. Sadly, some of Costa Rica's younger writers see Dobles and his generation as part of a historical and literary movement that lacked imagination, locked in, as they were, by a realistic narrative model and a prescriptive political position. These are the critics who feel that realism and/or socialism are outworn, outdated, and inferior narrative and political models, and as such, must be superseded by newer approaches to "reality," broader and more universal visions and narrative modes.

Underlying this criticism is the tension and ambivalence felt by national authors between "regional" and "universal" literature, perceived as opposite and mutually exclusive categories. This conflict arises from those unstated and still prominent modernist assumptions that privilege "universal" literature and presuppose it to mean the Anglo/European canon, that is, literature emanating from the metropolis. Costa Rican writers, thus, find themselves caught in a paradox: how can they aspire to universal literary values if they are by definition always and inevitably part of the periphery? Fortunately for the third world, postmodern literary criticism has largely deconstructed the privileged status of "universal" literature. Still, it is only natural that younger writers should want to look beyond their national borders for new ideas and models. Thus far, they are still experimenting, to the extent that they have been criticized for experimenting for the sake of experimentation[1] and for failing as yet to fulfill the promise for narrative heralded by Dobles and his generation.

Certainly, part of the Dobles legacy is the historical impact his writing has had on the narrative of his country. He is, clearly, a foundational writer in terms of Costa Rican literary history, but the historical importance of his narrative is less important, in my view, than his creation, confirmation, and codification of a national identity still fully apparent today. The fundamental factor underlying studies of Costa Rican nationalism is the importance of the land. At the beginning of the century, even the oligarchy depended on their huge coffee production and the success of an agro-export economic model. It became increasingly clear, however, that the small farmer was being driven away from his land and that even the oligarchy was in economic trouble due to a variety of factors—takeovers by foreign investors, the international decline of the agro-export model and industrialization of the agro (e.g., The United Fruit Company), growing urbanization, and the constant subdivision of land through inheritance. The Generation of 1940, already deeply influenced by socialist ideas, began to write, not only of the land but also of the economic, social, and psychological problems associated with land ownership, distribution, and loss.

This approach was fairly typical throughout Central America and the Spanish-speaking Americas at this time since the region, in general, was suffering from similar socioeconomic conditions. The main variation from country to country concerned who was affected by land loss, land takeovers, and redistribution. Countries like Guatemala, that have large indigenous populations, were particularly preoccupied about the Indian's complex relationship to the land. Other countries, like Nicaragua, focused on the control that the military exerted over the economy. Costa Ricans, on the other hand, worried more about their *campesinos*, the backbone of the agricultural system.

Nevertheless, "la tierra" (that is, who has it and who does not) cannot alone account for why Costa Ricans feel or imagine that other people in their country are like them and that "foreigners" are not. Costa Rica's sense of difference from the rest of Central America undoubtedly emanates from a variety of factors, but one of its distinguishing features has been a persistent ambivalence toward outside influences, toward modernity, and toward tradition. It is this ambivalence that I have observed in the Costa Rican linguistic tendency, so aptly manipulated by Dobles, to agree and disagree at the same time; what I have indicated throughout this study as "sí pero no" or "same but different."

Dobles' most important contribution to this discourse on national identity has been to recreate this hybrid voice and to encourage the myth that all Costa Ricans are fundamentally, essentially, and originally *campesinos*. In doing so, he has given value and agency, if only in the imagination, to Costa Rica's largest economic resource and richest national symbol. In Dobles' *campesino* opposing constructs paradoxically merge: that is, Costa Ricans are traditional but modern, closed but open, peaceful but fierce, rural but urban, simple but wise, crafty but uncomplicated, religious but tolerant. The list is both infinite and arbitrary.[2] Underlying all the modifiers, however, is a sense of hybridity, in that Costa Ricans are neither one nor the other of these descriptors within a set of opposing binomials nor a unique synthesis of the two,[3] but rather both extremes at once, a hybrid or a "bonding in difference." As Costa Rican philosopher (and incidentally a nephew of Fabián Dobles) Jaime González Dobles affirms: "El problema final es un asunto de balance" [The final problem is one of balance].[4] Dobles' fictional creations represent these idiosyncratic, hybrid *campesinos* who are caught in a blatantly colonial situation and who are trying to make the best out of a losing proposition. Costa Ricans not only believe in these images, but as Anderson explains are "continually reassured that the imagined world is visibly rooted in everyday life."[5] The pastoral Eden or Arcadia that Dobles recreates in his novels of the small farmer in an original and socially just environment is now part of every Costa Rican's mythical history. This imagined version of the Costa Rican *campesino*, therefore, is not only a part of the cultural landscape but also a projection of a national self.

Dobles, himself, was a prime example of this "sí pero no" image. He was and was not a *campesino*. He lived in the city, came from an upper-class family, and was well educated. By all objective accounts, he was most definitely not a country farmer. Yet even at age seventy, he still firmly identified himself as a *campesino* in his essence:

> el ambiente de pájaros y riachos y potreros y árboles y verdes y lluvias y vientos y vacas y caballos, pero sobre todo el mundo de hombres y mujeres y campesinos con su habla costarricense pura, que todo junto se vino conmigo del campo a la ciudad.[6]

> [the atmosphere of birds and streams and pastures and trees and greenery and rains and winds and cows and horses, but above all, the world of men and women and *campesinos* with their pure Costa Rican speech, that all together came with me from the countryside to the city.]

Dobles was and was not a Marxist. His politics revolved around social justice; he was a member of the Costa Rican Communist Party, but he was a nationalist first and foremost[7] and ardently defended the small landowner. More important, he was and was not a realist. While his work clearly falls under the category of realism, his experimentation with language goes far beyond a mimetic rendering of speech. In sum, then, he was a product of his Eurocentric training and education as well as that of his region and nation, an example of hybridity at its most fundamental level.

Costa Rica's young writers are still so preoccupied with finding new aesthetic means of expression that they have tended to reject the old in favor of the new. Alfonso Chase, who claimed that "para mi generación la vida y la obra de Fabián Dobles han sido símbolo y bandera"[8] [for my generation, the life and work of Fabián Dobles have been a symbol and a banner], also sees Costa Rica's younger writers as being a self-absorbed generation, unable or unwilling to deal with their environment: "El creador costarricense ha vuelto a refugiarse en su propio yo, como una manera de manifestar su inconformidad con el cuerpo social en el que tiene que desenvolver su trabajo"[9] [The Costa Rican creator has taken refuge in his own "self," as a way to show his disagreement with the social body in which he must work]. Rodrigo Soto, one of Costa Rica's younger writers, explains in a letter to Dobles, the fundamental differences that separate the two groups of writers:

Ninguno de ustedes hablaba de mi mundo: ese mundo al que yo empezaba a abrir los ojos, urbano y torrencial, transformado dramáticamente por la industria, el consumo y los medios de comunicación masiva. Sentía que no había nada en común entre la realidad que usted y sus compañeros de generación pintaban, y aquella en la que yo crecía. Con la arrogancia propia de quien no ha hecho nada, me daba el lujo de despreciarlos. "Esos rocos en su mundo campesino, bucólico y perdido, nada saben de esto," mascullaba frente a los libros de Cortázar, Sábato o Vargas Llosa . . .[10]

[None of you spoke of my world: that world that I had begun to see, urban and torrential, transformed dramatically by industry, consumerism, and mass communication. I felt that the reality that you and your generation painted and the one I grew up in had nothing in common. With the arrogance of one who has done nothing himself, I gave myself permission to look down on all of you. "Those old geezers in their countrified, bucolic and lost world, they don't know anything about this," I muttered in front of books by Cortázar, Sábato or Vargas Llosa . . .]

Magical realism, the "boom" writers of the 1960s, and postmodern literary criticism, all of which have dominated the academy for the last thirty years, have clearly influenced a new generation of writers in Costa Rica—writers who have merit and who hold promise, but who have not yet produced their own mature narrative.[11] Perhaps they are participating too hard by opposition and have not completely integrated their past or explored the depths of their national psyche. As Soto goes on to clarify:

> Una cosa es el parricidio, el intento de contraponer una concepción del quehacer literario a la que desarrolló la generación precedente, y otra muy distinta la omisión, el desconocimiento y la ignorancia. Nosotros crecimos en esta última posición. Y digo "nosotros" porque esos sentimientos los compartíamos todos o casi todos los que empezábamos a escribir a principios de los años ochenta.

> [One thing is patricide, the attempt to counter and replace the ideas about literary work that the preceding generation developed, and another very different thing is omission, not knowing, ignorance. We grew up with the latter position. And I say "we" because all of us, or almost all of us, who began writing in the eighties shared those sentiments.]

Certainly they have not explored the tantalizing possibilities that Dobles' language and his imagined *campesino* have to offer in the reformulation and intertextualization of national identity.

As an outsider trying to make sense of national personality quirks that Costa Ricans often take for granted, I am constantly reminded that most Costa Ricans feel they are, at heart, *campesinos,* (like the "labriego sencillo" of their national anthem), even though they live in an increasingly modern and urbanized world. Moncho, Tata Mundo, ñor Espíritu Santo, and Ignacio, are all metonymically part of "ese que llaman pueblo" that still forms the core of Costa Rican national identity today. Even Costa Rican women participate in this illusion when they identify with Dolores and the other *campesina* women from Dobles' novels—women they see as "sencilla, sana, fértil, mientras que la citadina es complicada, enferma, estéril"[12] [simple, healthy, fertile while the city woman is complicated, sick, steril]. This "alma campesino"[13] [campesino soul], which most Costa Ricans claim to possess, underlies their sense of humor and their oral tradition, their joking and storytelling. Most important, however, the *campesino* image provides the key to Costa Rica's style of postcolonial resistance. Dobles codifies the most sacred values of his community by privileging the uneducated *campesino* over the cultured oligarchy, the poor over the rich, the country over the city, the regional over the universal, and the Third World over the First World. Of all his *campesino* creations, Tata Mundo, is one of the most compelling, an archetype that, as Costa Rican dramatist Daniel Gallegos claims, essentially defines Costa Rica:

> [Tata Mundo] con sus raíces en la tierra, sencillo pero altivo e incorruptible en su verdad, generoso pero firme y fuerte en sus valores, sin perder nunca un ápice de compasión por sus semejantes, pero implacable en señalar el deterioro que causa la lucha del hombre contra el hombre.[14]

> [(Tata Mundo) rooted in the earth, humble yet arrogant and incorruptible in his righteousness, generous but firm and strong in his values, never once losing an iota of compassion for his fellow men but implacable in showing the deterioration that causes the struggle of man against man.]

It is no mere coincidence that the underlying linguistic structure of Gallegos' description is "sí pero no" ("sencillo pero altivo . . . generos pero firme . . . fuerte . . . pero implacable").

My suspicion is that as contemporary Costa Rican writers struggle with what it means to be Costa Rican, they will reexamine the nuances of their own language and in so doing rediscover Dobles' contribution to their cultural heritage. As Soto himself recognizes, "la literatura de un país no es una cosa lineal que se construye sólo desde el pasado hacia el presente, depende también de la lectura y elaboración que cada generación hace de la tradición y el pasado" [a country's literature is not a linear path that is constructed only from the past to the present; it depends as well on the reading and the elaboration that each generation makes of tradition and the past]. Surely, Costa Rica's new writers will discover opportunities to intertextualize Dobles' work, as they already have done with other writers[15] and with legendary figures like La llorona and La cegua or popular folk tales like Little Red Riding Hood,[16] and they will create new narrative and critical modes to understand the nation and themselves.

Dobles, as he aged, began to look more and more like his fictional

creation, Tata Mundo, and he always claimed to be writing himself
even as he wrote his country. Perhaps his greatest legacy, therefore,
is to future Costa Rican writers, who will undoubtedly learn that telling an authentic story in Costa Rica inevitably entails learning how
to reread and rewrite national identity. Dobles will be remembered
most for creating a space for Costa Rican speech through his novels
about the Costa Rican *campesino* and his relationship to the land. In
a final homage, Daniel Gallegos compares Fabián Dobles, his friend
and fellow writer, to an old oak tree, perhaps leaving us his most
befitting epitaph:

> cómo sus raíces profundas habían extraído de la tierra esa sabiduría,
> cómo su curtido tronco podía compararse a su hombría de bien, las
> ramas a su generosidad siempre pródiga al amigo, cómo la altura que
> alcanzó nunca lo separó del resto de esa humanidad que tanto amó. En-
> tonces pienso que puedo mirar la montaña y encontrar ahí su espíritu.[17]

> [How the deep roots extracted wisdom from the earth, how the weather-
> beaten trunk could be compared to his uprightness, the branches to his
> always prodigious generosity to a friend, how the height he reached
> never separated him from that humanity that he so loved. Then I think
> that I can look at the mountains and find his spirit there.]

Notes

PROLOGUE

1. Cf. Magda Zavala and Seidy Araya, *La historiografía literaria en América Central (1957–1987)* (San José: Editorial Fundación UNA, 1995).

2. See for example Linda J. Craft, *Novels of Testimony and Resistance* (Gainesville: University of Florida Press, 1997).

3. The first-person voice of one of the most famous and controversial testimonial narratives, Rigoberta Menchú with Elisabeth Burgos, *Me llamo Rogoberta Menchú y así me nació la conciencia* (Havana: Casa de las Américas, 1983), translated by Ann Wright as *I, Rigoberta Menchú: An Indian Woman in Guatemala* (London: Verso, 1984).

4. Carmen Naranjo is perhaps the only exception to this marginalization since she has been active within international feminist discourse.

5. Dobles was jailed twice following the Costa Rican Civil War of 1948. In addition, his novel *Los leños vivientes* (1962), originally titled *Hombres de tres tiempos,* was pulled from publication in 1954 by Imprenta Trejos Hnos because of its political content. Later, Dobles was fired from his teaching job at the Liceo Costa Rica on 10 March 1962 after returning from a trip to Cuba. He was accused of using the classroom as a political forum, an accusation he vehemently denied in print in area newspapers. For more information see chapter 1 of this study.

6. See, for example, Alfonso Chase, "Crónica de los Días: Aproximaciones a la última novela de Fabián Dobles," *El Centavo* 14, no. 143 (December 1989): 16–22; Amalia Chavarri, "*Los años, pequeños días*: Una lectura a través de categorías mítico-simbólicas," *Káñina* 17, no. 2 (1993): 21–28; Emma Gamboa, "Prólogo a *El sitio de las abras,*" in *Obras completas,* vol. 2 (San José: EUCR/EUN, 1993); Ann González, "Fabián Dobles y la novela de los recuerdos," *Káñina* 22, no. 3 (1998): 23–28; Resti Moreno Ortega, "Fabián Dobles: Su proyección intelectual. Entre el compromiso y la solidaridad con el pobre," *Senderos* 19 (1997): 409–52 and "Fabián Dobles: Vida y testimonio de un hombre—narrador y poeta—'Bueno' *In Memoriam* (1918–1997)," *Senderos* 19 (1997): 61–118 and "Fabián Dobles y la generación del 40," *Senderos* 20 (May–August 1998): 229–65; Alvaro Quesada, "Fabián Dobles en la narrativa costarricense," *Obras completas,* vol. 1 (San Jose: UCR/EUNA, 1993) and "Tradición e innovación: La novela de Fabián Dobles," *Semanario Universidad,* 1 July 1994, p. 3–4 and *Breve historia de la literatura costarricense* (San José: Editorial Porvenir, S.A., 2000); Ronald Solano Jiménez, "Crítica literaria en Costa Rica: De las *Historias de Tata Mundo,*" *Anuario de Estudios Centroamericanos* 18, no. 1 (1992): 85–95 and "¡Qué no sabía Tata Mundo! Narración, Saber, Seducción," *Revista Girasol* 1 (1996): 81–88; Margarita Rojas and Flora Ovares, *La casa paterna: escritura y nación*

155

en Costa Rica (San José: Editorial Universidad de Costa Rica, 1993) and *100 años de literatura costarricense* (San José: Farben Grupo Editorial Norma, 1995).

7. See Claudio Bogantes-Zamora, *La narrativa socialrealista en Costa Rica* (Aarhus, Denmark: Aarhus University Press, 1990); also see earlier histories of Costa Rican literature such as Abelardo Bonilla Baldares, *Historia y antología de la literatura costarricense*, 2nd ed. (San José: Editorial Costa Rica, 1967); Virginia Sandoval de Fonseca, *Resumen de literatura costarricense* (San José: Editorial Costa Rica, 1978); Jorge Valdeperas, *Para una nueva interpretación de la literatura costarricense* (San José: Editorial Costa Rica, 1979); and particularly Manuel Picado Gómez, *Literatura, ideología, crítica: Notas para un estudio de la literatura costarricense* (San José: Editorial Costa Rica, 1983) who criticizes what he calls the critics of verisimilitude and exposes the fallacies of so-called realism for the contemporary postmodern reader and critic.

8. See John Beverly, *Subalternity and Representation: Arguments in Cultural Theory* (Durham: Duke University Press, 1999) and *Literature and Politics in the Central American Revolutions* (Austin: University of Texas Press, 1990); also see Rita Ramos Alcida, *Indigenism: Ethnic Politics in Brazil* (Madison: University of Wisconsin Press, 1998) and Doris Sommer, *Foundational Fictions: The National Romances of Latin America* (Berkeley: University of California Press, 1991).

9. See Bill Ashcroft, Gareth Griffiths, and Helen Tiffin, *The Empire Writes Back: Theory and Practice in Post-Colonial Literatures* (London and New York: Routledge, 1989) as well as their *The Post-Colonial Studies Reader* (London and New York: Routledge, 1995); also Ranajit Guha, *Dominance without Hegemony: History and Power in Colonial India* (Cambridge: Harvard University Press, 1977) and *A Subaltern Studies Reader, 1986–1995* (Minneapolis: University of Minnesota Press, 1997); also Benedict Anderson, *Imagined Communities: Reflections on the Origin and Spread of Nationalism* (London: Verso, 1983).

10. See Alfred Arteaga, *An Other Tongue: Nation and Ethnicity in the Linguistic Borderlands* (Durham: Duke University Press, 1994).

11. "Bonding in Difference, interview with Alfred Arteaga (1993–1994)," in *The Spivak Reader*, ed. Donna Landry and Gerald Maclean (London and New York: Routledge, 1996), p. 24; also in *An Other Tongue*, ed. Alfred Arteaga (Durham: Duke University Press, 1994), pp. 273–85.

12. Term coined by Salman Rushdie.

13. See Ngugi Wa Thiong'o, "The Language of African Literature," in *Decolonising the Mind: The Politics of Language in African Literature* (London: James Currey, 1981); also the section on language in *The Post-Colonial Studies Reader*, ed. Bill Ashcroft, et al. (London and New York: Routledge, 1995).

14. Unpublished interview with Dobles by Mariannick Guennec, 1994; see also "Cuento que no comemos," *La Nación*, 1 September 1994, and "Alerta, ustedes," in *Cultura y signos: La humanidad y su entorno hoy,* ed. College of General Studies (San José: University of Costa Rica, 1994). Unless otherwise noted, all translations into English from this and any other source are mine.

15. Dobles, "Defensa y aliento de una literatura," *Obras completas*, vol. 2 (San José: EUCR/EUNA, 1993). All quotations from this essay refer to this volume and are identified by page number in parentheses in the text.

16. The irony here of turning an English word into Spanish—"*snobismo*"—probably was unintentional. Dobles certainly would have been careful not to use such a term in his fiction. Clearly, he did not monitor so closely what he said on the spur of the moment in an interview.

17. Ronald Solano, "Crítica literaria en Costa Rica: De las *Historias de Tata Mundo*," *Anuario de Estudios Centroamericanos* 18, no. 1 (1992): 92.

18. Fabián Dobles, letter to Mariannick Guennec, 25 September 1995.

19. Fredric Jameson, "Third-World Literature in the Era of Multinational Capitalism," *Social Text* 15 (1986): 69.

20. Alfonso Chase, "En el centro luminoso del sol," *La Prensa Libre,* 3 April 1997.

21. See in particular Alvaro Quesada Soto, *Breve historia de la literatura costarricense* and Margarita Rojas, Flora Ovares, et al., *La casa paterna: Escritura y nación en Costa Rica.*

22. Aurelia Dobles, "Cuento que no es cuento," *La Nación,* 18 April 1996.

23. Edward W. Said, *Orientalism* (New York: Pantheon Books, 1978).

24. Benedict Anderson, *Imagined Communities: Reflections on the Origin and Spread of Nationalism* (New York: Verso, 1983).

25. See representatives of the Chicago School of criticism or the Neo-Aristotelians, specifically Wayne C. Booth, *The Rhetoric of Fiction* (Chicago: University of Chicago Press, 1961). See also E. D. Hirsch, *The Validity of Interpretation* (New Haven and London: Yale University Press, 1967) and Patrick Parrinder, *Authors and Authority* (New York: Columbia University Press, 1991).

26. See Steven Seidman, introduction to *The Postmodern Turn* (Cambridge: Cambridge University Press, 1994) for a comprehensive synthesis of the claims and defining characteristics of postmodernism and poststructuralism.

27. See Seidman's discussion of standpoint theory: "This holds that knowledge is always produced from a specific social position exhibiting particular interests, values, and beliefs," p. 10.

28. Dobles, "Defensa," p. 365.

29. Miguel Arturo Ramos, "Fabián Dobles: 'Nunca escribo sólo por entretener,'" *La República*, 9 April 1985.

30. Dobles, letter, translation mine.

31. See theory on autobiography, e.g., James Olney, ed., *Autobiography: Essays Theoretical and Critical* (Princeton: Princeton University Press, 1980).

32. Dobles, "Consideraciones sobre la literatura," in *Obras completas,* vol. 2 (San José: EUCR/EUNA, 1993), p. 398.

33. Resti Moreno Ortega, "Fabián Dobles: Su proyección intelectual," *Senderos* 19 (1997): 416.

34. Charles Bernheimer, introduction to *Comparative Literature in the Age of Multiculturalism* (Baltimore: John Hopkins University Press, 1995), p. 12.

35. James Clifford, "Traveling Cultures" in *Cultural Studies,* ed. Lawrence Grossberg, Cary Nelson, and Paula Treichler (London and New York: Routledge, 1992), p. 109.

Chapter 1. Introduction

The Central American Context

1. Benedict Anderson, *Imagined Communities: Reflections on the Origin and Spread of Nationalism* (New York: Verso, 1983).

2. Carlos Meléndez, *Historia de Costa Rica* (San José: Editorial Universidad Estatal a Distancia, 1999, p. 97.

3. See, for example, Jaime González Dobles, *La patria del Tico* (San José: Editorial Logos, 1995). He in turn refers to other studies by Luis Barahona, Abelardo Bonilla, and Constantino Láscaris to name only a few.

4. The reasons for the scarcity of large indigenous populations in Costa Rica are more fully explored in chapter 3 of this study.

5. Carlos Fuentes, *La nueva novela hispanoamericana* (Mexico: Editorial Joaquín Mortiz, 1969), pp. 11–12 (translation mine; unless otherwise noted all translations from English to Spanish in this chapter are mine).

6. Virginia Sandoval de Fonseca, *Resumen de literatura costarricense* (San José: Editorial Costa Rica, 1978), p. 22.

7. See José Donoso, *The Boom in Spanish American Literature: A Personal History*, trans. Gregory Kolovakos (New York: Columbia University Press, 1977).

8. See the next section (The Life and Times of Fabián Dobles) for more information on this contest.

9. Paul W. Borgeson, Jr., "El Salvador," in *Handbook of Latin American Literature*, ed. David William Foster, 2nd ed. (New York: Garland Publishing, Inc., 1992), p. 590.

10. Alfonso Chase, ed., *Narrativa contemporánea de Costa Rica* (San José: Ministerio de Cultura, Juventud y Deportes, 1975), p. 61.

11. Rima de Vallbona, "Costa Rica," in *Handbook of Latin American Literature*, edited by David William Foster, 2nd ed. (New York: Garland Publishing, Inc., 1992), pp. 221–22.

12. See Alfonso Chase, introduction to *Narrativa contemporánea de Costa Rica* (San José: Ministerio de Cultura, Juventud y Deportes, 1975), p. 73. "Creo que la literatura moderna, la narrativa contemporánea, se inicia en nuestra patria como un esfuerzo prolongado y profesional, con este concurso de novela" [I believe that modern literature, contemporary narrative, begins in our country as a prolonged and professional effort with this novel competition].

13. See Magda Zavala and Seidy Araya, *La historiografía literaria en América Central (1957–1987)* (Heredia, Costa Rica: Editorial Fundación UNA, 1995), especially chapter 1 for a thorough review and analysis of the various histories of Costa Rican literature, beginning with Abelardo Bonilla's *Historia y antología de la literatura costarricense*. 2nd ed. (San José: Editorial Costa Rica, 1967), which sets the standard for the discipline. Also see Claudio Bogantes-Zamora, *La narrativa socialrealista en Costa Rica* (Aarhus, Denmark: Aarhus University Press, 1990); as well as other histories of Costa Rican literature such as Virginia Sandoval de Fonseca, *Resumen de literatura costarricense* (San José: Editorial Costa Rica, 1978); Jorge Valdeperas, *Para una nueva interpretación de la literature costarricense* (San José: Editorial Costa Rica, 1979); and particularly Manuel Picado Gómez, *Literatura, ideología, crítica: Notas para un estudio de la literatura costarricense* (San José: Editorial Costa Rica, 1983) who criticizes what he calls the critics of verisimilitude and exposes the fallacies of so-called realism for the contemporary postmodern reader and critic.

14. See Alvaro Quesada, *Breve historia de la literatura costarricense* (San José: Editorial Porvenir, S.A., 2000) for a succinct analysis of how Dobles and his generation or "promoción" revamped the concept of national identity by reversing the social, political, and ethical views of the first group of Costa Rican writers he calls the "Olimpo."

15. See Victor Manuel Arroyo Soto, *El habla popular en la literatura costarricense* (San José: Publicaciones de la Universidad de Costa Rica, 1971) for a linguistic analysis of Costa Rican speech in the national literature.

16. Edmundo Desnoes, "Nacer en Español," in *An Other Tongue*, ed. Alfred Arteaga (Durham: Duke University Press, 1994), p. 264.

17. Desnoes, pp. 265, 270, and 263.

18. Bruce Novoa, "Dialogical Strategies, Monological Goals: Chicano Literature," *An Other Tongue*, p. 231.

The Life and Times of Fabián Dobles (1918–1997)

19. Margarita Dobles, "Poeta y filósofo de la piedra y la madera," *Revista Nacional de Cultura* 10 (February 1991): 58–62.

20. Personal conversations between 1 January and 15 June 2000.

21. Resti Moreno, "Fabián Dobles: Vida y testimonio de un hombre—narrador y poeta—'Bueno' In Memoriam (1918–1997)," *Senderos* 19 (1997): 64–65.

22. Dobles quoted in "Un maestro de la realidad," by Argentinean Pablo Ananía, unpublished family document.

23. Francisco Araya, "Fabián Dobles: 'Escribo con el corazón,'" *Rumbo*, 26 April 1988.

24. Carmen Lyra (also spelled Lira) was the pseudonym of Isabel Carvajal, especially remembered for her adaptations of stories from the oral tradition for children, *Cuentos de mi tía Panchita* (1920).

25. Magón was the pseudonym of Manuel González Zeledón (1864–1936), the major exponent of Costa Rican *costumbrista* fiction.

26. Carlos Morales (dir.), "Tertulia literaria: Café de las cuatro," *Forja: Suplemento de Semanario Universidad*, 31 October–6 November, p. 3.

27. Unpublished interview with Dobles by Mariannick Guennec, 1994.

28. Guennec, interview.

29. José León Sánchez, "En el San Juan hay tiburón," *La República*, 26 November 1967, p. 33.

30. Both men were trained in the Universidad de Chile. Azofeifa became a well-known poet and Monge Alfaro became the rector of the University of Costa Rica.

31. Fabián Dobles, letter to Mariannick Guennec, 25 September 1995.

32. Cf. *La Razón*, 16 December, 1940, p. 5 and *La Hora*, 16 December 1940, pp. 1, 2, and 6; the text of the decision is reprinted in *Obras completas*, vol. 1, pp. 35–37.

33. Roberto Brenes Mesén, Joaquín García Monge, Rogelio Sotela, Alejandro Alvarado Quirós, and Marco Aurelio Zumbado.

34. Martin Erickson, "Trends in Central American Literature," in *Intellectual Trends in Latin America* (Austin: University of Texas Press, 1945), pp. 125–26.

35. Moreno, p. 87.

36. His sister Margarita, who was a Figuerista, went personally to Don Pepe to request that Edgar Cardona, the Minister of Defense, release Fabián. Since the charge was hiding weapons, they first searched the grounds of his home where they found a compost heap instead of the alleged weapons.

37. Guennec, interview, p. 10.

38. Dobles, letter.

39. Dobles, letter.

40. Morales, p. 5.

41. Dobles, letter.

42. Dobles, letter.

43. He almost lost his house at one point since he had not been able to pay the mortgage in over a year.

44. Moreno, p. 91.

45. Dobles, letter.

46. Dobles, letter, Dobles' emphasis. Clearly, Dobles does not agree and is aware of the subversive nature of these stories, a point I will argue in chapter 4 of this study.

47. Cf. Fabián Dobles, *Obras completas*, vol. 1, p. 28. Dobles recalls writer Lilia Ramos' eyewitness account of a truck loaded with boxes of Dobles' novel from the Almacén Nacional Escolar that stored copies originally bought by the Ministry of Education to help with printing costs. The truck was sent to the Crematorio Municipal despite Ramos' protests.

48. Guennec, interview, p. 9.

49. Moreno, p. 95.

50. Moreno, p. 100.

51. "Fabián Dobles contesta al fascismo," *Adelante*, 18 March 1962; also the same article under "Fabián Dobles defiende su cátedra," *La Nación*, 18 March 1962.

52. Dobles, letter.

53. Guennec, interview, p. 11.

54. Araya, p. 29.

55. (Lima, Perú: Editora Latinoamericana, 1955). See also *El cuento costarricense* (México, D.F.: Ediciones de Andrea, 1964); *América cuenta* (Caracas, Venezuela: Editorial Arte, 1965); *Die Sonnenfinsternis und andere Erzählungen aus Mittelamerika* (*El eclipse de sol y otros cuentos de Centroamérica*) (Tübingen, West Germany: Horst Eerdmanns Verlag, 1969); *Moderne latein-amerikanische Prosa* (Berlin: Verlag Volk und Welt, 1969); *Antología de cuentos Premios León Felipe* (Mexico, D.F.: Finisterre Editor, 1972); *El cuento actual latinoamericano* (Mexico, D.F.: Ediciones de Andrea, 1973); *Narradores centroamericanos contemporáneos* (Guayaquil, Ecuador: Editorial Ariel Universal, 1973); *Perfeccione su español* (Moscow: 1988); *Paz para el mundo* (Moscow: 1988); *And We Sold the Rain: Contemporary Fiction from Central America*, ed. Rosario Santos (New York: Four Walls Eight Windows, 1988); *Contemporary Short Stories from Central America* (Austin: University of Texas Press, 1994); *Costa Rica: A Traveler's Literary Companion*, ed. Barbara Ras (San Francisco: Whereabouts Press, 1994); *Déluge de soleil* (Ediciones Vericueto and UNESCO, 1996).

56. His sister Margarita recalls that the judges were most impressed by the style of the brief "por bello y convincente. Es una pieza literaria, sabia" [beautiful and convincing. It is a literary, wise piece]. Personal conversations between 1 January and 15 June 2000.

57. Guennec, interview, p. 3.

58. *Obras completas*, vol. 3, p. 359.

59. See for example: Alfonso Chase, "Crónica de los Días: Aproximaciones a la última novela de Fabián Dobles," *El Centavo* 14, no. 143 (December 1989): 16–22; Amalia Chavarri, "*Los años, pequeños días*: Una lectura a través de categorías mítico-simbólicas," *Káñina* 17, no. 2 (1993): 21–28; Emma Gamboa, "Prólogo a *El sitio de las abras*," in *Obras completas*, vol. 2 (San José: EUCR/EUN, 1993); Ann González,

"Fabián Dobles y la novela de los recuerdos," *Káñina* 22, no. 3 (1998): 23–28; Resti Moreno Ortega, "Fabián Dobles: Su proyección intelectual. Entre el compromiso y la solidaridad con el pobre," *Senderos* 19 (1997): 409–52 and "Fabián Dobles: Vida y testimonio de un hombre—narrador y poeta—'Bueno' *In Memoriam* (1918–1997)," *Senderos* 19 (1997): 61–118 and "Fabián Dobles y la generación del 40," *Senderos* 20 (May–August 1998): 229–65; Alvaro Quesada, "Fabián Dobles en la narrativa costarricense," in *Obras completas*, vol. 1 (San Jose: UCR/EUNA, 1993) and "Tradición e innovación: La novela de Fabián Dobles," *Semanario Universidad*, 1 July 1994, pp. 3–4 and *Breve historia de la literatura costarricense* (San José: Editorial Porvenir, S.A., 2000); Ronald Solano Jiménez, "Crítica literaria en Costa Rica: De las *Historias de Tata Mundo*," *Anuario de Estudios Centroamericanos* 18, no. 1 (1992): 85–95 and "!Qué no sabía Tata Mundo! Narración, Saber, Seducción," *Revista Girasol* 1 (1996): 81–88; Margarita Rojas and Flora Ovares, *La casa paterna: Escritura y nación en Costa Rica* (San José: Editorial Universidad de Costa Rica, 1993) and *100 años de literatura costarricense* (San José: Farben Grupo Editorial Norma, 1995), and most recently Carlos Cortés, *La invención de Costa Rica* (San José: Editorial Costa Rica, 2003), particularly the chapter titled "Fabián Dobles: Autorretrato con memoria," pp. 137–43.

60. Carlos Cortés, "Fabián Dobles: Las *Obras completas* son como un parto," *La Nación*, 5 July 1993.

61. Rodrigo Soto, "Letter to Fabián Dobles," *Revista Nacional de Cultura* (May 1993).

62. Alfonso Chase, "En el centro luminoso del sol," *La Prensa Libre*, 3 April 1997.

63. Dobles, letter, Dobles' emphasis.

64. Morales, "Tertulia literaria," p. 2.

65. Alfonso Chase, back cover of Fabián Dobles, *Y otros cuentos* (Heredia, Costa Rica: EUNA, 1999).

CHAPTER 2. THE EARLY NOVELS

1. E.V.V. (probably Emilio Valverde Vega), "Apuntes sobre 'AGUAS TURBIAS' de FABIÁN DOBLES," unpublished family document. Unless otherwise noted, all translations in this chapter from Spanish into English from this and any other source are mine.

2. Ibid, E.V.V.'s emphasis.

3. The text of the decision was published in *La Razón*, 16 December 1940. Also see the introductory chapter of this study on the contest's controversial decision.

4. Interview with Virginia Grütter, *Libertad*, 15–21 March 1985, p. 12.

5. *Obras completas*, vol. 1, p. 91. All future quotations from the novels in this chapter refer to this volume in the *Obras completas* and will be indicated by page number in parentheses in the text.

6. An analysis of this novel's urban/rural conflicts can be found in Claudio Bogantes-Zamora, *La narrativa socialrealista en Costa Rica 1900–1950* (Aarhus, Denmark: Aarhus University Press, 1990), pp. 210–29.

7. León Pacheco, "Ese que llaman pueblo," *La Nación*, 26 July 1968.

8. Alfonso Orantes, "Un libro de Fabián Dobles," *El Diario de Hoy*, 27 June 1943.

9. Iver Romero, "Leyendo 'Ese que llaman Pueblo,' January 1943, unpublished family document.

10. Abelardo Bonilla, "Un juicio sobre 'Ese que llaman pueblo' la novela de Fabián Dobles, 25 September 1942. (Newspaper not identified—family clipping.)

11. See Ronald Solano, "Crítica literaria en Costa Rica: De las *Historias de Tata Mundo*," *Anuario de Estudios Centroamericanos* 18, no. 1 (1992): 85–95 discussed more specifically in chapter 4 of this study.

12. See Bogantes-Zamora's analysis of Dobles' experimentation with point of view and his judgment that the narrative techniques in this novel represent "un avance importante" [an important advance] in Costa Rican literature. *La narrativa socialrealista en Costa Rica 1900–1950*, p. 219.

CHAPTER 3. THE CONTROVERSIAL NOVELS

1. The 1946 and 1971 editions read "A Miguel, mi padre." Later editions, which added an important introduction by Osvaldo Sauma, neglected to include the dedication. It was reinstated in the *Obras completas*.

2. Margarita Dobles, Ph.D. in Education, M.A. in Psychology from Stanford University, California is an expert on children's literature and adolescent psychology. In private conversations between 1 January and 15 June 2000.

3. An unnamed reviewer, for instance, says "Obra muy diferente a sus otros relatos, *Una burbuja en el limbo* es probablemente la más sorprendente y discutida de sus novelas" [A very different work from his stories, *Una burbuja en el limbo* is probably the most surprising and controversial of all his novels] in "Nuevo Libro de la Editorial Costa Rica," *Diario de Costa Rica*, 15 September 1971). Unless otherwise noted, all translations in this chapter from Spanish into English from this and any other source are mine.

4. Alberto Cañas, "Chisporroteos," *La República*, 8 March 1994, p. 17A.

5. Alberto Cañas, "Chisporroteos," *La República*, 10 January 1972.

6. Alfonso Chase, "Novela de la libertad," *La Nación*, 14 April 1996.

7. Chase.

8. Osvaldo Sauma, "Semblanza del Loco Ríos," *La Nación*, 22 May 1995.

9. Ministerio de Educación Pública, "Literatura para séptimo año," in *Programa de Estudios: Tercer Ciclo: Español* (San José: El Ministerio, 1995), p. 26. This program began under the administration of José (Pepe) Figueres' son and stayed in effect until 2002. Actually, Dobles' novel is not absolutely required in this plan. It is part of Option 1 (of two options) that teachers must choose to follow during the year. According to a friend in the field and anecdotal accounts (no numbers available), most teachers chose Option 1 for the novel, which meant their students read Dobles' novel, to avoid having to teach Melville's *Moby Dick*, which was in Option 2 (see pp. 26–27).

10. See the chapter of this study on *Los años, pequeños días* (1989).

11. His sister Margarita claims that biographical elements from both Fabián's life and his father's childhood are conflated in this novel to create Ignacio's character. Specifically, the incident of Nacho in the tree, threatening to urinate on his uncle if he does not leave him alone and the idea of having two uncles for Ignacio: one

good and one bad—both come from stories Dr. Dobles told Fabián about his side of the family.

12. Carlos Meléndez, *Historia de Costa Rica,* 2nd ed. (San José: Editorial Universidad Estatal a Distancia, 1983, reprint, 1999), pp. 89–118.

13. Those against annexation argued for a republican system following the Bolívar model. But as Meléndez explains, "Es conveniente hacer resaltar aquí, que tanto monárquicos como republicanos tenían la clara conciencia de que nuestro territorio centroamericano debería agregarse a otra juridicción mayor, como estado protector, puesto que la experiencia les había enseñado que de lo contrario podríamos ser fácil presa de cualquier potencia europea que resoliese apoderarse de nuestro territorio" (95) [It is best to emphasize here that both monarchists and republicans clearly believed that our Central American territory should join a larger jurisdiction as a protected state, given that experience had taught that otherwise we would become easy prey for any European power that decided to take over our territory.]

14. See the first section "Formación de la provincia de Costa Rica," in Meléndez, pp. 11–89.

15. Dobles, *Una burbuja en el limbo,* in *Obras completas,* vol. 2, pp. 122–23. All future quotations from this novel come from this volume and will be indicated by page number in parentheses in the body of the text.

16. Alfred Arteaga, *An Other Tongue: Nation and Ethnicity in the Linguistic Borderlands* (Durham: Duke University Press, 1994), pp. 17–18. "In response to colonialism, there are several general reactions available for the colonized Other. Very generally, the reactions can be described according to different criteria as either autocolonial, nationalist, or hybrid . . .

> *Autocolonialism* . . . requires the Other's adoption of the hegemonic discourse to the extent that colonizer permits and to the extent that the Other is able to predicate it. The Other assimilates both discourse and the relationships it systematizes, so to the degree the discourse suppresses, the autocolonist effaces or denigrates him/herself from within . . .
>
> *Nationalism* opposes the authority of the colonial discourse with the authority of an alternate discourse . . . The alien, colonially defined world is rejected in favor of the native, nationalistically defined world . . .
>
> *Hybridization,* or cultural mestizaje, differs from both autocolonialism and nationalism in that it is inherently polyglot. Hybridized discourse rejects the principle of monologue and composes itself by selecting from competing discourses. Further, there is no detritus of difference; distinct elements remain so, relating in a dialogue of dissimilarity."

17. See the paradoxical concept of *sí pero no* discussed in chapter 2 of this study.

18. See David Lloyd's discussion of Norma Alarcon's "beautiful formulation, to be chicano/a is to say at once 'I am a citizen, I am not a citizen.' To adhere to what is called an ethnic culture is to refuse the cultural formation of the citizen; to be formed as a citizen is to undertake the impossible task of negating one's given ethnicity." "Adulteration and the Nation," in *An Other Tongue: Nation and Ethnicity in the Linguistic Borderlands,* ed. Alfred Arteaga (Durham: Duke University Press, 1994), p. 81.

19. The image is precolonial although the historical period is anachronistically that of early independence.

20. Dobles quoted in "*Una burbuja en el limbo*: Novela de Fabián Dobles," *La Tribuna,* 27 August 1946.

21. See Amalia Chaverri F., "Título y transformación," *La Nación*, 15 November 1987, pp. 1D and 4D.

22. The clash here is represented in his family by his father who ultimately gives up trying to change him and lets him be and his aunt, the stern and severe religious fundamentalist who openly hates Ignacio and never gives up her mission to punish him.

23. See for example Gerald Vizenor, "The Ruins of Representation: Shadow Survivance and the Literature of Dominance," in *An Other Tongue: Nation and Ethnicity in the Linguistic Borderlands*, ed. Alfred Arteaga (Durham: Duke University Press, 1994), pp. 139–67. Our definitions of shadow, however, are not identical. He uses the term to deconstruct representations of Native American history and literature: "The shadow is that sense of intransitive motion to the referent; the silence in memories. Shadows are neither the absence of entities nor the burden of conceptual references. The shadow is the silence that inherits the words; shadows are the motions that mean the silence, but not the presence or absence of entities. Archshadows are honored in memories and the silence of tribal stones. Shadows and the postmodern are the natural trace of liberation in the ruins of representation," p. 140.

24. See Michael G. Cooke, "Rhetoric of Obliquity," in *An Other Tongue: Nation and Ethnicity in the Linguistic Borderlands*, ed. Alfred Arteaga (Durham: Duke University Press, 1994), pp. 169–84; "There are never enough colonizers to complete or maintain the silent partners," p. 170.

25. The "casa típica" in Costa Rica is a white adobe house with a blue stripe along the bottom and a red tiled roof—the incarnation of the red, white, and blue striped Costa Rican national flag.

26. See chapter 4 of this study.

27. See chapter 1 of this study.

28. José Fabio Garnier, "Cien novelas costarricenses (no. 89): *Una araña verde*, Novela de Fabián Dobles," *La Nación*, 27 May 1950.

29. Dobles, unpublished letter to Mariannick Guennec, 25 September 1995, p. 8.

30. See chapter 4 on Dobles' short stories in this study.

31. José Piedra, "*Los leños vivientes*: La última y mejor novela de Fabián Dobles," *Adelante*, 18 March 1962.

32. Dobles, *Los leños vivientes* in *Obras completas,* vol. 3. All future quotations from this novel come from volume 3 and will be indicated by page number in parentheses in the body of the text.

33. See Doris Sommer, *Foundational Fictions: The National Romances of Latin America* (Berkeley: University of California Press, 1991).

34. Alberto Cañas, "Chisporroteos," *La República*, 8 March 1994, p. 17A.

35. See, for example, Doriam Díaz Matamoros, "Recuerdos del 48," *Semanario Universidad*, 23 August 1996, p. 4 and "De don Fabián Dobles," *Semanario Universidad*, 3 August 1996, p. 19.

36. See chapter 1 of this study for further historical and contextual information about this period in Costa Rican history and its effect on Dobles' personal life.

37. The Communist Party was constitutionally banned after the Nationalists came to power.

38. "Reales" here is a loaded term meaning not only realities, the problem of

multiple realities, but also money, a financial problem, as well as royalties, a reference to the Spanish colonial past that has left the Costa Rican writer with a language that was not born of his own reality but imposed on it.

39. Gayatri Chakravorty Spivak, "Can the Subaltern Speak?" in *The Post-Colonial Studies Reader*, ed. Bill Ashcroft, Gareth Griffiths, and Helen Tiffin (New York and London: Routledge, 1995), pp. 29–35.

40. The mention of "maíz" [corn] harkens back to the Mayan culture and the *Popol Vuh*, which claims that humankind originated from corn and that it forms the life blood of humanity.

41. Certainly the religious overtones of the name John the Baptist reinforce the themes of oppression and resistance. It should be remembered that Calderón's government was allied not only with the Communists, but also with the Catholic Church. Pepe Figueres' right-wing nationalist forces ultimately were opposed to the pro-governmental position of the Catholic Church.

CHAPTER 4. THE NOVEL OF SHORT STORIES

1. This edition was illustrated with woodcuts by Costa Rica's well-known artist Francisco (don Paco) Amighetti. Both Dobles and Amighetti donated the proceeds from this edition to help the Republican (anti-Franco) veterans of the Spanish Civil War.

2. All translations of story titles come from Henry's translation.

3. The number was expanded to twenty-five in the *Obras completas*. The additional story was titled significantly "La última de Tata Mundo" [Tata Mundo's Last Story].

4. *Historias de Tata Mundo*, special ed., illustrated in color by Luis Daell (San José: EUNED, 1993).

5. *La República*, 24 March 1955.

6. Seymour Menton, *El cuento costarricense* (Lawrence: University of Kansas Press, 1964), 27, quoted in several of the initial reviews.

7. *Diario de Costa Rica*, 29 December 1957.

8. Ronald Solano Jiménez, "Crítica literaria en Costa Rica: De las *Historias de Tata Mundo*," *Anuario de Estudios Centroamericanos* 18, no. 1 (1992): 85.

9. Solano, p. 86.

10. Solano, pp. 85–95.

11. See, for example, Rodrigo Soto, "Más allá de Tata Mundo," *Ancora: Suplemento Cultural de la Nación*, 9 January 2000.

12. *Y otros cuentos* (San José: Editorial de la Universidad Nacional, 1999). Each story was selected for inclusion in this last collection by Dobles himself shortly before his death.

13. Ronald Solano Jiménez, "¡Qué no sabía Tata Mundo! Narración, Saber, Seducción," *Revista Girasol* 1 (1996): 81–88.

14. Fabián Dobles, *Historias de Tata Mundo*, in *Obras completas*, vol. 4, p. 159. All citations from the Tata Mundo stories are taken from this volume and are referenced by page number in the text in parentheses. All the translations for the citations come from Joan Henry, trans., *The Stories of Tata Mundo* (San José: Editorial de la Universidad de Costa Rica, 1998) and are indicated by page number in the

text in parentheses. In this particular case, however, the translation is mine since Henry left these two paragraphs completely out of her rendering of the story.

15. The trickster figure is a staple of oral storytelling practices, prominent as well in other Latin American folk literature (e.g., Juan Bobo from Puerto Rico), in African and African American literature and in literature of the Southern United States.

16. Guido Ortiz Mangel, "Treinta años de vida literaria de Fabián Dobles," *Diario de Costa Rica*, 15 May 1971. Ortiz also calls Tata Mundo Dobles' "alter-ego."

17. Dobles, "Cuento que no comemos," *La Nación*, 1 September 1994. Dobles here is punning on the familiar folk saying "Dime con quien andas y te digo quien eres" [Tell me who you associate with and I'll tell you who you are].

18. Aurelia Dobles, "Cuento que no es cuento," *La Nación*, 18 April 1996.

19. The "vosotros" form, second-person familiar, plural, is only commonly used today in Spain and is one of the most notable differences between Latin American and Peninsular Spanish. Note that "cultured" in this comment is clearly associated with Penninsular, i.e., European, values.

20. Lorenzo Vives, "Historias de Tata Mundo," *Diario de Costa Rica*, 21 June 1955, p. 4.

21. Dobles, "Cuento."

22. Dobles, "Cuento." His comment here is aimed against Costa Rica's Ministry of Education's mandate to teach English at all levels in the school system, "para proporcionarles a los futuros turistas angloparlantes buenos y obsecuentes guías—léase serviciales lacayitos—cuando nos 'favorezcan' con sus dólares de visitantes" [in order to provide future English-speaking tourists with good and humble guides—read little obedient servants—when they "favor" us with their visiting dollars].

23. My translation. Henry's is "Pitchblack night" (15).

24. My translation; this line is missing in Henry's version.

25. Specifically, a kind of tropical snake.

26. My translation; Henry leaves the story title as "Bejuco."

27. This title is actually a made-up word.

28. Translation mine; Henry leaves the title unchanged from Spanish.

29. The son of Fabián's younger brother, Alvaro.

30. Literally, the cat with shoes.

31. See Carlos Cortés, *La invención de Costa Rica* (San José: Editorial Costa Rica, 2003) for his deconstruction of the myth of Juan Santamaría as national hero, pp. 29–34.

32. Personal conversation with Cecilia Dobles, 29 February 2000.

33. Literally, the one from sand.

34. The pun on his name is clearly intentional—Flaco Arroyo [Thin Stream].

35. All of these translations are mine since Henry does not conserve the water imagery in hers.

36. Translation mine; Henry does not consistently keep the water imagery and mistranslates "tarantas" as "tarantula" rather than scatterbrained.

37. Translation mine; Henry does not conserve the agricultural imagery.

38. Translation mine; I disagree with Henry's rendering of "el saco de huseos fuertes con su poco de cabeza lista que era su mujer" as "his wife, who was strong and clever" (213).

39. Translation mine; Henry mistranslates "largas" as big.

40. Literally, Mass.

41. Translation mine; Henry eliminates the land metaphor.

42. See for example, "La luz en la oscurana" where the father explains why he accepts another's child as his own, "me traje conmigo al otro . . . porque el cipotillo de nada tenía la culpa" (257) [I've even brought the other child with me . . . because it wasn't his fault (191)].

43. Alberto Cañas, "Chisporroteos," *La República,* 19 September 1971.

44. Translation mine; Henry mistranslates this passage: "you're young to be contracting out your lives" (173).

45. Menton, *El cuento costarricense,* p. 28.

46. Alcida Rita Ramos, *Indigenism: Ethnic Politics in Brazil* (Madison: University of Wisconsin Press, 1998), p. 285.

47. A "Tata Mundo" story is included in a seventh grade reader. See Mario Fernández L., *Textos de lectura y comentarios para sétimo año,* 2nd ed, (San José: Editorial Fernández Arce, 1980), pp. 70–72.

CHAPTER 5. OTHER STORIES AND COLLECTIONS

1. María Amoretti, "La cuentística de Fabián Dobles," *Revista de filología y lingüística de la Universidad de Costa Rica* 2, no. 3 (1976): 41. Unless otherwise noted, all translations in this chapter from Spanish into English from this and any other source are mine.

2. *Obras completas,* vol 4 (San José: Editorial de la Universidad de Costa Rica y Editorial de la Universidad Nacional, 1993), p. 20. All the citations from Dobles' stories, unless otherwise specified, come from the *Obras completas,* vol. 4 and will be indicated by page number in parentheses in the text.

3. José León Sánchez, "En el San Juan hay tiburón," *La República,* 26 November 1967, p. 33; see also the introduction to this study.

4. Resti Moreno Ortega, "Fabián Dobles: Vida y testimonio de un hombre—narrador y poeta—'Bueno' In Memoriam (1918–1997)," *Senderos* 19 (1997): 95.

5. Alberto Cañas, "Chisporroteos," *La República,* 13 February 1966.

6. (San José: EUNED) with a prologue by Jorge Charpentier.

7. Rodolfo Cerdeño, "Violín contra chatarra," *La Nación,* 22 May 1993.

8. See the section on Dobles' life in chapter 1 of this study; Dobles' imprisonment after the Civil War of 1948 and the loss of his teaching job in 1962 after a visit to Cuba are two examples.

9. An untranslatable, made-up word.

10. The title refers to the job of taking the sap from the gum tree.

11. Cerdeño, Cerdeño's emphasis.

12. Semantically, the *and* and *but* function alike, combining into a hybrid concept what are otherwise binary and mutually exclusive terms (either/or).

13. Alberto Cañas, "Chisporroteos," *La República,* January 1971.

14. Flora Ovares and Margarita Rojas, "Fragmento del prólogo a antología de cuentos de Costa Rica traducidos al francés," *Ancora: La Nación,* n.d.

15. Ovares and Rojas.

16. *Paracuentos* are included in vol. 5 of the *Obras completas*. All citations will refer to this volume number and be included in the text in parentheses.

17. *Obras completas,* vol. 2, p. 368.

CHAPTER 6. THE MATURE NOVELS

1. See the bibliography on Fabián Dobles under the section: Theses. Also see Carlos Morales, "Fabián Dobles: Un estudio sobre *El sitio de las abras,*" *Cuadernos Universitarios,* FEUCR, no. 1 (1974); Michael White, *"El sitio de las abras:* Una novela de Fabián Dobles," *Káñina* 5, no. 1 (1981): 17–27; Carlos Molina and Edwin Salas, "Pasado y presente en *El sitio de las abras,*" *Letras* 6–7 (July–December 1980–January–June 1981): 159–82, and "Un estudio sobre 'El sitio de las abras,'" unpublished university lecture, Biblioteca Tinoco de la Universidad de Costa Rica as well as more recent studies by Flora Ovares and Margarita Dobles in *La casa paterna: Escritura y nación en Costa Rica* (San José: Editorial Universidad de Costa Rica, 1993, and *100 años de literatura costarricense* (San José: Farben Grupo Editorial Norma, 1995); Claudio Bogantes-Zamora, *La narrativa socialrealista en Costa Rica* (Aarhus, Denmark: Aarhus University Press, 1990), pp. 230–56; and Alvaro Quesada *Breve historia de la literatura costarricense* (San José: Editorial Porvenir, S.A., 2000).

2. Eliodoro Domínguez, "Fabián Dobles: Verdadero escritor costarricense," *La Nación,* 7 November 1946.

3. *"El sitio de las abras* de Fabián Dobles: La novela agraria de Costa Rica," *Ultima Hora,* 12 September 1947. Unless otherwise noted, all translations in this chapter from Spanish into English from this and any other source are mine.

4. I would argue, however, that because of the social reforms enacted during the administration of Costa Rican President Calderón Guardia, the history of land struggle cannot be so superficially compared between Costa Rica and Guatemala, or anywhere else, for that matter.

5. "Crítico español opina sobre una novela de Fabián Dobles," *Diario de Costa Rica: Suplemento,* 6 July 1952.

6. See for example, Inés Trejos de Steffen, "'El sitio de las abras' por Fabián Dobles," *La Prensa Libre,* 30 November 1970; Gerardo César Hurtado, "'El sitio de las abras,' de Fabián Dobles," *La Prensa Libre,* 12 May 1971, or Emilia Prieto, "'El sitio de las abras' de Fabián Dobles," *Diario de Costa Rica,* 16 May 1971.

7. Alberto Cañas, "Chisporroteos," *La República,* 5 April 1997.

8. Alberto Cañas, "Chisporroteos," *La República,* 2 May 1971.

9. Carlos Catania, "'El sitio de las abras,' de Fabián Dobles," *La Nación,* 22 July 1973; emphasis mine.

10. Doris Sommer, "Irresistible Romance: The Foundational Fictions of Latin America," in *Nation and Narration,* ed. Homi K. Bhabha (New York and London: Routledge, 1990), pp. 78, 75.

11. Sommer, p. 90.

12. *El sitio de las abras,* in *Obras completas,* vol. 2, p. 192. All citations from the novel are taken from this volume and are referenced by page number in the text in parentheses.

13. The magical number seven is by no means fortuitous. Seven is the building block of time—the week, the length of time it took God to create the universe.

14. Costa Rica is linguistically feminine, a point Dobles himself makes in "Mujeres de Costa Rica: Palabras dichas en el Instituto Costarricense-Soviético, en reciente homenaje a escritoras," *Obras completas,* vol. 3, p. 364; "Costa Rica, país con nombre femenino" [Costa Rica, a country with a feminine name].

15. Michael G. Cooke, "Rhetoric of Obliquity," in *An Other Tongue: Nation and Ethnicity in the Linguistic Borderlands,* ed. Alfred Arteaga (Durham: Duke University Press, 1994), p. 171.

16. See Dobles, "Mujeres," p. 365.

17. Michael White, "*El sitio de las abras*: Una novela de Fabián Dobles," *Káñina* 5, no. 1 (1981): 21.

18. Most of the social legislation (including socialized medicine) enacted during Calderón's presidency has remained in effect, an unusual phenomenon in Latin America. Even after the Costa Rican Civil War of 1948 when Calderón was ousted along with his Catholic/Communist coalition, successive governments still have been unable or unwilling to reverse this legislation.

19. Cf. my earlier objection to generalizing the history of land struggle in Costa Rica to all of Central and South America.

20. Sommer, p. 82.

21. Alberto Cañas, "Chisporroteos," *La República,* ca. 1968. (Neither the family clipping nor the library clipping at the University of Costa Rica was dated).

22. See "De don Fabián Dobles," *Semanario Universidad,* 3 August 1996, p. 19. Joan Henry has already translated Dobles' last novel *Los años, pequeños días* [*Years Like Brief Days*], 1996 and *Historias de Tata Mundo* [*The Stories of Tata Mundo*], 1998.

23. Frederic Jameson, "Third World Literature in the Era of Multinational Capitalism," *Social Text* 15 (Fall 1986): 65–88.

24. See Aijaz Ahmad, "Jameson's Rhetoric of Otherness and the 'National Allegory,'" *The Post-Colonial Reader,* ed. Bill Ashcroft, Gareth Griffiths, and Helen Tiffin (New York and London: Routledge, 1995) who argues convincingly against three worlds theory and Jameson's restrictive use of "national." Ahmad's reply to Jameson originally appeared in *Social Text* 17 (Fall 1987).

25. Clearly, on the periphery whether one speaks of one world or three worlds theory.

26. "Bonding in Difference, Interview with Alfred Arteaga (1993–1994)," in *The Spivak Reader,* ed. Donna Landry and Gerald Maclean (New York and London: Routledge, 1996); also in *An Other Tongue: Nation and Ethnicity in the Linguistic Borderlands,* ed. Alfred Arteaga (Durham: Duke University Press, 1994).

27. Dobles, *En el San Juan hay tiburón,* in *Obras completas,* vol. 3, p. 169. All future quotations from this novel refer to this volume and are included in the text in parentheses.

28. C., "En el San Juan hay tiburón," *Contrapunto,* 18 February 1985. Only this reviewer notes the symbolism of the deaf mute and, from my point of view, misreads the equivalence, equating Gugú with "nuestro pueblo" [our people], that is the Costa Rican people. The rest of the allegory falls apart if this is the case. The reviewer does make a valid point, however, that "técnicamente [el mudo] es el personaje central de la novela, pues enlaza los distintos momentos de su desarrollo" [technically (the deaf mute) is the central figure in the novel since he ties the various moments of the novel's development together].

29. "Patria libre o morir" [Freedom or death] was the battle cry of the Sandinistas.

30. Cf. H. Fernando Bullón, *Postmodernidad y la iglesia evangélica* (San José, Costa Rica: El Instituto Internacional de Evangelización a Fondo, 2000).

31. Michael Foucault, *Power/Knowledge: Selected Interviews and Other Writings 1972–1977*, trans. Colin Gorden et al., ed. Colin Gordon (New York: Pantheon, 1980), p. 82.

32. Literally big eggs or big balls, referring to the size of a man's testicles. This slang is typical throughout Central America to refer to another man without using his name.

CHAPTER 7. THE LAST NOVEL

Earlier versions of this chapter appeared in "Fabián Dobles and the Maze of Memory," *World Literature Today* (Summer 1999): 485–88 and "Fabián Dobles y la novela de recuerdos," *Káñina* 12, no. 3 (December 1998): 23–28.

1. Carlos Rivera, "Los años pequeños días para Fabián Dobles," *Contrapunto*, 2 November 1989, p. 16. All translations in this chapter, except for quotations from Dobles' last novel, are mine.

2. Shortly before his death he remarked to his sister Margarita that he still lacked one novel that should be about "las hermanas" [the sisters], but that he would not live long enough to be able to write it. Conversations with Margarita Dobles between 1 January and 15 June 2000.

3. See reviews listed in the bibliography for this novel.

4. See Juan Durán Luzio, "Desafíos de una traducción," *La Nación*, 25 August 1996, pp. 4–5.

5. For example, Dobles' maternal grandmother Micaela Solera, known to her grandchildren and great-grandchildren as Mamita Quela, and his maternal grandfather Santiago Rodríguez, called Papá Santiago, had eight children besides Fabián's mother, Carmen Rodríguez Solera, three of whom were the unmarried aunts in the novel: Lucila, Marta and Otilia. Another daughter, Margarita, married José Manuel Peralta, the rich uncle who appears in the novel. Fabián had six sisters, all of whom appear briefly in the novel: Carmen is the eldest, and Rosario is the married sister who saves Fabián as he tries to escape his angry brother Miguel. Alicia, my mother-in-law, is the daughter with the voice of a lark who almost dies as a young woman in the typhoid epidemic that Fabián recounts. Susana is another of Fabián's older sisters along with Margarita of the doll-bathing incident. Both Margarita and he, only about two years apart in age and virtually inseparable, are sent away to San Ramón during the typhoid epidemic. His elder brother Miguel, who has such a pivotal role in the novel, managed Papá Santiago's farm and business and had a passion for horses that Fabián faithfully represents. Dobles' two younger brothers, Alejo and Alvaro, and his baby sister Marielos are not even born for most of the novel's childhood memories. See the introduction to this study for further biographical information relating to this novel.

6. Alfonso Chase, "Crónica de los días: Aproximaciones a la última novela de Fabián Dobles," *El Centavo* 14, no. 143 (December 1989): 16; article reprinted as

"Lectura de *Los años, pequeños días*: La última novela de Fabián Dobles," *Contrapunto*, 16 November 1989, pp. 12–13.

7. See Amalia Chaverri F., "*Los años, pequeños días* (Una lectura a través de categorías mítico-simbólicas), *Káñina* 17, no. 2 (1993): 21–28.

8. Fredric Jameson, "Third-World Literature in the Era of Multinational Capitalism," *Social Text* 15 (1986): 69.

9. Chase, "Crónica," p. 17.

10. See Steven Seidman, introduction to *The Postmodern Turn: New Perspectives on Social Theory* (Cambridge: Cambridge University Press, 1994), pp. 1–23 for a comprehensive synthesis of the defining characteristics of postmodernism.

11. James Olney, ed., *Autobiography: Essays Theoretical and Critical* (Princeton: Princeton University Press, 1980), p. 4.

12. Hayden White, "The Historical Text as Literary Artifact," *The Tropics of Discourse: Essays in Cultural Criticism* (Baltimore: Johns Hopkins University Press, 1978). I have reversed White's thesis here to argue that Dobles' novel—a "literary artifact"—also works as a historical (autobiographical) text.

13. See Michel Foucault, "Genealogy and Social Criticism," *The Postmodern Turn: New Perspectives on Social Theory*, ed. Steven Seidman (Cambridge: Cambridge University Press, 1994), pp. 39–45.

14. According to his sister Margarita in conversations between 1 January and 15 June 2000.

15. Fabián Dobles, *Los años, pequeños días*, in *Obras completas*, vol. 5, p. 39. All citations from the novel are taken from this volume and are referenced by page number in the text in parentheses. All the translations for this novel come from Joan Henry, trans., *Years Like Brief Days* (London: Peter Owen, 1996) and are indicated by page number in the text in parentheses.

16. Famous Latin American folksinger.

17. Olney, p. 26.

18. The sister that, according to the novel (66), almost drowned Fabián as a little boy pretending he was a doll and giving him a bath. As it happens, Margarita disputes this version and counters Fabián's memory with her own recollection. She remembers washing her baby doll with a friend when Fabián came too close to the washtub and fell in. The fact that this narrative incident provokes a challenge to Fabián's story parallels a similar phenomenon that takes place in the novel with Miguel's challenge to Fabián's letter. My argument here is that both Fabián's discourse and the counterdiscourses it provokes both within and outside the novel represent a fundamental decentering of the scientific respect for objective history.

CHAPTER 8. CONCLUSION

1. See Alfonso Chase, introduction to *Narrativa contemporánea de Costa Rica* (San José: Ministerio de Cultura, Juventud y Deportes, 1975), p. 112. "Es una literatura experimental, sujeta a los vaivenes de la experimentación por la experimentación" [It is an experimental literature, subject to the ups and downs of experimentation for the sake of experimentation]. All translations in this chapter are mine.

2. See Jaime González Dobles, *La patria del Tico* (San José: Editorial Logos,

1995), pp. 54–58: "el costarricense de siempre" [the typical Costa Rican], pp. 54–58.

3. See Abelardo Bonilla, "Abel y Caín en el ser histórico de la nación costarricense," in *Ensayistas Costarricenses*, ed. Luis Ferrero (San José: A. Lehmann, 2nd ed., 1972). Bonilla asserts that the Costa Rican character displays the opposing positive and negative characteristics of the two Biblical brothers. This idea is supported in the notion of "el quijotismo" discussed by both González Dobles and Barahona as "ese estilo trágico de vivir una doble vida" [that tragic style of living a double life" quoted in González Dobles, *La patria del Tico*, p. 68.

4. González Dobles, *La patria del Tico*, p. 60.

5. Benedict Anderson, *Imagined Communities: Reflections on the Origin and Spread of Nationalism* (New York: Verso, 1983), p. 33.

6. Isabel Aguilar-Umaña, "Interview with Fabián Dobles," *Tragaluz* 16 (2 May 1987): 13.

7. See former President Luis Alberto Monge's comment on Costa Rica's special brand of communism: "Hasta el partido comunista nuestro adopta básicamente una actitud liberal" [Even our communist party has adopted basically a liberal attitude], quoted in González Dobles, *La patria del Tico*, p. 62.

8. Alfonso Chase, "En el centro luminoso del sol," *La Prensa Libre*, 3 April 1997.

9. Chase, *Narrativa contemporánea de Costa Rica*, p. 113.

10. Rodrigo Soto, letter to Dobles, May 1993, a document in the Dobles estate.

11. See *Para no cansarlos con el cuento: Narrativa costarricense actual*, ed. Carlos Cortés, Vernor Muñoz, and Rodrigo Soto (San José: Editorial Universidad de Costa Rica, 1989). In addition, see *Narrativa contemporánea de Costa Rica*, ed. Alfonso Chase, vol. 2 (San José: Ministerio de Cultura, Juventud y Deportes, 1975). Other contemporary writers not included in either of these volumes are Linda Berrón, Alfredo Aguilar, Tatiana Lobo, Rima de Vallbona, and Anacristina Rossi.

12. Margarita Rojas and Flora Ovares, *100 años de literatura costarricense* (San José: Farben Grupo Editorial Norma, 1995), p. 131.

13. González Dobles, *La patria del Tico*, p. 56 referring to Eugenio Rodríguez Vega's view of national identity in his essay "Debe y haber del costarricense."

14. Daniel Gallegos, "Fabián Dobles: *In Memoriam*," *Revista Nacional de Cultura* 30 (August 1997): 4.

15. One such intertextualization has been the recent publication of *Cundila* by Costa Rican historian Iván Molina (San José: Varitec, 2002), a novel that plays with the idea that a second unpublished part exists of *El Moto*, Costa Rica's first novel published in 1900 by Joaquín García Monge.

16. See for example, Rafael Angel Herra, "Había una vez dos veces," in *Para no cansarles con el cuento*, pp. 17–29.

17. Gallegos, p. 4.

Bibliography

Literary Works by Fabián Dobles not included in the Bibliography of his Complete Works, *Obras Completas* (1993)

Aguas turbias. 3rd ed. Heredia: Editorial de la Universidad Nacional, 1995.

Los años, pequeños días. 3rd ed. San José: Farben Grupo Editorial Norma, 1993.

"The Bridge." Translated by Steve Hellman. In *Clamor of Innocence: Stories from Central America*, edited by Barbara Paschke and David Volpendesta, 150–55. San Francisco: City Lights Books, 1988.

Una burbuja en el limbo. 6th rep. San José: Editorial Costa Rica, 1995.

Cuentos. Prologue by Carlos Morales. San José: EDUCA, 1996; 2nd ed., 1997.

"Dos Venganzas," *Frente Estudiantil*, 16 August 1939. (A short story).

En el San Juan hay tiburón. 3rd ed. Heredia: Editorial de la Universidad Nacional, 1996.

Ese que llaman pueblo. 7th ed. San José: Editorial Costa Rica, 1995.

Historias de Tata Mundo. 13th ed. San José: Al Día, 1995; 14th ed. Edited and illustrated by Carlos Barboza. Pamplona: EUNATE, 2000.

"El Iluminado," *Crónica*, November 1942. (A short story).

Los leños vivientes. 3rd ed. Heredia: Editorial de la Universidad Nacional, 1996.

Obras Completas. 5 vols. San José: Editorial de la Universidad de Costa Rica and Editorial de la Universidad Nacional, 1993. Reprint, 1997. (The only difference is that Dobles dedicated the reprint of his *Obras Completas* to his wife Cecilia).

"El puente." In *Déluge de soleil*, translated by Flora Ovares and Margarita Rojas. Ediciones Vericueto y la UNESCO, 1996.

"Self-Defense." Translated by Asa Zatz. In *And We Sold the Rain: Contemporary Fiction from Central America*, edited by Rosario Santos, 191–200. New York: Four Walls Eight Windows, 1988.

El Sitio de las abras. Prologue by Emma Gamboa. 10th ed. San José: Editorial Costa Rica, 1999.

The Stories of Tata Mundo. Translated by Joan Henry. San José: Editorial de la Universidad de Costa Rica, 1998.

"The Targuá Tree." Translated by John Incledon. In *Costa Rica: A Traveler's Literary Companion*, edited by Barbara Ras, 37–42. San Francisco: Whereabouts Press, 1994.

"The Trunk." Translated by Leland H. Chambers. In *Contemporary Short Stories from*

Central America, edited by Enrique Jaramillo Levi y Leland H. Chambers, 171–73. Austin: University of Texas Press, 1994.

Y otros cuentos. Illustrated by Claudio Carazo. Back cover commentary by Alfonso Chase. San José: Editorial de la Universidad Nacional, 1999.

Years Like Brief Days. Translated by Joan Henry. London: UNESCO Publishing/Peter Owen Publishers, 1996.

Essays by Fabián Dobles not included in his complete works, *Obras Completas* (1993).

"A dos libros me refiero." *Repertorio Americano* 48, no. 3 (February 1953): 46.

"Acuerdo Gorbachov Reagan: Un hecho de enorme magnitud." *La Nación,* 18 December 1987, p. 2.

"Album de Figueroa." *La Nación: Viva,* 31 January 1995. (On José María Figueroa Oreamuno).

"Alerta, ustedes." *Cultura y signos: La humanidad y su entorno hoy.* Edited by the Escuela de Estudios Generales. San José: Universidad de Costa Rica, 1994.

"Comentariando." *Surco* 16, no. 5 (November 1940): n.p.

"Cuento que no comemos." *La Nación,* 1 September 1994, p. 15 A.

"Defensa y realidad de una literatura." *La Prensa Libre,* 14 February 1998. (Reprint of an essay written in January 1945 and included in *Obras Completas* under the title "Defensa y aliento de una literatura," vol. 2, pp. 361–62.

"Dijo su nombre." (Commentary on *Yerbamar,* a work of poetry written by both Fabián Dobles y Mario Picado). Unidentified family newspaper clipping, ca. 1966.

"Don Fabián Dobles se refiere a ataques al partido socialista." *La República,* 6 November 1960. (An article by Dobles with the following editorial disclaimer: "No comparte este diario las apreciaciones políticas y económicas-sociales que contiene" [This newpaper does not share the political and socioeconomic views contained here]).

"Dos fotografías y un problema social." *Surco* 4 (27 October 1940): n.p.

Duncan, Quince. *El negro en la literatura costarricense.* Prologue by Dobles. San José: Editorial Costa Rica, 1975.

"Entender lo que se lee." *Prensa Libre,* 19 February 1994.

"Fabián Dobles contesta." *Diario de Costa Rica,* 16 May 1971, p. 12.

"Fabián Dobles contesta al fascismo." *Adelante,* 18 March 1962. Also see the same essay under the title "Fabián Dobles defiende su cátedra." *La Nación,* 18 March 1962.

"Fabián Dobles replica." *La Hora,* 22 November 1973, p. 5.

"!Goles, goles!" *La Nación,* 4 May 1972.

"Isabel Carvajal se nos volvió inmortal." *Libertad,* 15 January 1988, pp. 8–9.

"Joaquín Gutiérrez, 'Puerto Limón,' y un seminario." Unidentified family newspaper clipping, ca. 1966. (Review of a novel by Gutiérrez).

"Manifiesto político hará oportunamente el Partido Socialista Costarricense." *La Nación*, 21 October 1960.

"Mi hija Catalina, hija del pueblo." *Libertad*, 20 February 1965.

"Nadie será sometido a torturas ni a penas o tratos crueles, inhumanos o degradantes." *La República*, 18 December 1960.

"¿Obras completas?" *Rumbo* 488 (26 April 1994): 46–47.

"Pintor que pinta ciudades." *La Nación*, 5 November 1994, p. 15 A.

"Protesta por 'nueva cacería de brujas.'" Unidentified family newspaper clipping. (Response to the charge of communist control over national cultural entities).

Rodríguez Gutiérrez, Rafael Armando. *Cuentos y leyendas costarricenses*. Prologue by Dobles. San José: Imprenta Tormo, 1966.

Salazar Ruiz, Milton. *Compañero*. Prologue by Dobles. San José: Imprenta Elena, 1964.

"Se ha ausentado un poeta: Ricardo Segura." *Brecha* 1, no. 12 (August 1957): 20.

"Somos Testigos." *Adelante*, 28 January 1962.

"La vida y la obra de Manuel Mora son indivisibles de la vida y la obra del Partido Vanguardia Popular: Carta de Fabián Dobles a su Hija." *La Nación*, 30 December 1983.

Interviews with Fabián Dobles

Aguilar-Umaña, Isabel. "Fabián Dobles: 'La literatura, una forma de sentirme útil.'" *Tragaluz* 16 (2 May 1987): 13–15.

Del Rosario, Agustín. "Como hombre y como escritor cumplo con la sociedad." *Dominical: El Panamá-América*, 19 March 1972.

"Entrevista con Fabián Dobles, Premio Magón 1968." *La República*, 13 April 1969, p. 23. (Includes bibliography and commentary).

"Fabián Dobles contesta." *Diario de Costa Rica*, 16 May 1965, p. 12.

"Fabián Dobles: Es el pueblo que nos rodea el que inspira y construye toda obra literaria." *Semanario Universidad: Suplemento Cultural Forja: Café de las 4*, 31 October/6 November 1986, pp. 1 and 5. (Also participating are: Carlos Morales, Abel Pacheco, Violeta Fernández, and Fernando Durán Ayanegui).

"Fabián Dobles: 'Mi militancia ha sido la de un escritor.'" *Libertad*, 29 January/4 February 1988.

Grütter, Virginia. "Entrevista al escritor Fabián Dobles, en ocasión de la segunda edición de su libro 'Aguas turbias.'" *Libertad*, 15–21 March 1985.

León Sánchez, José. "Fabián Dobles: Premio nacional de novela 1967." *Eco Católico*, 5 May 1966.

Tovar, Enrique. "'Sólo los snobs complejudos pueden creer que hacemos el ridículo': Fabián Dobles." *La República*, 28 March 1971, p. 9.

Vargas, Roberto. "Entrevista: Fabián Dobles: 'Uno escribe para vivir, no para sobrevivir.'" *Etcétera* 3 (July 1993): 13–15.

———. "Tatamundo se fue a rodar tierras." *La Nación: Ancora: Suplemento Cultural de la Nación*, 5 May 1996, p. 3.

REVIEWS

Ese que llaman pueblo (1942)

1942

Bonilla, Abelardo. "Un juicio sobre 'Ese que llaman pueblo' la novela de Fabián Dobles." Unidentified family newspaper clipping, 25 September 1942.

Brenes, F. "'Ese que llaman pueblo,' un libro que honra las letras patrias." Unidentified family newspaper clipping, 1942.

Echeverría Loría, Arturo. "Nota sobre una novela 'Ese que llaman pueblo." Unidentified family newspaper clipping, 1942.

Garnier, José Fabio. "Cien Novelas Costarricenses: *Ese que llaman pueblo.*" *La Nación.* Unidentified family newspaper clipping, ca. 1942.

Lyra, Carmen. "'Ese que llaman pueblo' por Fabián Dobles." Unidentified family newspaper clipping, ca. 1942.

"Novela de Fabián Dobles titulada 'Ese que llaman pueblo.'" Unidentified family newspaper clipping, ca. 1942.

Roldán Espinoza, Juan. "Una novela de Fabián Dobles." *La Prensa Libre,* ca. 1942.

Segura Méndez, Manuel. "No constituye ciertamente una novela . . ." *La Prensa Libre,* ca. 1942.

1943

Orantes, Alfonso. "Un libro de Fabián Dobles." Unidentified family newspaper clipping, 1943.

"Un excelente libro de Costa Rica." *El Imparcial* (Guatemala), 16 April 1943.

1960

Cañas, Alberto F. "Cinco novelas costarricenses: 'Ese que llaman pueblo.'" *La República,* 3 April 1960, p. 18.

1968   Reviews of the 2nd ed.

Cañas, Alberto F. "Chisporroteos." *La Nación,* 25 August 1968.

Franck, Carlos. "*Ese que llaman pueblo,* novela de Fabián Dobles." *La Prensa Libre,* 16 July 1968, p. 25.

Pacheco, León. "Ese que llaman pueblo." *La Nación,* 26 July 1968, p. 15.

1977

Jiménez, Floria. "La novela de Fabián Dobles 'Ese que llaman pueblo.'" *La República,* 8 August 1977.

1995   Review of the 3rd ed.

"*Ese que llaman pueblo.*" *La Nación,* 7 November 1995.

Aguas turbias (1943)

1940

"3 novelas merecieron el 1er premio." *La Razón,* 16 December 1940. (Also included in *Obras Completas*).

1984

"Aparecen nuevas publicaciones." *La Nación*, 22 June 1984.

Una burbuja en el limbo (1946)

1946

"Una burbuja en el limbo: Novela de Fabián Dobles." *La Tribuna*, 27 August 1946.

1954

Foción. "Una novela de Fabián Dobles." *La Nación*, 13 February 1954, p. 4.

Quijano, Alfonso. "Al margen de 'Una burbuja en el limbo.'" *La Nación*, 11 February 1954, p. 4.

1971

"Una burbuja en el limbo." *La Nación*, 6 September 1971. (Advertisement for the book by Editorial de Costa Rica).

"Nuevo libro de la Editorial Costa Rica." *Diario de Costa Rica*, 15 September 1971, p. 4.

1972

Cañas, Alberto F. "Chisporroteos." *La República*, 16 January 1972, p. 8.

Hurtado, Gerardo César. "'Una burbuja en el limbo,' de Fabián Dobles." *La Prensa Libre*, 30 September 1972, p. 8.

Trejos de Steffen, Inés. "'Una burbuja en el limbo' por Fabián Dobles." *La Prensa Libre*, 3 January 1972, p. 18.

1987

Chaverri F., Amalia. "Título y transformación." *La Nación*, 15 November 1987, p. 1D.

1995   Review of the fifth reprint

Sauma, Osvaldo. "Semblanza del Loco Ríos." *La Nación: Viva*, 22 May 1995, p. 15.

1996

Chase, Alfonso. "Novela de la libertad." *La Nación*, 14 April 1996, p. 6D.

El sitio de las abras (1950)

1947

"*El sitio de las abras* de Fabián Dobles, la novela agraria de Costa Rica." *Ultima Hora*, 12 September 1947.

1950

"Cien novelas costarricenses: *El sitio de las abras.*" *La Nación,* 24 May 1950.

1952

"Crítico español opina sobre una novela de Fabián Dobles." *Diario de Costa Rica: Suplemento,* 6 July 1952.

1970

Trejos de Steffen, Inés. "'El sitio de las abras' por Fabián Dobles." *Prensa Libre,* 30 November 1970, p. 3D.

1971

Azofeifa, Isaac Felipe. "Héroes y malvados en *El sitio de las abras.*" *Semanario Universidad,* 5 July 1971.

Cañas, Alberto F. "Chisporroteos." *La República,* 2 May 1971, p. 8.

Hurtado, Gerardo César. "*El Sitio de las abras,* de Fabián Dobles." *La Prensa Libre,* 12 March 1971, p. 24.

Prieto, Emilia. "*El sitio de las abras* de Fabián Dobles." *Diario de Costa Rica,* 16 May 1971, p. 14.

1973

Catania, Carlos. "'El sitio de las abras,' de Fabián Dobles." *La Nación,* 22 July 1973, p. 16.

1975

Blanco Segura, Ricardo. "Libros: *El sitio de las abras.*" *La Nación,* 18 May 1975, p. 2A.

1990

"Libros." *La Nación: Viva,* 19 January 1990, p. 16.

2000

Fernández Alvarez, Guillermo. "Frutos de la Madurez." *La Nación: Ancora,* 19 March 2000. (Review of a new collection of twentieth-century authors from Editorial Costa Rica that includes *El sitio de las abras*).

Los leños vivientes (1962)

1950

Garnier, José Fabio. "Cien Novelas Costarricenses: Una araña verde." *La Nación,* 27 May 1950.

1962

Piedra, José. "'Los leños vivientes': La última y mejor novela de Fabián Dobles." *Adelante,* 18 March 1962.

1979

Morales, Carlos A. "En librerías: *Los leños vivientes; Ese que llaman pueblo.*" *Semanario Universidad,* 19–25 October 1979, p. 18.

1996

Díaz Matamoros, Doriam. "Recuerdos del 48." *Semanario Universidad,* 23 August 1996, p. 4.

En el San Juan hay tiburón (1967)

1967

Cañas, Alberto F. "Chisporroteos." *La República,* 3 December 1967, p. 8.

León Sánchez, José. "En el San Juan hay tiburón." *La República,* 26 November 1967.

Ruiz, Juan. "'En el San Juan hay tiburón' de Fabián Dobles." *La Prensa Libre: Suplemento Arte y Literatura,* 1967.

1968

Aguilera Malta, Demetrio. "En el San Juan hay tiburón." *La Prensa Libre,* 10 April 1968, p. 20.

Cañas, Alberto F. "Chisporroteos." *La República,* 25 August 1968, p. 9.

"En el San Juan hay tiburón." *La República,* 18 February 1968, p. 18.

Pacheco, León. "Novelas y novelistas costarricenses." *La Nación,* 22 July 1968.

"Salarrué elogia obra de Fabián Dobles." Unidentified family newspaper clipping, ca. 1968.

1978

Marín Cañas, José. "En el San Juan hay tiburón." *La Nación: Ancora,* 29 October 1978, p. 4.

1985

C. "En el San Juan hay tiburón." *Contrapunto,* 18 February 1985.

Los años, pequeños días (1989)

1989

Cañas, Alberto F. "Chisporroteos." *La Prensa Libre,* 10 October 1989.

Fernández, Victor Hugo. "Fabián Dobles, la novela del paisaje interior." *La Nación: Ancora,* 15 October 1989, pp. 1D–2D.

Jones, Fernando. "Caprichos: *Los años, pequeños días.*" *La Prensa Libre,* 18 December 1989.

Marín, Mario Alberto. "Fabián Dobles: *Los años, pequeños días,*" *Contrapunto,* 2 November 1989, p. 17.

"Nueva novela de Fabián Dobles." *La Prensa Libre,* 13 November 1989, p. 13.

"Nuevo libro: *Los años, pequeños días.*" *La República*, 3 October 1989.

"Presentaron la nueva novela de Fabián Dobles." *La Nación*, 11 November 1989.

Rivera, Carlos. "*Los años, pequeños días* para Fabián Dobles." *Contrapunto*, 2 November 1989, p. 16.

1990

"*Los años, pequeños días*: Fabián Dobles abre nuevas perspectivas a la literatura." *La Nación*, 1990.

Cardona, Alfredo. "Fabián Dobles: Su último libro." *Semanario Universidad*, 20 April 1990, p. 7.

Cerutti, Franco. "La última novela de Fabián Dobles." *La Nación*, 12 December 1990.

"¿Ha leído usted? *Los años, pequeños días?*" *La Prensa Libre*, 1990.

Prensa Libre, 8 December 1990. (Brief mention of *Los años, pequeños días*).

1991

Catania, Carlos. "Lecturas de los últimos meses." *La Nación*, 1991.

Cortés, Carlos. "'Los años, pequeños días': Autorretrato con memoria." *La Nación*, 10 February 1991, pp. 8D–9D.

"Los años, pequeños días." *La Prensa Libre*, 22 October 1991, p. 9.

1993 Review of the 2nd ed.

"Juegos del tiempo." *Semanario Universidad*, 18 July 1993, p. 4.

1996

López Castellanos, Victor. "*Los años, pequeños días*: Rincón de la Biblioteca." *Co-Latino*, 11 (19 October 1996).

Review of the English translation. *La Nación*, 25 August 1996.

1997

Hood, Edward Waters. "Dobles, Fabián. *Years Like Brief Days.* Trans. Joan Henry. London: Peter Owen, 1996." *World Literature Today* 71, no. 2 (Spring 1997): 360–61.

Reviews: Stories

1947

Cañas, Alberto F. "La rescoldera." *La Nación*, 28 March 1947, p. 2.

1954

"La Rescoldera de Fabián Dobles." *La Nación*, 11 February 1954, p. 4.

1955

Abad, Dr. Andrés J. "Escritor argentino opina sobre 'Tata Mundo.'" *La Nación*, 17 November 1955, p. 17.

Blu, Aldo. " 'Historias de Tata Mundo': Un libro de Fabián Dobles, escritor costarricense." *Repertorio Americano*, from *El Deber* (Chile), 26 August 1955.

Cañas, Alberto F. "Chisporroteos." *La República*, 16 October 1955.

Fernández, Guido (Don Guy). "Historias de Tata Mundo." *Diario de Costa Rica*, 1 May 1955, p. 17.

"Historias de Tata Mundo: Un nuevo libro del escritor y poeta Fabián Dobles." *La República*, 24 March 1955.

Vives, Lorenzo. "Historias de Tata Mundo." *Diario de Costa Rica*, 21 June 1955, p. 4.

1956

Salazar Ruiz, Milton. "Historias de 'Tata mundo.' " *Novedades*, 6 March 1956.

1957

Didier Solís, Marta. "A propósito de las nuevas historias de Tata Mundo." *La República*, 15 September 1957, p. 1.

"La Enciclopedia Británica incluye un libro de Fabián Dobles entre los mejores de 1956." *Diario de Costa Rica*, 29 June 1957, p. 11.

"El Maijú." *Diario de Costa Rica*, 7 July 1957.

Yabrudy, Alejandro. "La vuelta de Tata Mundo." *La República*, 25 August 1957, p. 16.

1966

Cañas, Alberto F. "Chisporroteos." *La República*, 13 February 1966, p. 2. (*La violín y la chatarra*).

Salazar Ruiz, Milton. "Historias de Tata mundo." *La Prensa Libre,* 16 December 1966, p. 8. Reprint in *Historias de Tata Mundo*, special edition, illustrated by Luis Daell, 178–79. San José: EUNED, 1994.

1967   Review of *Historias de Tata Mundo* and *El Maijú* in one volume

Cañas, Añberto F. "Chisporroteos." *La República*, 5 February 1967, p. 2.

1971   Review of *Cuentos de Fabián Dobles*

Cañas, Alberto F. "Chisporroteos." *La República*, 19 September 1971, p. 8.

1972   Review of the 1971 edition with prologue by Azofeifa

Tovar, Enrique. "Historias de Tata Mundo." *La República*, 30 April 1972, p. 26.

1977

Morales, Carlos. "Historias de Tata Mundo: Cuentos." *Semanario Universidad.* Undated family newspaper clipping.

1978   Review of the 6th ed. illustrated by César Valverde

Bustos Arratia, Miriam. "Las sabrosas *Historias de Tata Mundo.*" *Contrapunto,* October 1978. Reprint in *Historias de Tata Mundo*, special edition, illustrated by Luis Daell, 195–97. San José: EUNED, 1994.

1983

"EDUCA editó cuentos de Fabián Dobles." *La Nación*, 14 May 1983, p. 4B.

Morales, Carlos. "En librerías 'Historias de Tata Mundo.'" *Semanario Universidad*, 1983. Reprint in *Historias de Tata Mundo*, special edition, illustrated by Luis Daell, 181. San José: EUNED, 1994.

1986

"La pesadilla y otros cuentos." *Semanario Universidad*, 4–10 April 1986.

1991

"Dobles, Fabián: 'Historias de Tata Mundo.'" *La Nación*, 5 September 1991.

1993   Reviews of the luxury edition of *Historias de Tata Mundo*

Cerdeño, Rodolfo. "Violín contra chatarra." *La Nación*, 22 March 1993.

Chacón, Lorna. "Tata Mundo con nuevo rostro." *Semanario Universidad*, 16 July 1993, p. 8.

Cortés, Carlos. "Tata Mundo se vuelve clásico." *La Nación: Viva*, 5 June 1993, p. 13B.

Gamboa, Emilia Mora. "Tata Mundo en acuarelas." La *República: Galería*, 9 September 1993, p. 4B.

González V., Sandra. "Historias de Tata Mundo." *La Prensa Libre*, 14 September 1993, p. 17.

Hoffman, Myriam. "Libros: Historias de Tata Mundo." *Tiempo*. Undated newspaper clipping, ca. 1993.

Madrigal, Mario. "Fabián Dobles." *La Nación*, 19 September 1993.

Morales, Carlos. "Monumento a Fabián Dobles." *Semanario Universidad*, 17 September 1993.

"'Tata Mundo' en soberbia edición." *La Prensa Libre*, 26 August 1993, p. 7.

1996

Dobles, Aurelia. "Cuento que no es cuento." *La Nación: Viva*, 18 April 1996, p. 5.

1999

Valembois, Victor. "Globalización literaria bien entendida." *La Nación: Ancora*. 25 April 1999, p. 8.

2000   Review of *Y otros cuentos*

Soto, Rodrigo. "Más allá de Tata Mundo." *La Nación: Ancora*, 9 January 2000, p. 5.

REVIEWS: THEATER

1976

"'Barrilete' promisora obra de Fabián Dobles." *Excelsior*, 27 August 1976, 2nd section, p. 3.

1983   Reviews of the stage production of *"El barrilete"*

"'El barrilete' alzará vuelo." *La Nación,* 13 September 1983.

"'El Barrilete': Exito de Fabián Dobles." *Libertad,* 11 September 1983.

Cañas, Alberto F. "El barrilete." *Semanario Universidad,* 23–29 September 1983.

Henchoz, Erika. "En 'El Barrilete' los sueños se frustran pero no son imposibles." *Semanario Universidad,* September 1983.

"El teatro como poesía y testimonio." *La Nación,* 4 September 1983.

Reviews: *Obras completas* (1993)

1993

Cortés, Carlos. "Fabián Dobles: 'Las obras completas son como un parto.'" *La Nación: Viva,* 5 June 1993, p. 13.

1994

Bravo, Vanessa. "!Que sigan incompletas! *La Nación,* 12 March 1994, p. 8B.

Cañas, Alberto F. "Chisporroteo." *La República,* 8 March 1994, p. 17A.

"*Obras completas* de Fabián Dobles." *La Nación,* 7 March 1994, p. 39A.

Miscellaneous articles about Fabián Dobles

Albán, Laureano. "Laureano juzga a Fabián Dobles, et. al." *Diario de Costa Rica,* 7 March 1971, pp. 15–16.

"El año de Fabián Dobles." *La Nación: Viva,* 22 March 1993, p. 10B.

Araya, Francisco. "Fabián Dobles: 'Escribo con el corazón.'" *Rumbo* 181 (26 April 1988): 25–27.

Artavia, Betania. "Fabián Dobles fue enterrado ayer: Voló la mejor pluma del 48." *Diario Extra,* 24 March 1997.

"Artistas del pueblo." *Libertad,* 6–12 December 1985, p. 11.

B.O.A. "Fabián Dobles en la novela costarricense." *La Nación,* 11 February 1954, p. 4.

Bermúdez, Manuel. "La memoria del sudor." *Semanario Universidad,* 5 February 1993, p. 5.

———. "Una tertulia con los cardinales literarios." *Semanario Universidad,* 25 August 1995.

———. "Cuatro caras de la juventud canosa." *Semanario Universidad,* 1 September 1996, p. 1D.

———. "La voz cerrera y dulce de los montes." *Semanario Universidad: Forja,* 4 April 1997, p.1.

"Bibliografía de Fabián Dobles." *Diario de Costa Rica,* 16 May 1971, p. 12.

Bravo, Vanessa. "Colección de lujo." *La Nación,* 8 March 1994, p. 8.

———. "Don Fabián . . . desde el alma." *La Nación: Viva*, 1 May 1994, p. 1B.

———. "*Al Día* entra en las letras." *La Nación*, 1 March 1995.

Bustos, Myriam. "Un viejo pícaro de la literatura costarricense." *Contrapunto*, 1 June and 16 June 1979.

Camacho, Gabriela. "Lo mágico de las leyendas." *La Prensa Libre*, 31 January 1996, p. 2.

Cañas, Alberto."Chisporroteos." *La República*, 25 April 1965, p. 2. (On *Yerbamar*).

———. "Chisporroteos." *La República*, 6 April 1969, p.9. (On the Premio Magón).

———. "Chisporroteos." *La Nación*, January 1971. (On the story "El puente").

———. "Chisporroteos." *La República*, 23 January 1993. (Wishing Dobles a happy 75th birthday).

———. "Chisporroteos." *La República*, 5 April 1997, p. 11A. (After the death of Dobles).

Cardona Peña, Alfredo. "El cuento centroamericano en alemán." *La Nación*, 10 July 1968, p. 16.

———. "El cuento costarricense en 1967." *La Nación*, 6 July 1969, p. 15.

———. "Escritora costarricense gana premio de $6000." *La Nación*, 13 February 1954, p. 4. (Dobles received an honorary mention for his "Cuentos y para-cuentos").

———. "Lejos de mi ánimo enjuiciar la literatura costarricense." *La Nación*, 24 January 1970, p. 40.

Carvajal, Erick. "Fabián Dobles en inglés." *La República: Galería*, 11 August 1996, p. 17A.

———. "Murió Fabián Dobles." *Al Día*, 23 March 1997.

Castegnaro, Marta. "Fabián Dobles." *La Nación*, 12 September 1980. (*Día Histórico* daily column).

Castro, Alberto. "Los escritores no debemos olvidarnos del pueblo: Coloquio con Alberto Cañas, Fabián Dobles, Mario Picado y José León Sánchez." *La Nación: Ancora*, 2 December 1973.

Cavallina, Karlissa. "El rostro de las 'Historias de Tata Mundo.'" *Seminario Universidad*, 10 September 1993, p. 16. (On the exposition of Luis Daell's watercolors that accompany the luxury edition of *Historias de Tata Mundo*, 1994).

———. "Soldado de las letras." *Semanario Universidad*, 28 May 1993, p. 14. (On Gutiérrez, Dobles and Cañas).

"Centro de Cine presentará próximamente filme 'Tatamundo.'" *La Nación*, 16 January 1985.

Chacón, Lorna. "¡Gracias, don Fabián!" *La República: Signos*, 13 March 1994, p. 3.

———. "Compromiso de transparencia." *La Nación*, 14 April 1997, p. 14A.

Charpentier, Jorge. "Fabián Dobles y Luis Daell: El arte de lo posible." *Esta Semana*, September 1993. (Reproduction of the presentation given 30 August 1993 at the inauguration of the exposition of Daell's watercolors that accompany *Historias de Tata Mundo*).

Chase, Alfonso. "Los que se fueron." *La Prensa Libre*, 17 June 1993.

———. "Novela de libertad." *La Nación: Ancora*, 14 April 1996, p. 6.

————. "En el centro luminoso del sol." *La Prensa Libre*, 3 April 1997, p. 13.

————. "Fabián Dobles: Verdad del tiempo." *La Nación: Ancora*, 22 May 1998, p. 2.

————. "Homenaje." *La Nación: Ancora*, 22 March 1998.

"Cine costarricense en exhibición en España." *Tiempo Libre*. Undated newspaper clipping.

"Cineastas italianos filman en San José relatos de autores costarricenses." *Diario de Costa Rica*, 10 May 1956.

"Conversación con pulso de poesía." *La Nación: Viva*, 9 June 1997, p. 8B.

"Correspondencia." *Esta Semana*, 17–23 November 1989.

Cortés, Carlos. "Fabián Dobles: Un personaje de leyenda." *La Nación: Ancora*, 9 June 1996.

————. "Dobles total." *La Nación*, 5 March 1994, p. 13A.

"Decía Tata Mundo." *Américas* 7, no.9 (September 1955): 19.

"De don Fabián Dobles." *Semanario Universidad*, 3 August 1996, p. 19. (On *En el San Juan hay tiburón* and *Los leños vivientes* published by EUNA).

"De los libros 'Viento-Barro.'" *Brecha* 2, no. 4 (December 1957): 18.

Dobles, Aurelia. "Abrazo de literatura y artes plásticas en el 'más costarricense de los libros.'" *Esta Semana*, 13–19 July 1993.

————. "Tomasito el volcánico." *La Nación: Ancora*, 17 January 1993, p. 3D. (Wishing him a happy 75th birthday).

————. "Las 'Obras Completas' de Fabián Dobles: Un legado en vida del autor." *Esta Semana*, 15–21 March 1994.

————. "Dobles en turco." *La Nación: Viva*, 20 July 1996, p. 6B.

————. "Tiros a marco." *La Nación: Ancora*, 10 November 1996, pp. 1–3.

Domínguez, Eliodoro. "Fabián Dobles, verdadero escritor costarricense." *La Nación*, 7 November 1946, p. 2.

Duverrán, Carlos Rafael. "El país le debe homenaje a Fabián Dobles." *Semanario Universidad*, 15 September 1989, pp. 7.

"Entre las 'Abras' y 'Tata Mundo.'" *Al Día*, 1 March 1995.

"Escritores centroamericanos enjuician Seminario del Libro." *La Nación*, 26 January 1968.

"Escritores del Istmo se reúnen en frontera." Unidentified family newspaper clipping.

"Fabián Dobles." *Ultima Hora*, 10 January 1947. (Commentary on the first four novels; the article includes samples of Dobles' poetry and the short story "Chuta Miranda").

"Fabián Dobles." *La República: Aprendamos*, no. 85 (30 May 1978): 10. (Biography plus the short story "El Targuá").

"Fabián Dobles." *La República*, 1 May 1984. (Biography).

"Fabián Dobles en la novela costarricense." *La Nación*, 11 February 1954, p. 4.

"Fabián Dobles al patrimonio universal." *La Nación: Viva*, 3 March 1995, p. 16B.

"Fabián Dobles nuevo académico de la lengua." *La Nación*, 2 October 1980.

"Fabián Dobles: Ritórnelo de la vida y los momentos." *La Nación: Ancora*, 19 January 1997, p. 5.

"Fabián Dobles vuelve a la pantalla grande." *La Nación,* 4 September 1983, p. 1B and p. 4.

"Fabián, ilustre hijo de Belén." *La Nación,* 9 June 1994, p. 2A.

Fernández, Guido. "Encuentro de memorias un martes 13." *La Nación: Revista Dominical,* 25 February 1996.

Fernández, Rocío. "1940: Un gran escándalo en las letras costarricenses." *Excelsior,* 29 February 1976, p. 8.

Fernández, Victor Hugo. "La abuela cuentacuentos." *La Nación,* 16 May 1993.

Formoso, Manuel. "Cuando el poeta ha muerto." *La Nación,* 15 June 1997, p. 15A.

Franck, Carlos. "Europa se interesa por la literatura Centroamericana." *La Prensa Libre,* 1967.

Fuentes, Laura. "Homenaje a dos maestros." *Semanario Universidad,* 13 October 1999, p. 14.

Gallegos, Daniel. "Fabián Dobles: *In Memoriam.*" *Revista Nacional de Cultura* 30 (August 1997): 3–4.

Gamboa, Francisco. "Fabián Dobles: Vida llena de contrastes." *La República: Suplemento Dominical,* 14 September 1958.

García H., Roberto. "Hasta luego, Tata Mundo." *La Nación,* 23 March 1997, p. 16A.

Garrido, Lenín. "Fuera y dentro, dentro y fuera." *La Nación,* 5 October 1968.

González, Gilda. "Señores de la palabra." *La Nación,* 29 May 1993, p. 16B. (On Dobles, Alberto Cañas, y Joaquín Gutiérrez).

Guevara, José David. "Ancoras para el mérito." *La Nación,* 21 December 1990.

Guier, Fernando. "Aquí y ahora." *Al Día,* 20 November 1994, p. 4.

Guiomar. "En 1918 le nació a Costa Rica un novelista de entraña." *Repertorio Americano* 38 (28 June 1941).

H. G., A. "Fabián Dobles: Premio Magón 1968." *Libertad.* Undated newspaper clipping, ca. 1968.

"Hablan los Premiados." *La Nación,* 3 April 1969.

Henchoz, Erika. "Don Fabián hereda sus versos en prosa." *La Nación,* 15 April 1997, p. 14A.

——— and Juan Ramón Rojas. "Un vistoso rincón social en obras de Fabián Dobles." *Semanario Universidad,* 2–8 September 1983.

Hilje Q., Luko. "Don Fabián." *Semanario Universidad,* 11 April 1997, p. 20.

Hurtado, Gerardo César. "Con Fabián Dobles." *Revista Artes/Letras* 2, no. 14 (1971).

———. "Ideología social de Fabián Dobles." *La Prensa Libre,* 4 December 1969, p. 28.

Hurtado, Victor. "Los suntuosos." *La Nación: Revista Dominical,* 28 September 1997.

Jara Jiménez, Eladio. "Vuelan las águilas." *La Nación,* 26 April 1997, p. 15A.

"Juegos de tiempo." *Semanario Universidad: Suplemento Los Libros,* 18 June 1993, p. 4.

Juncos, Carmen. "Periscopio." *La República: Galería,* 9 April 1997, p. 16A

———. "El cuento centroamericano en alemán." *La Nación,* 10 July 1968, p. 16.

León Sánchez, José. "Premio nacional de novela 1967." *La Prensa Libre,* 5 May 1968, p. 30.

————. "De Fabián Dobles a Solzhenitsin: Los caminos de la duda." *La República*, 8 August 1982, p. 7.

Lobo, Tatiana. "Me voy a perder el partido." *La Nación*, 27 March 1997.

López Vallecillos, Italo. "Bibliografía de Fabián Dobles." *Diario de Costa Rica*, 16 May 1971, p. 13.

Marín, Mario Alberto. "Fabián Dobles: *Los años, pequeños días*." *Contrapunto*, 2 November 1989.

Marín Cañas, José. "Fabián Dobles, Magón 1968." *Diario de Costa Rica*, 16 May 1971, pp. 11–12.

————. "Escritor." *La Nación*, 12 December 1973, p. 3B; 16 December 1973, p. 3B; 19 December 1973, p. 3B; 6 January 1974, p. 3B.

"Memoria viva de los maestros." *La Nación: Viva*, 28 May 1997, p. 7.

Mena, Rosibel. "El San José que se esfumó." *La Prensa Libre*, 16 September 1995, pp. 4–5.

Molina, Ma. Cecilia. "Mamita Maura." *La República*, 17 April 1988, p. 7.

Molina S., Julio. "Allá . . . en el sitio de las Abras." *Prensa Libre*, 21 July 1993, p. 12. (A visit to Dobles' homestead, which is named after the title of his novel).

Monge B., Carlos L. "Talento y remembranzas." *La Prensa Libre*, 31 August 1995, p. 2.

Mora Rodríguez, Arnoldo. "75 años de Joaquín y Fabián." *La República*, 21 June 1993, p. 19A.

Morales, Carlos. "Esa sensación de lo nuestro." *Semanario Universidad: Suplemento Cultural Forja*, 3 November 1995.

Morales, Francisco. "Fabián Dobles." *Extra*, 1 September 1992.

Morvillo F., Mabel. "Tránsito normativo de Fabián Dobles: La nostalgia luminosa." *Aportes* 80 (August 1991): 31–33.

"More than a Writer, a Forger of Dreams/Más que un escritor, un forjador de sueños." *Join Us* (1993–1994): 56.

Muñoz Campos, Fabio. "Fabián Dobles, un escritor con alma de campesino." *Contrapunto*, no. 43 (16 July 1980).

"Norma Loaiza, premio nacional de periodismo." Undated newspaper clipping, ca. 1968. (Mention of Dobles, winner of the Premio Magón).

"Noticia de autor: El año de Fabián Dobles." *La Nación*, 22 March 1993.

"Novelas, novelistas y comentarios." *La Hora*, 23 November 1973, p. 4.

"Nueva novela de Fabián Dobles." *La Prensa Libre*, 13 November 1989.

"Nuevo libro de Fabián Dobles." *Brecha* 1, no. 11 (July 1957): 27.

"Novela de Fabián Dobles será publicada en Guatemala." Unidentified family newspaper clipping. (On the manuscript of "Hombres de tres tiempos").

"Obra de Fabián Dobles será estudiada en El Salvador." *La Nación*, 14 April 1973, p. 28.

Ortíz Mangel, Guido. "Treinta años de vida literaria de Fabián Dobles." *Diario de Costa Rica*, 15 May 1971, p. 11.

Ortíz Pacheco, José Joaquín. "Señores Fabián Dobles, Alberto Cañas, Isaac Felipe Azofeifa y compañeros." *La Nación*, 6 February 1979, p. 39A.

Ovares, Flora, and Margarita Rojas. "Esencia y escritura." *La Nación: Ancora.* Undated family newspaper clipping.

Pacheco, Abel. "Comentarios." *La República*, 2 April 1997. (Memories of don Fabián).

Pacheco, León. "Novelas y novelistas costarricenses." *La Nación*, 22 July 1968, p. 15.

Palacino, Amalia, and Vanessa Bravo. "Manantiales de palabras." *La Nación*, 26 March 1994.

Parra Aravena, Ana María. "Partió don Fabián." *La República*, 23 March 1997, p. 2A.

———. "El viaje de Tata Mundo." *La República*, 24 March 1997, p. 2A.

———. "Lejos de lo rural." *La República: Suplemento Galería*, 25 March 1997, p. 14A.

Pinto, Julieta. "La presencia de Fabián Dobles." *La Nación*, 22 April 1997, p. 14A.

Prego, Irma. "Adiós, Fabián Dobles." *La Prensa Libre*, 5 April 1997, p. 13.

"La presencia de Vanguardia en el ámbito de la cultura es un hecho indiscutible." *Libertad*, 17–23 June 1976.

Quesada, Laura. "De la mano con el autor." Unidentified family newspaper clipping, ca. 1993.

Quesada, Ricardo F. "Sanción sí, crítica no." *La Nación*, 13 February 1954, p. 4.

Quiros J., Maribelle. "Escritor a disgusto." *La Nación*, 17 July 1992, p. 8B.

———. "Hacedores de cultura." *La Nación*, 8 October 1992.

———. "Adición a la poesía." *La Nación: Viva*, 11 February 1993, p. 18.

Ramos, Miguel Arturo. "Fabián Dobles: 'Nunca escribo sólo por entretener.'" *La República*, 9 April 1985.

"Realizan película sobre cuentos de Fabián Dobles." *La República*, 10 September 1983, p. 19.

Rivera, Arnoldo. "Hospitalizado Fabián Dobles." *La Nación*, 18 January 1997, p. 8A.

———. "Falleció Fabián Dobles." *La Nación*, 23 March 1997, p. 16A.

Rodríguez, Julio. "Obituario." *La Nación*, 12 April 1997, p. 15.

Rojas, Ana. "Fabián Dobles: Dueño de la palabra." *La República: Semanario Cultural Signos*, 12 December 1993, pp. 1–2.

Salas Zamora, Edwin. "Tres novelas de Fabián Dobles." *Semanario Universidad: Forja*, 2–8 June 1978, p. 17.

Salazar Martínez, Francisco, "Cumbres de la palabra." *La Nación*, 10 November 1991. (Poetry in honor of Joaquín Gutiérrez, Isaac Felipe Azofeifa y Fabián Dobles).

Sancho, Eugenia. "Sin embargo, no se ha ido." *La Nación: Heredia Hoy* (Monthly newspaper from the province of Heredia), April 1997, pp. 1–2.

Sancho Rodríguez, Floriberto. "El sitio de las abras, Huasipungo y Mamita Yunai." *La Nación*, 15 August 1973.

"Se filma en cinemascope un cuento de Fabián Dobles: 'Matatigres.'" 1955; reprint in *Historias de Tata Mundo*, special edition, illustrated by Luis Daell, 172. San José: EUNED, 1994.

"Los 60 años de Fabián Dobles." *Libertad*, 3–9 March 1978.

Simón, Luis. "Vértice." *La Prensa Libre*, 5 May 1997. (Eulogy).

Soto, Rodrigo. "Carta a Fabián Dobles." *Revista Nacional de Cultura* (May 1993).

Sterloff, Virginia. "La conferencia de la semana." *La Nación*, 13 August 1971, p. 54.

———. "Novelística de Fabián Dobles." *La Prensa Libre*, 28 June 1974, p. 20.

"Treinta años de vida literaria: 'Cuentos de Fabián Dobles.' " *Semanario Universidad*, ca. 1970.

Tovar, Enrique. "Fabián Dobles, aspirante al premio Rómulo Gallegos." *La Nación*, 8 May 1991.

V.C., B. "Certamen nacional: Hablan los premiados." *La Nación*, 3 April 1969, p. 6.

Valverde, César. "Fabián, dilecto amigo." *La Nación*, 4 April 1997, p. 15 A.

Vargas Montero, E. "Literatos en Costa Rica." *Diario de Costa Rica*, 9 October 1960, p. 18.

"Votos razonados para premios nacionales." *La Nación*, 19 abril 1969. (On Dobles' award of El premio Magón).

Yurkivich, Saúl. "Cinco novelas costarricenses al concurso Latinamericano de Estados Unidos." *La Hora*, 16 December 1940.

Critical Studies on Fabián Dobles

Amoretti Urtado, María Gertrudis. "La cuentística de Fabián Dobles." *Revista de filología y lingüística de la Universidad de Costa Rica* 2, no.3 (1976): 39–47.

Azofeifa, Isaac F. "Sobre las *Historias de Tata Mundo*." In *Historias de Tata Mundo*. 5th ed. San José: Editorial Lehmann, 1971.

Chase, Alfonso. "Crónica de los Días: Aproximaciones a la última novela de Fabián Dobles." *El Centavo* 14, no.143 (December 1989): 16–22.

———. "Lectura de *Los años pequeños días*: La última novela de Fabián Dobles." *Contrapunto*, 16 November 1989, pp. 12–13.

Chaverri F., Amalia. "*Los años, pequeños días*: Una lectura a través de categorías mítico-simbólicas." *Káñina* 17, no. 2 (1993): 21–28.

"Un estudio sobre 'El sitio de las abras.' " Unpublished manuscript in the file on Dobles collected by the Tinoco Library at the University of Costa Rica.

Coppella, Yolanda. "Una burbuja en el limbo." Conferencia de Castellano No. 12, 2 September 1976.

Durán Luzio, Juan. "Desafíos de una traducción." *La Nación*, 25 August 1996, pp. 4–5.

Gamboa, Emma. "Prólogo a *El sitio de las abras*." In *Obras Completas*, vol. 2. San José: EUCR/EUN, 1993, 167–81.

García Monge, J. "Prólogo." In *El Maijú y otras historias de Tata Mundo*. San José: Editorial Trejos Hnos, 1957.

González, Ann Brashear. "Fabián Dobles and the Maze of Memory." *World Literature Today* (Summer 1999): 485–88.

———. "Fabián Dobles y la novela de los recuerdos." *Káñina* 22, no. 3 (1998): 23–28.

———. "El Legado de Tata Mundo." *Istmo: Revista virtual de estudios literarios y cultu-*

rales centroamericanos, no. 3 (January–June 2002), http://www.denison.edu/istmo/articulos/tata.html

Hurtado, Gerardo César. "Ideología social de Fabián Dobles." *La Prensa Libre*, 4 December 1969.

Menton, Seymour. *El cuento costarricense*. México, D.F.: Ediciones Andrea, 1964.

Molina, Carlos, and Edwin Salas. "Pasado y presente en *El sitio de las abras*." *Letras* 6–7 (July–December 1980–January–June 1981): 159–82.

Morales, Carlos. "Fabián Dobles: Un estudio sobre *El sitio de las abras*." *Cuadernos Universitarios*, FEUCR, no. 1 (1974).

Moreno Ortega, Resti. "Fabián Dobles: Su proyección intelectual. Entre el compromiso y la solidaridad con el pobre." *Senderos*, 19 (1997): 409–52.

———. "Fabián Dobles: Vida y testimonio de un hombre—narrador y poeta—'Bueno'" *In Memoriam* (1918–1997)." *Senderos*, 19 (1997): 61–118.

——— "Fabián Dobles y la generación del 40." *Senderos* 20 (May-August 1998): 229–65.

Quesada, Alvaro. "Fabián Dobles en la narrativa costarricense." *Obras Completas*, vol. 1. San Jose:UCR/EUNA, 1993, pp. 11–23.

———. "Tradición e innovación: La novela de Fabián Dobles." *Semanario Universidad*, 1 July 1994, pp. 3–4.

Rodríguez, Camilo. "Poesía escondida." *Rumbo* 616 (14 October 1996): 36.

Sauma, Osvaldo. "Poesía de fuego y combate." *La Nación: Ancora*, 22 May 1994, p. 2D.

Solano Jiménez, Ronald, "Crítica literaria en Costa Rica: De las *Historias de Tata Mundo*." *Anuario de Estudios Centroamericanos* 18, no. 1 (1992): 85–95.

———. "!Qué no sabía Tata Mundo! Narración, Saber, Seducción." *Revista Girasol* 1 (1996): 81–88.

White, Michael. "*El sitio de las abras*: Una novela de Fabián Dobles." *Káñina* 5, no.1 (1981): 17–27.

Unpublished Family Documents

Abreu-Gómez, Ermilo. Letter to Kathleen Walker, Director of the *Revista Américas*. 2 February 1956. (On the story "Adelante").

Ananía, Pablo. "Fabián Dobles: Un maestro de la realidad."

Boccanera, Jorge. "Fabián Dobles: Siempre me ha picado la lengua." February 1996.

Dobles, Fabián. Copy of letter sent to Mariannick Guennec. San Isidro de Heredia, 25 September 1995.

Durán Luzio, Juan. "Sobre la traducción al inglés de *Los años pequeños días*, de Fabián Dobles." (Earlier draft of an article that was published in *La Nación*, see the section on critical articles in this bibliography).

De Elliott, Lic. Yolanda. "Notas sobre las *Historias de Tata Mundo* y su autor." Universidad de Costa Rica, Facultad de Ciencias y Letras, Departamento de Estudios Generales, Cátedra de Castellano.

Guennec, Mariannick. "Entrevista con Fabián Dobles, 1994." (Letter to Dobles containing the typescript of an interview with him).

Henry, Joan. Letter to Fabián Dobles. 1 June 1996.

Romero, Iver. "Leyendo 'Ese que llaman pueblo' de Fabián Dobles." January 1943.

V.V., E. (probably Emilio Valverde Vega). "Apuntes sobre 'Aguas turbias' de Fabián Dobles."

Zamora, Carlos Francisco. "Presentación para Vernissage Exposición de Acuarelas de Luis Daell, Ilustrativas del Libro *Historias de Tata Mundo* de Fabián Dobles." 30 August 1993.

THESES

Chan Wong, Hilda. "Visión del relato *Los leños vivientes* de Fabián Dobles a partir de método estructural." Licenciatura thesis. Universidad de Costa Rica, San Pedro de Montes de Oca, 1979.

Mora López, Jorge L. "*Una burbuja en el limbo,* Ignacio Ríos: Su conflicto con la familia y con el medio." Licenciatura thesis. Universidad de Costa Rica, San Pedro de Montes de Oca, 1977.

Moya Portuguéz, Boris. "Estudio sobre *Historias de Tata Mundo* de Fabián Dobles." Licenciatura thesis. Universidad de Costa Rica, San Pedro de Montes de Oca, 1977.

Salas Zamora, Edwin. "*El sitio de las abras,* de Fabián Dobles." Licenciatura thesis. Universidad de Costa Rica, San Pedro de Montes de Oca, 1975.

Solano Jiménez, Ronald. "Leer al detalle, literatura, psicoanálisis, teoría literaria." Licenciatura thesis. Universidad de Costa Rica, San Pedro de Montes de Oca, 1991.

Solano Sánchez, Karla. "Bio-bibliografía de Fabián Dobles." Licenciatura thesis. Escuela de Bibliotecología Universidad de Costa Rica, San Pedro de Montes de Oca, 1998. (References from the University of Costa Rica's file on Dobles plus articles from 1995–2000 available from the internet).

Valverde Vega, Jorge Luis. "Persistencia de rasgos naturalistas en tres novelas costarricenses." Licenciatura thesis. Universidad Nacional, Heredia, Costa Rica, 1991.

Vargas Méndez, María Auxiliadora. "La elipsis temporal y la evolución ideológica en *El sitio de las abras.*" Licenciatura thesis. Universidad de Costa Rica, San Pedro de Montes de Oca, 1986.

White, Michael Gerard. "Costa Rican Realism through Two Novels of Fabián Dobles: *Ese que llaman pueblo* and *El sitio de las abras.*" Master's thesis, Tulane University, 1979.

OTHER REFERENCES TO FABIÁN DOBLES

Advertisement for Banco Nacional with Dobles' photograph. *La República*, 18 April 1994.

Newspaper advertisement with Dobles' photograph for CCSS.

Announcement of the presentation of *Years Like Brief Days*. *La Nación: Viva*, 12 May 1996.

Letter to Fabián Dobles from Juan M. Rojas B. *La Nación*, 7 September 1994.

Letter from Fabián Dobles. *La Nación*, 22 July 1996. (Dobles' commentary on Costa Rica's Olympic swimming champion, Silvia Pol).

Letter from Fabián Dobles to Pablo Casals and the director of *Brecha*. *Brecha* 1, no. 9 (May 1957).

"Don Fabián aclara." *La Nación: Ancora*, 12 May 1996.

"Ese oficio de escribir" (cassette recording of Dobles). EUNED. Oficina de Extensión Cultural, 1990.

Congratulations for winning the Premio Ancora 1990. *La Nación*, 6 January 1991.

Undated newspaper photograph of Dobles with Julio Cortázar, *Excelsior*.

Photograph of Dobles, et al. Caption reads "Tres siglos, dos años y cuatro vasos." *Seminario Universidad*, n.d.

Photograph of Dobles with García Monge and other Costa Rican authors. Caption reads "El pensamiento de García Monge." *La Nación: Ancora*, April 1975.

Photograph of Dobles with the Cultural Attaché, Lic. Carlos Ortega Guerrero, in the Mexican Embassy. *La Prensa Libre*, ca. 10 February 1992.

Unidentified newspaper photograph of current employees including Dobles of the Patronato Nacional de la Infancia. ca. 1940.

Unidentified newspaper photograph of Dobles with the Ambassador from Venezuela, Francisco Salazar Martínez. n.d.

González Feo, Mario. "Mis tres ángeles." *El Espectador*. Undated newspaper clipping. (Dobles, his wife Cecilia and brother Alvaro act in this comedy).

"Grata visita." *Boletín Informativo "Calufa."* Colegio Carlos Luis Fallas. Departamento de Español. April 1993.

"Homenaje del 'Bloque' para Fabián Dobles." Unidentified newspaper clipping, ca. 1968. (Includes photograph of Dobles with his three daughters).

Report by Dobles, who represented Costa Rica at the World Assembly for Peace in Finland, 1955. *Paz*, August 1955.

"*Obras Completas* de Fabián Dobles." San José: IPS, ca. 1993.

M., M.M. "Mis Tres Angeles." Unidentified newspaper clipping. (Review of this comedy in which Dobles played the part of Jules.)

Mention of the participation of Dobles in adapting a play by Molnar to San José of the 1920s: "una versión literaria que adaptara el lenguaje de la pieza al medio costarricense" [a literary vision that adapts the language of the play to the Costa Rican medium]. Unidentified newspaper clipping, n.d.

Muñoz Ledo, Jesús Cabrera. "*Los años, pequeños días.*" *Noticias de México*, ca. 8 November 1989. (Announcement of the presentation of this novel in Casa de México).

Unidentified and undated newspaper clipping of Dobles with photograph in response to the death of an unidentified Roberto.

UNED pamphlet announcing the luxury edition of *Historias de Tata Mundo*, 1993. (Includes information on Dobles by Alberto Cañas and on the illustrator, Luis Daell, by Carlos Guillermo Montero).

ADDITIONAL REFERENCES

Alcida, Rita Ramos. *Indigenism: Ethnic Politics in Brazil.* Madison: University of Wisconsin Press, 1998.

América cuenta. Caracas: Editorial Arte, 1965.

Anderson, Benedict. *Imagined Communities: Reflections on the Origin and Spread of Nationalism.* New York/London: Verso, 1983.

Antología de cuentos Premios León Felipe. Mexico, D.F.: Finisterre Editor, 1972.

Arrollo Soto, Victor Manuel. *El habla popular en la literatura costarricense.* San José: Publicaciones de la Universidad de Costa Rica, 1971.

Arteaga, Alfred. *An Other Tongue: Nation and Ethnicity in the Linguistic Borderlands.* Durham: Duke University Press, 1994.

Ashcroft, Bill, Gareth Griffiths, and Helen Tiffin. *The Empire Writes Back: Theory and Practice in Post-Colonial Literatures.* London and New York: Routledge, 1989.

————. *The Post-Colonial Studies Reader.* London and New York: Routledge, 1995.

Bernheimer, Charles. Introduction to *Comparative Literature in the Age of Multiculturalism.* Baltimore: John Hopkins University Press, 1995.

Beverley, John. *Literature and Politics in the Central American Revolutions.* Austin: University of Texas Press, 1990.

————. *Subalternity and Representation: Arguments in Cultural Theory.* Durham: Duke University Press, 1999.

Bhabha, Homi K. *Nation and Narration.* New York and London: Routledge, 1990.

Bogantes-Zamora, Claudio. *La narrativa socialrealista en Costa Rica.* Aarhus, Denmark: Aarhus University Press, 1990.

Bonilla Baldares, Abelardo. *Historia y antología de la literatura costarricense.* 2nd ed. San José: Editorial Costa Rica, 1967.

————. "Abel y Caín en el ser histórico de la nación costarricense." In *Ensayistas Costarricenses,* edited by Luis Ferrero. San José: A. Lehmann, 1972.

Booth, Wayne C. *The Rhetoric of Fiction.* Chicago: University of Chicago Press, 1961.

Borgeson, Jr., Paul W. "El Salvador." In *Handbook of Latin American Literature,* edited by David William Foster, 2nd ed. New York: Garland Publishing, Inc., 1992.

Bullón, H. Fernando. *Postmodernidad y la iglesia evangélica.* San José: El Instituto Internacional de Evangelización a Fondo, 2000.

Chase, Alfonso, ed. *Narrativa contemporánea de Costa Rica.* San José: Ministerio de Cultura, Juventud y Deportes, 1975.

Clifford, James. "Traveling Cultures." In *Cultural Studies,* edited by Lawrence Grossberg, Cary Nelson, and Paula Treichler. London and New York: Routledge, 1992.

Contemporary Short Stories from Central America. Austin: University of Texas Press, 1994.

Cortés, Carlos. *La invención de Costa Rica.* San José: Editorial Costa Rica, 2003.

Cortés, Carlos, Vernor Muñoz, and Rodrigo Soto, eds. *Para no cansarlos con el cuento: Narrativa costarricense actual.* San José: Editorial Universidad de Costa Rica, 1989.

Craft, Linda J. *Novels of Testimony and Resistance.* Gainesville: University of Florida Press, 1997.

El cuento actual latinoamericano. Mexico, D.F.: Ediciones de Andrea, 1973.

Dobles, Margarita. "Poeta y filósofo de la piedra y la madera." *Revista Nacional de Cultura* 10 (February 1991): 58–62.

Donoso, José. *The Boom in Spanish American Literature: A Personal History*. Translated by Gregory Kolovakos. New York: Columbia University Press, 1977.

Erickson, Martin. "Trends in Central American Literature." *Intellectual Trends in Latin America*. Austin: University of Texas Press, 1945.

Fernández L., Mario. *Textos de lectura y comentarios para sétimo año*. 2nd ed. San José: Editorial Fernández Arce, 1980.

Foucault, Michael. *Power/Knowledge: Selected Interviews and Other Writings 1972–1977*, trans. Colin Gorden et al., ed. Colin Gordon. New York: Pantheon, 1980.

Fuentes, Carlos. *La nueva novela hispanoamericana*. Mexico: Editorial Joaquín Mortiz, 1969.

González Dobles, Jaime. *La patria del Tico*. San José: Editorial Logos, 1995.

Guha, Ranajit. *Dominance without Hegemony: History and Power in Colonial India*. Cambridge: Harvard University Press, 1997.

———, ed. *A Subaltern Studies Reader, 1986–1995*. Minneapolis: University of Minnesota Press, 1997.

Hirsch, E. D. *The Validity of Interpretation*. New Haven and London: Yale University Press, 1967.

Jameson, Fredric. "Third-World Literature in the Era of Multinational Capitalism." *Social Text* 15 (1986).

Landry, Donna, and Gerald Maclean, eds. *The Spivak Reader*. London and New York: Routledge, 1996.

Meléndez, Carlos. *Historia de Costa Rica*. 2nd ed. 1983. Reprint, San José: Editorial Universidad Estatal a Distancia, 1999.

Menton, Seymour. *El cuento costarricense*. Lawrence: University of Kansas Press, 1964.

Ministerio de Educación Pública. "Literatura para séptimo año." In *Programa de Estudios: Tercer Ciclo: Español*. San José: El Ministerio, 1995.

Moderne latein-amerikanische Prosa. Berlin: Verlag Volk und Welt, 1969.

Molina, Iván. *Cundila*. San José: Varitec, 2002.

Narradores centroamericanos contemporáneos. Guayaquil: Editorial Ariel Universal, 1973.

Olney, James, ed. *Autobiography: Essays Theoretical and Critical*. Princeton: Princeton University Press, 1980.

Panorama del cuento centroamericano. Lima, Perú: Editora Latinoamericana, 1955.

Parrinder, Patrick. *Authors and Authority*. New York: Columbia University Press, 1991.

Paz para el mundo. Moscow, 1988.

Perfeccione su español. Moscow, 1988.

Picado Gómez, Manuel. *Literatura, ideología, crítica: Notas para un estudio de la literatura costarricense*. San José: Editorial Costa Rica, 1983.

Quesada Soto, Alvaro. *Breve historia de la literatura costarricense*. San José: Editorial Porvenir, 2000.

Ramos, Alcida Rita. *Indigenism: Ethnic Politics in Brazil.* Madison: University of Wisconsin Press, 1998.

Ras, Barbara, ed. *Costa Rica: A Traveler's Literary Companion.* San Francisco: Whereabouts Press, 1994.

Rojas, Margarita, and Flora Ovares. *La casa paterna: Escritura y nación en Costa Rica.* San José: Editorial de la Universidad de Costa Rica, 1993.

———. *100 años de literatura costarricense.* San José: Farben Grupo Editorial Norma, 1995.

Said, Edward W. *Orientalism.* New York: Panthean Books, 1978.

Sandoval de Fonseca, Virginia. *Resumen de literatura costarricense.* San José: Editorial Costa Rica, 1978.

Santos, Rosario, ed. *And We Sold the Rain: Contemporary Fiction from Central America.* New York: Four Walls Eight Windows, 1988.

Seidman, Steven. Introduction to *The Postmodern Turn: New Perspectives on Social Theory.* Cambridge: Cambridge University Press, 1994.

Sommer, Doris. *Foundational Fictions: The National Romances of Latin America.* Berkeley: University of California Press, 1991.

Die Sonnenfinsternis und andere Erzählungen aus Mittelamerika (El eclipse de sol y otros cuentos de Centroamérica). Tübingen, West Germany: Horst Eerdmanns Verlag, 1969.

Thiong'o, Ngugi Wa. "The Language of African literature." In *Decolonising the Mind: The Politics of Language in African Literature.* London: James Currey, 1981.

Vallbona, Rima de. "Costa Rica." In *Handbook of Latin American Literature,* edited by David William Foster. 2nd ed. New York: Garland Publishing, Inc., 1992.

Valdeperas, Jorge. *Para una nueva interpretación de la literature costarricense.* San José: Editorial Costa Rica, 1979.

White, Hayden. "The Historical Text as Literary Artifact." *The Tropics of Discourse: Essays in Cultural Criticism.* Baltimore: Johns Hopkins University Press, 1978.

Zavala, Magda, and Seidy Araya. *La historiografía literaria en América Central (1957–1987).* San José: Editorial Fundación UNA, 1995.

Index